Contents

iii

iv *Contents*

Spiritual Exercises Based on Paul's Epistle to the Romans

Joseph A. Fitzmyer, S.J.

William B. Eerdmans Publishing Company
Grand Rapids, Michigan / Cambridge, U.K.

This edition 2004 by Wm. B. Eerdmans Publishing Co.
255 Jefferson Ave. S.E., Grand Rapids, Michigan 49503 /
P.O. Box 163, Cambridge CB3 9PU U.K.
www.eerdmans.com

IMPRIMI POTEST
Eduardus Glynn, S.J.
Praepositus Provinciae Marylandiae

NIHIL OBSTAT
Reverend Isidore Dixon, S.T.D.
Censor Deputatus

IMPRIMATUR
Reverend Msgr. William E. Lori, S.T.D.
Vicar General for the Archdiocese of Washington
9 September 1994

The *nihil obstat* and *imprimatur* are official declarations that a book or pamphlet is free of doctrinal or moral error. No implication is contained therein that those who have granted the *nihil obstat* and the *imprimatur* agree with the content, opinions, or statements expressed.

Printed in the United States of America

09 08 07 06 05 04   7 6 5 4 3 2 1

Library of Congress Cataloging-in-Publication Data

Fitzmyer, Joseph A.
   Spiritual exercises based on Paul's epistle to the Romans / Joseph A. Fitzmyer.
      p.   cm.
   Includes bibliographical references and index.
   ISBN 0-8028-2673-3
   1. Bible. N.T. Romans — Commentaries. 2. Spiritual exercises. I. Title.
BS2665.3.F54   1995
248.3 —
dc20   95-8650
                                                                         CIP

The Publisher gratefully acknowledges use of the following materials: excerpts from the poetic English translation of the Pentecost sequence, ©1964 United States Catholic Conference (formerly National Catholic Welfare Conference), Washington, D.C. 20017. Used with permission; excerpts from the Anchor Bible series (no. 33), *Romans: A New Translation with Introduction and Commentary*, by Joseph A. Fitzmyer, S.J., with permission from DOUBLEDAY, a division of Bantam Doubleday Dell Publishing Group, Inc.; excerpts from *The Spiritual Exercises of Saint Ignatius: A Translation and Commentary*, by G. E. Ganss, Chicago, Illinois: Loyola University, 1992, published by the Institute of Jesuit Sources, St. Louis, Missouri; excerpts from the *Revised Psalms of the New American Bible*, ©1991 by the Confraternity of Christian Doctrine, Washington, D.C. 20017. Used with permission. All rights reserved.

Preface

This book was published originally in 1995, and the opportunity of reprinting it gives me the chance to revise the preface to it. The book came into being from the realization that the Pauline teaching in the Epistle to the Romans has often been neglected in modern treatments of Christian spirituality. For instance, one looks in vain in a recent dictionary of spirituality for an article on Paul or Pauline spirituality, not to mention one on Romans and the influence it could have on that aspect of human life.[1] So I tried to remedy that neglect by casting Paul's teaching in the Epistle to the Romans in a form that people who are accustomed to making a spiritual retreat would find more suitable to their reflection or meditation.

Centuries ago, the author of the Second Letter of Peter counselled his readers, "Consider the forbearance of the Lord as salvation, as our beloved brother Paul, according to the wisdom given to him, also wrote to you, speaking of these things, as he does in all his letters. There are in them some things hard to understand that the ignorant and unstable distort to their own destruction, just as they do the other Scriptures" (3:15-16). The author seems to be referring to Rom 2:4, where Paul speaks of the wealth of God's "kindness, forbearance, and patience" in a context of the day of divine judgment. The things that are "hard to understand" in Paul's letters are undoubtedly part of the reason why Pauline spiritual teaching is often neglected. And yet there is much in the Epistle to the Romans that can be understood quite easily, for Paul himself once said in another letter, "We write for you nothing but what you can read and understand; I hope that you will understand completely" (2 Cor 1:13).

One should also recall, however, the story of the Ethiopian eunuch, whom Philip the evangelist encountered reading the

1

fourth Servant Song of Isaiah 53. When Philip asked him whether
he understood the words of Isaiah that he was reading, the Ethiopian replied, "How should I be able, unless someone guides me?"
(Acts 8:31). Having written a detailed commentary on the Epistle
to the Romans, I then attempted to recast Paul's teaching in the
Epistle in a more reflective form in this book.

The title of this book includes the words "Spiritual Exercises," and readers who are familiar with *The Spiritual Exercises of
Saint Ignatius of Loyola*[2] will recognize that the two words are borrowed from the title of his booklet, which has been of tremendous value in helping people to grow spiritually in union with
God through Jesus Christ. It is not, however, my intention to put
Paul's Epistle to the Romans into a Procrustean bed. Anyone who
reads and studies the Pauline epistles today realizes what a gold
mine they are for personal spiritual growth. In particular, Paul's
Epistle to the Romans, if read critically yet meditatively, is a tremendous source for prayer and reflection on the human condition and about a Christian's relationship to God. Almost all the is-
sues that surface in the Ignatian *Spiritual Exercises* as components
or problems of that human condition are treated in Paul's writings, and most of them in the Epistle to the Romans. One may
have to substitute Pauline modes of abstract expression for
Ignatian contemplations or meditations on concrete incidents in
the Gospel stories of the life and ministry of Jesus of Nazareth,
and one will not find passages in the Pauline letters corresponding to the "contemplations" or "mysteries" of the Second, Third,
and Fourth Weeks of the Ignatian *Exercises*. The thrust of the Epistle to the Romans, however, is such that one can follow it and find
in this epistle the Pauline way of putting many of the things that
preoccupy Ignatius in his *Spiritual Exercises,* for there is a striking
affinity in both writings.

In a sense, the purpose of the two writings is different, and
this has to be kept in mind. For Ignatius, the *Spiritual Exercises*
were mainly conceived as a means to make an "election," a means
of making a choice about one's state in life, how one should live
in the future, or as a means "of seeking and finding God's will in
the ordering of our life for the salvation of our soul" (§1.4). Such
a purpose will not be found in the Epistle to the Romans. This
Paul wrote rather to introduce himself to the Christians of Rome,

whom he hoped to visit in the coming months, and to set forth for them his understanding of the Christian gospel, his missionary reflections on the power of God's gospel. The Ignatian *Spiritual Exercises*, however, are often made with a less fundamental purpose in mind, simply as a means to renew or revitalize one's spiritual life, for instance, in the annual retreat made by many persons (priests, religious, or layfolk). It is mainly for such persons that this set of exercises based on the Epistle to the Romans is now being offered. Many of the topics that Paul discusses in this epistle are easily adapted to such renewal and revitalization. Even though Paul has presented his discussion of them in letter form, they can easily be used as the basis of meditation, for exercitants who use the epistle can easily imagine Paul addressing themselves, and the application of his ideas to themselves can be the source of fruitful meditation, consideration, and reform of one's life.

It is not my purpose, then, to bend the Epistle to the Romans to the structure of the Ignatian *Spiritual Exercises*. That is why I have entitled this treatment *Spiritual Exercises Based on the Epistle to the Romans*. I shall borrow at times from Ignatius elements of his exercises and query the Pauline text accordingly, but my concern above all is to let Paul speak to modern exercitants. After the first introductory exercise, which is generic, the others will follow the buildup of the Epistle to the Romans itself. When elements in the Ignatian *Exercises* are similar to or echo Pauline ideas, reference will be made to them in order that an Ignatian focus may also color the meditation on the words and teaching of Paul, because that focus is not totally alien to Paul.

On occasion, passages will be cited from other Pauline letters that bolster up what the Apostle may say in Romans, for, even if Romans is the best formulation of most of Pauline teaching, there are items that he does not treat in this letter, and sometimes he formulates things better in other writings. Such passages will be introduced at times to enhance the meditation on Romans. An effort will be made, however, not to introduce considerations from other New Testament writers, lest the Pauline character of the meditations be obscured or the thrust of Romans be tampered with. Even though John or Luke may teach something similar at times, or perhaps even phrase things better than Paul has, to import such extraneous material would obscure the Pauline thrust, which has its own importance.

It will not be possible to meditate on all the intricacies of the dense text of the Epistle to the Romans. My intention, then, is to select and highlight those aspects of the text of the Epistle that lend themselves readily to a series of twenty-four meditations so that the exercitant who uses this book will indeed capture the spirit and teaching of Romans, if not all its detail. Each exercise is subdivided into numbered paragraphs, which will provide separate sections on which the exercitant may find it profitable to pause and reflect. There is certainly food for meditation in almost all of them, even when I have not sought explicitly to suggest the pertinence or application of a given paragraph by adding reflective comments. The number of twenty-four exercises is used as a convenient way of dividing the topics for meditation into three exercises a day for an eight-day retreat. The exercises vary in length, and they can obviously be combined at times, should one want to use them for a retreat of less than eight days. If one should use the exercises for a shorter retreat, one should concentrate on the exercises based on Romans 1–8 (Exercises 1-18), since those that follow (Exercises 19-24) are of less importance; but in no case should Exercises 14-18 be omitted.

The one who uses this book will be able to find further explanation of what may be puzzling in Paul's text in my commentary on the Epistle.[3] What is being presented here should be used along with that commentary, because it fills out the meaning of the Pauline ideas that this book seeks to present in meditative form. The translation of Romans used in this book is drawn from that commentary. At the end of each exercise a reference will be given to corresponding pages in that commentary, which will be profitable for further reading and reflection. Exercitants will also do well to familiarize themselves with the synthetic sketch of "Pauline Teaching in Romans" found in the Introduction to the commentary (pp. 103-43).

Having often used the Epistle to the Romans in my own retreats in recent years, I have been trying to make the meditations and reflections on this important Pauline letter serve a more immediate spiritual goal. This is why I have fitted each exercise with questions, questions that arise from topics in the sections of the

Epistle on which the foregoing considerations have been made, and questions that may spark further personal application. At the end of each there is also a "colloquy" (the term is borrowed from Ignatius' use of it). It is often a psalm that echoes some of the ideas in the preceding exercise. The exercitant may find it more profitable to substitute some other form of colloquy.

Acknowledgements: I am indebted to the Permissions Department of Doubleday, a division of Bantam Doubleday Dell Publishing Group, Inc., of New York, for the right to use here the translation of the Epistle to the Romans, which is found in my commentary, mentioned above, and also to use some of the comments and notes in this new and different form.

I am also indebted to the Confraternity of Christian Doctrine of Washington, DC, for permission to quote a number of psalms from *The Revised Psalms of the New American Bible* (New York: Catholic Publishing Co., 1991); and to the Institute of Jesuit Sources of St. Louis, MO, for permission to quote passages of the Ignatian exercises from George E. Ganss, *The Spiritual Exercises of Saint Ignatius: A Translation and Commentary* (Chicago, IL: Loyola University, 1992).

I must also express my gratitude to J. R. Donahue, S.J., who read through an early draft of this book and gave me wise counsel, and to Messrs. William B. Eerdmans, Jr., Samuel E. Eerdmans, and Michael Thomson for their interest in the book and their desire to see it reprinted.

Joseph A. Fitzmyer, S.J.
Professor Emeritus, Biblical Studies
The Catholic University of America
Washington, DC 20064

Resident at:
Jesuit Community, Georgetown University
Washington, DC 20057-1200

*Spiritual Exercises
Based on Paul's
Epistle to the
Romans*

EXERCISE 1

The Purpose of Spiritual Exercises

1.1 In his introductory observation Ignatius of Loyola speaks of the purpose of the *Spiritual Exercises* as a way of "preparing and disposing our soul to rid itself of all disordered affections and...of seeking and finding God's will in the ordering of our life for the salvation of our soul" (§1.4). Again he speaks of it as "the conquest of self and the ordering of one's life, without reaching a decision through some disordered affection" (§21.1). As Ignatius had compared his "spiritual exercises" to various bodily exercises (§1.3: talking a walk, traveling on foot, running), so Paul does, perhaps even more expressively. In effect, Ignatius' formulation is an echo of what Paul wrote to the Christians of Corinth,

> Do you not know that runners in the stadium all run in the race, but only one wins the prize? Run so as to win. Every athlete exercises discipline in every way. They do it to win a perishable crown, but we an imperishable one. Thus I do not run aimlessly; I do not fight as if I were shadowboxing. No, I drive my body and train it, for fear that, after having preached to others, I myself should be disqualified (1 Cor 9:24-27).

Paul recognizes that our human life resembles a race, run in pursuit of a goal, and the runner must discipline the body to curtail his or her disordered affections or inordinate attachments. Paul alludes to the prize that a runner in a race seeks to win, the "garland" made of leaves, bestowed in token of athletic prowess and victory in ancient Greek games and contests, especially at Olympus, Delphi, Nemea, and Isthmia (cf. 2 Tim 2:5; 1 Tim 4:8).[4] But those crowns soon withered and died, for they were made of perishable substance. But the "imperishable crown," of which Paul speaks, is none other than eternal life, what is called elsewhere in the New Testament the "crown of life" (Jas 1:2; Rev 2:10). It denotes what Ignatius meant by the "salvation of our soul," a later, especially medieval way of phrasing the purpose of human life. Whether we live so as to save our soul or to win an imperishable crown, it is all summed succinctly in Paul's counsel, "Run so as to win." (The goal proposed to us is clear, but we must reflect and meditate on it more in order to discipline ourselves to attain such a goal and to let that goal motivate the activity of our lives as it should.) For there is always the danger of running "aimlessly," of which Paul warns us.

The metaphor is changed, when Paul speaks of "shadow-boxing." For Paul realizes that one can be merely beating the air, as one is so engaged in other pursuits, even that of preaching to others, that one can forget about one's own goal in life. In this regard one can be merely shadowboxing. One has to cope with reality, and what more existential question is there in life than the goal of it all? This, then, is the purpose of the spiritual exercises we are engaged in. They are to recall to us (the seriousness of the pursuit in which we are involved.)

1.2 Paul once wrote to the Christians of Philippi:

> It is not that I have already achieved it or have already attained perfect maturity, but I continue in my pursuit in hope that I may possess it, since I have indeed been taken possession of by Christ [Jesus]. Brothers, I for my part do not consider myself to have taken possession. Just one thing: forgetting what lies behind but straining forward to what lies ahead, I continue my pursuit toward the goal, the prize of God's upward calling, in Christ Jesus. Let us, then, who are "perfectly mature" adopt this attitude. If you have a different attitude, this too God will reveal to you. Only, with regard to what we have attained, continue on the same course (Phil 3:12-16).

Here Paul formulates the goal of Christian life a little differently. It is still something to be pursued, something to be run after, but he now speaks of it in terms of "perfect maturity." Toward such a goal, he realizes, most Christians are striving, but they have not yet taken possession of it. There is also the other side of the coin: the goal is not so much something to be possessed as it is to be taken into possession by Christ himself. Paul is trying to formulate the way Christ Jesus should dominate the life of a Christian. That is the goal for which one strives, "the prize of God's upward calling, in Christ Jesus." One reaches, then, "perfect maturity" when one is possessed by Christ, when Christ takes possession of the Christian.

Yet Paul knows that some individuals may have a "different attitude," an inordinate attachment in life preventing them from attaining such a goal, preventing them from being possessed by Christ. He assures us that "God will reveal" that too to us, if we continue in the same pursuit and on the same course. This, then, becomes the purpose of such "straining forward" in Paul's mind; in effect, it is the purpose of the course of spiritual exercises that one is beginning.

For we set before ourselves the goal of all human life, and propose that goal to ourselves in our meditations. In such exercises we return to what is basic and fundamental. We look too for the attitude that is "different," for the area in which we must discipline the body, for the inordinate attachments or disordered affections that prevent us from seeking and finding the will of God. We know that we cannot dispose our lives on our own. We may seek to free ourselves of self and inordinate affections and to regulate our lives in conformity with Christ Jesus, who seeks to make us his own. But this we cannot do by pulling ourselves up by our own bootstraps. Freedom from self and unruly attachment is nothing else but an openness to God who himself will reveal that "different attitude," and to the grace that is now inviting us to consider it.

1.3 This too is what Paul means when he counsels us, "Work out your salvation with fear and trembling" (Phil 2:12b). To achieve salvation or to save our souls is no easy task in human life. One has to labor at it, and there is that element of life that Paul calls "fear and trembling," because no one can be sure that the goal has been attained. Our striving toward such a goal must be an anxious concern. For that reason Paul immediately adds, "For God is the one who, for *his* good purpose, is at work in you both to desire and to work" (Phil 2:13). With all that "fear and trembling," which has to accompany our striving, God is at work in us with prevenient grace, especially when we undertake such spiritual exercises. God will inspire us to desire what is good for us and enable us to do what we are to do, in order to discover that different attitude. Paul thus calls us as Christians to cooperate with the grace of God to be given to us during the course of such exercises. "I am convinced that he who began a good work in you will bring it to completion at the day of Jesus Christ" (Phil 1:6). So Paul assures us of the divine concern that is operative in our lives

1.4 With such advice Paul wrote to the Christians of Corinth and Philippi, but in the epistle he sent to the Christians of Rome he invokes an eschatological consideration when he counsels,

> The night is far spent, and day has drawn near. Let us cast off, then, the deeds of darkness and don the armor of light, that we may conduct ourselves with decency as befits the daylight, not in orgies or drunkenness, not in debauchery or sexual excess, not in quarreling or jealousy. Put on rather the Lord Jesus Christ and give no more thought to the desires of the flesh (Rom 13:12-14).
>
> For none of us lives for himself, and none of us dies for himself. If we live, we live for the Lord; and if we die, we die for the Lord. So whether we live or die, we belong to the Lord (Rom 14:7-8).

Paul's formulation in Romans is much more figurative and christological. Indeed, it makes Ignatius' comparison with physical exercises sound almost philosophical. But in reality the two are saying the same thing about the conduct of human life. The Pauline way of stating the goal of that conduct suffuses and gives added meaning to Ignatius' way.

The first quotation from Romans comes from the eschatological comment that Paul makes in chap. 13, immediately after he has set forth the relation of Christians to civil authorities (13:1-7) and the way that love must dominate Christian life, as it fulfills the law (13:8-10). Having commented on these two facets of life, Paul adds his exhortation about human life as vigilance and decent conduct that befits the daylight (13:11-14). He makes use of the apocalyptic contrast of day and night, of light and darkness, as symbols of ethical conduct, of good and evil. He thus counsels us to rid ourselves of all inordinate attachments and disordered affections: to "cast off the deeds of darkness and don the armor of light." He gives examples of such disordered affections or "deeds of darkness": orgies, drunkenness, debauchery, sexual excess, quarreling, and jealousy. One could easily add other similar deeds that plague all our lives. He urges us to put on the Lord Jesus Christ as armor against such "desires of the flesh." Putting on the Lord Jesus will mean allowing him to dominate our lives, letting him take possession of us.

When Augustine, the African teacher of rhetoric, tells of his conversion to Christianity, he describes something that happened to him in Milan: When he heard a child singing in a nearby house, "Tolle lege, tolle lege" ("Take up and read; take up and read"), he picked up a scroll lying at his feet and his eyes fell upon vv. 13-14 of this passage in Romans (*Confessions* 8.12; CSEL 33. 194-95). Thus God's grace came to him in the song of a Milanese child, and these verses of Romans 13 sparked the conversion of the great Christian whose teaching has shaped western theology. Those same words can have a similar effect in our lives.

The second quotation comes from the section in Romans in which Paul comments on what is expected of Christians living together in solidarity as members of a Christian community, on the love owed by the strong to the weak in it. In speaking of that solidarity, he again states the goal of Christian life: "Whether we live or die, we belong to the Lord" (14:8), for none of us lives for himself or herself alone. Belonging to the Lord makes demands on how we conduct ourselves in relation to others; this calls for ridding ourselves of inordinate attachments also in relation to others.

The Pauline passages quoted contain further details for our meditation and reflection. They must suffuse our thinking in this preliminary consideration of what we are about in such a course of exercises. They must enable us to beg God for the grace of disposition, for the grace to see what the "different attitude" or disordered affection is that is withholding us from attaining our goal of perfect maturity, our goal of being possessed by Christ.

Questions: How conscious am I of the real goal of my life? Of orienting all that I do to the attaining of that goal? Of the discipline needed to achieve it? Is "perfect maturity" in Christian life something that I have ever thought of? Have I been running aimlessly? Do I consider that I have been living for the Lord? Do I have possibly a "different attitude"? One that I ask God to make known to me during the course of these exercises?

COLLOQUY: PSALM 25

> I wait for you, O LORD;
> > I lift up my soul to my God.
> In you I trust; do not let me be disgraced;
> > do not let my enemies gloat over me.
> No one is disgraced who waits for you,
> > but only those who lightly break faith.
> Make known to me your ways, LORD;
> > teach me your paths.
> Guide me in your truth and teach me,
> > for you alone are God my savior.
> For you I wait all the long day,
> > because of your goodness, LORD.
> Remember your compassion and love, O LORD;
> > for they are ages old.
> Remember no more the sins of my youth;
> > remember me only in light of your love.
> Good and upright is the LORD,
> > who shows sinners the way,
> Guides the humble rightly,
> > and teaches the humble the way.
> All the paths of the LORD are faithful love
> > toward those who honor the covenant demands.
> For the sake of your name, LORD,
> > pardon my guilt, though it is great.
> Who are those who fear the LORD?
> > God shows them the way to choose.
> They live well and prosper,
> > and their descendants inherit the land.
> The counsel of the LORD belongs to the faithful;
> > the covenant instructs them.
> My eyes are ever upon the LORD,
> > who frees my feet from the snare.
> Look upon me, have pity on me,
> > for I am alone and afflicted.

Relieve the troubles of my heart;
    bring me out of my distress.
Put an end to my affliction and suffering;
    take away all my sins.
See how many are my enemies,
    see how fiercely they hate me.
Preserve my life and rescue me;
    do not let me be disgraced, for I trust in you.
Let honesty and virtue preserve me;
    I wait for you, O LORD.

God's Gospel Concerning His Son (1:1-15)

✓ **1:1 Paul, a slave of Christ Jesus, called to be an apostle, set apart for God's gospel—2 which he promised long ago through his prophets in the sacred Scriptures, 3 concerning his Son who was born of David's stock by natural descent, 4 but established as the Son of God with power by a spirit of holiness as of his resurrection from the dead, Jesus Christ our Lord, 5 through whom we have received the grace of apostleship to promote a commitment of faith among all the Gentiles on behalf of his name, 6 among whom you too were called to belong to Jesus Christ—7 to all the beloved of God in Rome, called to be his dedicated people, grace and peace to you from God our Father and the Lord Jesus Christ.** ✓

8 First of all, I give thanks to my God through Jesus Christ for all of you, because your faith is proclaimed in all the world. 9 Now the God, whom I worship with my spirit in the evangelization of his Son, is my witness that I constantly make mention of you.

10 I beg always in my prayers that somehow, by God's will, I may at length succeed in coming to you. 11 I yearn to see you in order to pass on to you some spiritual gift that you may be strengthened—12 or rather that we may be mutually encouraged by each other's faith, both yours and mine. 13 I do not want you to be unaware, brothers, of how often I have proposed to come to you though I have been hindered up to now, in order to reap some fruit also among you as among the other Gentiles. 14 Both to Greeks and to barbarians I am

indebted, both to the wise and to the unlearned! [15] Hence my eagerness to preach the gospel also to you who are in Rome.

2.1 In the prescript of the epistle to the Romans Paul sends his greetings to the Christians of Rome, identifying himself in a very formal way, which he does not do in most other letters, because he realizes that many of them do not know him personally.

Paul refers to himself as "a slave of Christ Jesus," by which he may mean his dedicated service to Christ as a Christian, but more probably he identifies himself as *doulos*, "slave," imitating the title used of Old Testament figures who served Yahweh in a special way (Moses, 2 Kgs 18:12; Joshua, Judg 2:8; Abraham, Ps 105:2; David, 2 Sam 7:5). Thus he stands in a line of illustrious forebears, servants of God, but he transfers that service to "Christ Jesus."

Paul also identifies himself as "one called to be an apostle" (1:1), i.e. someone sent by divine authority as an emissary commissioned for an exclusive mission. This he explains in the third designation of himself, "set apart for God's gospel" (probably alluding to the call of such Old Testament figures as the Servant in Isa 49:1 or Jeremiah in Jer 1:5): "He who had set me apart before I was born and had called me through his grace was pleased to reveal his Son to me, so that I might preach him among the Gentiles" (Gal 1:15-16). Thus Paul acknowledged "the grace of apostleship" (1:5) that he had received, his call and commission "to promote a commitment of faith among all the Gentiles on behalf of his name" (1:6). As "the apostle of the Gentiles" (11:13), Paul was keenly aware of this special mission. He was "set apart" and "called" by God, who even graced him with a revelation of his own Son, all for the sake of a mission. As such, he writes to the Christians of Rome, whom he recognizes as predominantly of Gentile background.

None of us shares that precise apostolic role in God's salvific plan that Paul had, but we too are called by God to carry out diverse functions in it, as Paul himself acknowledged in writing to the Christians of Corinth, "Everyone should live as the Lord has assigned, just as God has called each one.... Everyone should continue before God in the state in which he was called" (1 Cor 7:17, 24). As Paul was aware that his apostolic commission was a "grace," so he invites his readers to realize the "grace" involved in the call that each of them has received from God. Such a realization is crucial at the beginning of a retreat or a course of spiritual exercises. It calls for an awareness of the special "grace" that each one may be receiving, a call to a level of greater faith and commitment to the service of God and his Son. For as Paul uses the word *charis*, it denotes primarily the "favor" that God has shown toward him and all others so endowed. For this is the "grace" of vocation, the grace by which God calls each individual to a certain function in the Christian community. It is what the theologians of later date would call *gratia gratis data*, the grace freely given for a function to be performed in the community. It is different from the *gratia gratum faciens*, the grace that makes one pleasing in God's sight, i.e. sanctifying grace. The two aspects are not the same, and the two may be present in an individual in differing degrees. In both cases there is the divine call for cooperation, for cooperation in one's personal holiness and sanctification, and for cooperation in the function or vocation to which one is called.

(2.2) In the course of this formal epistolary introduction Paul enunciates some of the fundamental teachings which he will develop in the course of the epistle. Among them is what he calls "the gospel of God," for this idea is basic to his whole approach to Christian life, nothing less than than the good news about Christ Jesus and what he has done for humanity.

For Paul, "the gospel" involves a new development in God's salvific plan for human life. The divine salvific plan for God's people saw realization in many forms in the course of Israel's history. Now, however, it has been made manifest that that plan also concerns Jesus of Nazareth. It came to a new and historic realization in the ministry, passion, death, resurrection, and exaltation of God's own Son. This is the gospel that Paul preaches, the good news that comes from God himself, the "gospel of God." It is only another way of saying what Ignatius would later call "the will of God in the ordering of our life" (§1.4). For God's will in the ordering of our lives is nothing other than the concrete implementation of the divine salvific plan.

Yet it is also "the gospel of his Son" (1:9), not only the good news about God's Son, but also the good news that that Son has brought to humanity (15:18-19). In other words, "gospel" is Paul's one-word summary of the Christ-event, the significance and meaning that the person and lordship of Jesus have for our existence and that of all human beings. It is the concrete formulation of God's will for the disposition of human life. That too is why Paul speaks so personally about it as "my gospel" (2:16). Similarly, it has to become for each of us "my gospel," the good news coming from God as guidance for my life and my conduct on this earth.

2.3 Paul realizes, moreover, that his preaching of this gospel has been a cultic, priestly act of worship offered to God (1:9; 15:16). In preaching it, he has been serving God in a way similar to what the priests of the Jerusalem Temple of old did in their daily and weekly service there. Their service was one of dedication and sacrifice to God in his awesome Temple presence, as they carried out their cultic rituals to the glory and worship of his name. The preaching of the gospel was for Paul likewise a cultic activity, one by which he adored and worshiped God. Similarly, the living out of the gospel in our own lives must become an act of worship that we too offer to God, in imitation of Paul. "Be imitators of me as I am of Christ" (1 Cor 11:1).

2.4 Paul related the gospel that he preached to the salvific plan of God. That gospel was for him something "promised long ago through his prophets in the sacred Scriptures" (1:2). What prophets of old had proclaimed included utterances which were translated in the Greek Old Testament as *euangelion* or with the verb *euangelizesthai*, the terms from which the Christian "gospel" eventually developed. For instance, Second Isaiah proclaimed consolation to those returning from Babylonian Captivity: "How beautiful upon the mountains are the feet of the one who brings glad tidings (*euangelizomenos agatha*), announcing peace, bearing good news, announcing salvation, and saying to Zion 'Your God is King!'" (52:7). In this way Paul sees the prophetic utterances of Israel's prophets as a *praeparatio evangelica*, a mode of preparing Israel and all humanity for the gospel, the good news of Christ Jesus. "I do all things for the sake of the gospel that I may share in its blessings" (1 Cor 9:23).

Because that gospel is related to God's salvific plan, it

concerns Jesus as God's Son "born of David's stock by natural descent" (1:3). In other words, the heritage of the Jewish people of old founded in the Davidic dynasty was likewise part of God's plan. His Son was destined to be born of David's royal stock, to bring to humanity a new mode of salvation. This has been brought even by a Jew of such illustrious background and heritage.

2.5 Sometimes Paul speaks of "the truth of the gospel," i.e. that truth that the gospel exercises in human life, which it seeks to norm. For the gospel is not only revelatory or proclamatory, but it is normative. In Gal 2:14 Paul rebuked even Peter publicly, because he was not walking according to "the truth of the gospel" (see also Gal 2:5). For there is "no other gospel" (Gal 1:7). "Even if we, or an angel from heaven, should preach to you a gospel contrary to that which we have preached to you, let him be anathema" (Gal 1:8).

2.6 In reflecting on "God's gospel," one should ponder "the commitment of faith," of which Paul speaks (1:5). For "faith" is the proper response of a human being to the gospel. It is the acceptance of the challenge with which the gospel accosts us. It begins as a listening to the "word" that is preached (10:8): "faith comes from what is heard" (10:17). It thus begins with an intellectual assent to the proclamation that "Jesus is Lord" (10:9): one has to profess with one's lips that Jesus is Lord and believe in one's heart that God raised him from the dead in order to be saved. But what began as intellectual assent has to end with the commitment of faith, with what is often called "the obedience of faith." This means the engagement of the whole person, a dedication stemming from the very depths of one's being.

2.7 In writing to the Christians of Rome, Paul flatters them by acknowledging their Christian commitment: "Your faith is proclaimed in all the world" (1:8). He gives thanks to God because of it. This thanksgiving addressed to God stresses for us the importance of faith in Christ Jesus as the response to the gospel, the radical role that the gospel has to play in Christian life. In writing to the Thessalonians, Paul said, "We also thank God constantly that, when you received the word of God which you heard from us, you accepted it not as the word of human beings, but as what it really is, the word of God, which is at work in you believers" (1 Thess 2:13). This too explains the reason why Paul, who has been hindered from coming to Rome earlier in his apostolic career, is now anxious to come there: "My eagerness to preach the gospel also to you who are in Rome" (1:15). He would want to preach it to us too.

2.8 God's gospel now invites us to meditate upon it and to listen to the message of his Son, descended from David's stock, and now established as "the Son of God with power by a spirit of holiness as of his resurrection from the dead" (1:4). For that is what the gospel of God proclaims to us. That gospel is going to reveal to us in these exercises how God's Son has been established "in power" on our behalf. "Thus it is written, 'The first man Adam became a living being'; the last Adam became a life-giving Spirit" (1 Cor 15:45). It is the risen Christ of whom Paul now speaks, and of the power that his resurrection has to vitalize our spiritual lives. This is how Christ influences us by his spirit of holiness and by his grace in the daily lives that we try to lead. That is why the entire message of the epistle to the Romans can be summed up as "God's gospel." Our task is to pray to be open to the message of that gospel, open to the power of his risen Son that it proclaims, and open to the graces that God will offer us through his Son in our response of faith.

2.9 Questions. How aware am I of the grace of God that has called me to my station in life? Do I really try to live as one so called and so graced? How operative has the good news of God's gospel been in my everyday life? Do I try to understand my daily tasks as a means of worshiping God as did Paul in preaching the gospel? Do I ever reflect on what the "commitment of faith" should mean in my response to God's gospel-invitation? Am I sufficiently disposed to hear the gospel as summoning me to a deepening of my faith? Am I as open to the challenge of that good news as were the Christians of Rome for whose faith Paul thanked God?

COLLOQUY: PSALM 19

> The heavens declare the glory of God.
>> the sky proclaims its builder's craft.
> One day to the next conveys that message,
>> one night to the next imparts that knowledge.

There is no word or sound;
    no voice is heard;
Yet their report goes forth through all the earth,
    their message, to the end of the world.
God has pitched a tent there for the sun;
    it comes forth like a bridegroom from his chamber,
    and like an athlete joyfully runs its course.
From one end of the heavens it comes forth;
    its course runs through to the other;
    nothing escapes its heat.
The law of the LORD is perfect,
    refreshing the soul.
The decree of the LORD is trustworthy,
    giving wisdom to the simple.
The precepts of the LORD are right,
    rejoicing the heart.
The command of the LORD is clear,
    enlightening the eye.
The fear of the LORD is pure,
    enduring forever.
The statutes of the LORD are true,
    all of them just;
More desirable than gold,
    than a hoard of purest gold.
Sweeter also than honey
    or drippings from the comb.
By them your servant is instructed;
    obeying them brings much reward.
Who can detect heedless failings?
    Cleanse me from my unknown faults.
But from willful sins keep your servant;
    let them never control me.
Then shall I be blameless,
    innocent of grave sin.
Let the words of my mouth meet with your favor,
    keep the thoughts of my heart before you,
LORD, my rock and my redeemer.

See further *Romans*, 227-52, 109-10, 112-13.

Through the Gospel the Uprightness of God Is Revealed (1:16-17)

¹⁶ Now I am not ashamed of the gospel. It is God's power unleashed for the salvation of everyone who believes, for the Jew first but also for the Greek. ¹⁷ For in it is revealed the uprightness of God, through faith and for faith, as it stands written, *The one who is upright shall find life through faith.* **ᵃ**
   ᵃ Hab 2:4

3.1 Paul now invites us to meditate on the content of God's gospel: on the uprightness of God revealed in it and what flows from that divine characteristic for the salvation of all human beings who are summoned to faith by it. In these two verses Paul announces the theme of the whole epistle: the revelation of God's uprightness in view of the salvation of all human beings who come to belief in God's gospel. These two verses continue the idea of the "preaching" of the gospel of v. 15. What Paul now proclaims in vv. 16-17 he will spell out in great detail in the following eleven chapters of the epistle, in 1:18–11:36.

The thesis of Romans, now before us in this exercise, is fundamental to Paul's way of thinking. As we reflect on it, it thrusts us back onto the basic content of the gospel, the new divine plan of salvation. It reads differently from "First Principle and Foundation," with which Ignatius prefaced his "First Week." That Ignatian prelude is a resolutely philosophical epitome of the whole of the *Spiritual Exercises.* But in a sense, it acts as does the thesis of Romans. It forces us to examine the fundamentals of our spiritual lives. Yet neither Ignatius nor Paul makes mention of Christ in their theses. When the title "our Lord" is used there by Ignatius, it is given in Old Testament style to "God" (as in Ps 8:2,10; Neh 10:30), who, if it were not for this Old Testament usage, could be the God of philosophers. The difference between the two theses stems from the context of the two writings, as Paul reflects on the missionary possibilities and spiritual ramifications of the gospel that he has been preaching and as Ignatius seeks to formulate for Renaissance man the goal of human life. Yet both of them, each in his own way, are striving to bring us back to basics, to the fundamentals of the spiritual life.

3.2 Paul begins with a gross understatement, "I am not ashamed of the gospel" (1:16). Given what it meant to him, how could he have been ashamed of it? For, as he explains, it is not just a message or a word that he is passing on to the Christians of Rome, even with his own guarantee. Rather, it is a *dynamis*, "a power," a power that God has unleashed in the world of humanity, a power that actively accosts human beings, challenging them to accept it with faith. Thus Paul stresses the dynamic character of "God's gospel." It is a force unleashed among humanity enabling human beings in a new way to come to salvation, to save their souls. Paul is not ashamed of proclaiming this gospel, because he openly announces it and acknowledges that it is his way of proclaiming how God has intervened anew on our behalf.

3.3 That gospel is also apocalyptic, because it reveals something about God. It tells humanity about God's "uprightness" or about God's "righteousness," a divine quality or attribute because of which God now seeks in a new way to bring about the salvation of humanity. In the Hebrew Scriptures of old, many attributes or qualities of God are described: God's love, mercy, uprightness, wrath, justice, fidelity, longsuffering, loving kindness, power. Of these Paul singles out in Romans mainly three, God's wrath, God's love, and God's uprightness or righteousness. He begins with divine uprightness, but will soon make mention of divine wrath (1:18).

The Greek expression *dikaiosynē theou* is often translated as "the righteousness of God," which is an acceptable rendering, provided it is rightly understood. To the ears of English-speaking persons, however, it may sound like God's self-righteousness, which is the last thing that Paul would mean by it. In the Old Testament God is often said to be *ṣaddîq*, "righteous, upright" (Ps 116:5; 119:137; 129:4; Deut 32:4), and his *ṣedeq* or *ṣĕdāqāh*, "righteousness, uprightness," is often mentioned (Isa 46:13; Ps 35:28; Job 36:3; Hos 2:21). It is the quality whereby Yahweh is depicted, when he is involved in a lawsuit with rebellious Israel, as judging it and displaying his "righteousness" or "uprightness" toward it. It is the quality that is characteristic of his judicial or forensic activity. Moreover, in the writings of the postexilic period, it acquires an added nuance, the quality whereby God acquits his sinful people, manifesting toward them his gracious, salvific power in a just judgment. In Isa 46:13 "my righteousness" and "my salvation" stand in poetic parallelism: "I am bringing on my righteousness; my salvation shall not tarry." See also Isa 51:5,6; 56:1; 61:10; Ps 40:9-10. In this sense Yahweh is reckoned as *ṣaddîq*, "upright" (Ezra 9:15; Neh 9:8) and "righteous" in all that he has done (Dan 9:14), i.e. in all the ways that he has dealt with rebellious Israel.

In this last Old Testament sense Paul introduces the phrase "the uprightness of God" into the very thesis of Romans. He sums up the gospel that he proclaims as a revelation of this acquitting and saving quality of God. In this sense of a divine attribute or quality this phrase will be used again in Romans on several occasions. The gospel, then, is a power that God has unleashed into the world of humanity because it makes known the powerful activity of the upright and righteous God who seeks to acquit us.

3.4 In 2 Cor 5:21 Paul uses *dikaiosynē theou* in another sense, denoting the term of the process of justifying human beings. There he says, "[God] made him [Christ Jesus] to be sin who knew no sin, so that in him we might become the uprightness of God." In this verse of 2 Corinthians Paul expresses abstractly what he might otherwise say concretely: so that in Christ we might become upright in God's sight. The term of that process is an effect of what Christ Jesus has done for us; because of him we achieve the status of uprightness or rectitude before God's tribunal, or we are made upright in God's sight. This means that Paul has used the phrase "the righteousness of God" in two ways, of an attribute or quality in God, and of the gift that he has bestowed on humanity in Christ Jesus. Because of this double meaning, commentators differ at times about how it should be interpreted, even in Rom 1:17 (and more so in Rom 10:3). But because of what Paul will say in 3:5 and in 3:21-22 and because the phrase stands in parallelism here to "God's wrath" (1:18), it is best understood (both here and elsewhere in Romans) as a quality or characteristic of God.

3.5 What is of importance for our meditation and consideration is the gracious aspect of God that Paul singles out. God's uprightness is said to be revealed "for the salvation of everyone who believes, for the Jew first but also for the Greek." A prerogative of Israel is thus recognized, its priority in the gracious salvific plan of God. For the God that Paul worships and honors by the proclamation of the gospel is the God of Israel. But he is at pains to emphasize the universality of God's salvation, "for the salvation of everyone who believes," and yet he also acknowledges the priority given to the Jew, because the people of Israel have been for centuries, even prior to the Christ-event, the Chosen People of God. Now, however, Paul speaks of God's salvific activity being exercised toward Jew and Greek alike, toward "everyone who believes" (1:17). The "Jew" is mentioned "first" to recall to us Christians the Jewish heritage of what is being manifested to humanity, the Jewish heritage in which we are invited by the gospel to participate, the Jewish heritage of salvation that we share. The favor that God accorded Israel of old is now extended to "the Greek," to the non-Jew in the human race, to "everyone who believes." But it is in every case God's favor or grace revealing his uprightness.

3.6 In the Old Testament God is often spoken of as the *môšîa'*, "savior" of Israel (Isa 45:15; Zech 8:7) or as providing for Israel human "saviors" (Judg 3:9; 6:36). By such a designation was meant that Yahweh provided deliverance from harm or evil, whether physical, psychic, cataclysmic, national, or moral (= sin). That "salvation" was usually understood in a terrestrial sense, but in time it developed an eschatological nuance. In this sense Paul takes over the notion of "salvation," a deliverance from eschatological and moral evil.

"For everyone who believes," i.e. who comes to faith. At this point in Romans Paul does not express the object of that faith. That will be spelled out in 3:21-31, where it becomes faith in Christ Jesus, the Savior of all humanity. The qualities of God as upright and as Savior, known already in the Old Testament, now take on a new mode of manifestation: they become manifest for everyone, Jew and Greek alike, who learns to live in faith. This is being proclaimed by Paul to us as well: God's gospel has unleashed a salvific power that can change our lives, if our faith can measure up to it and accept it.

3.7 Paul adds a puzzling phrase, "through faith and for faith." It seems to mean that the entire process of salvation is now one of faith, of faith from start to finish. The double prepositional usage *ek* ("from")...*eis* ("to") often expresses a passage from one degree to another. Paul may well mean that God's new economy of salvation is shared in more and more by a faith that grows: from a beginning or inceptive faith to a more perfect or culminating faith. Or he may mean "through faith (and) for faith," understanding the first preposition (*ek*) as instrumental and the second (*eis*) as expressing purpose: the means by which a person shares in salvation is faith, and the purpose of the divine plan itself is to bring people to faith. In any case, it reveals the Pauline emphasis on the need of faith as the response to God's gospel in Christian life. For faith is something that cannot be neglected or trivialized in the spiritual life of a Christian. Thus Paul is inviting us to examine the extent to which we allow faith to play in our lives.

3.8 Finally, to bolster up his analysis of God's gospel and its call for a vital faith, Paul quotes Hab 2:4, "The one who is upright shall find life through faith." Paul had used the same verse in Gal 3:11b, and this repeated use of it, especially when he deals with justification, reveals how important that Old Testament verse was for his understanding of the gospel.

In the Book of Habakkuk, the words were uttered by the prophet to stress the value of the observance of the law as a form of fidelity to Yahweh. The Hebrew text of Habakkuk says, "But the righteous one shall live by his fidelity." The words formed part of Yahweh's reply to the complaint of the prophet about the continuing oppression of Judah. Chaldean invaders, who were about to enter the land of Judah and whose god was their might, were contrasted with the almost defenseless people of Judah, whose deliverance lay in fidelity to Yahweh. God thus assured Habakkuk that at the coming invasion the upright Judahite would find life through fidelity to Yahweh.

3.9 Such an understanding of Habakkuk's words received a significant interpretation in the Qumran community of Jews in the last pre-Christian centuries. After Hab 2:4 is quoted, the Qumran commentary on Habakkuk continues: "The interpretation of it concerns the observers of the law in the house of Judah, whom God shall deliver from the house of judgment because of their striving and their fidelity to the Teacher of Righteousness" (1QpHab 7:5–8:3). In this case, that Palestinian Jewish community understood the prophet's words to promise life not only for observance of the law, but also for fidelity to the teaching and person of a Jewish leader, otherwise unknown, but often referred to in Qumran writings as the Teacher of Righteousness. Paul's application of Habakkuk's words to the new form of deliverance that God is now providing through the teaching and person of a new Jewish leader thus stands within a genuine Jewish tradition of interpretation.

3.10 The Greek Old Testament changed the meaning of Habakkuk's words, and this in two ways. Some manuscripts of the Septuagint read: "But the righteous one shall live by my fidelity," i.e. by God's fidelity to his promises to assure "life" for the one who is upright or righteous. But other manuscripts read: "My righteous one shall live by fidelity," i.e. the one righteous in my [God's] sight shall find "life," or deliverance from the invaders. When, however, Paul quotes Habakkuk, he cites the text according to neither the Hebrew nor the Greek version. He not only drops the possessive pronoun, but understands Greek *pistis* not as "fidelity," but as "faith" in his own Christian sense, and he takes "life" to mean not deliverance from death or invasion, but a share in the risen life of Christ, as will become apparent later in Romans. In this way, Paul has wrested the words of Habakkuk from their context and made them serve his thesis of salvation through faith. In quoting Habakkuk, Paul illustrates what he wrote in Gal 3:8, "Scripture, foreseeing that God would justify the Gentiles through faith, preached the gospel beforehand to Abraham, saying, 'In you shall all the nations be blessed.'" By citing Habakkuk, Paul gives a concrete example of what he said in his introductory verses about

"God's gospel, which he promised long ago through his prophets in the sacred Scriptures" (1:2).

3.11 This quotation from the Old Testament thus emphasizes the role of faith in the economy of salvation that God has now initiated. For Paul and for all of us, faith has made a tremendous difference. Allegiance and fidelity to God has now taken on a new form. It is a call for an allegiance to God in a new dimension, which Paul will further explain in 3:21-31. Paul thus summons us again to examine the role of faith in our lives and in our daily conduct as our response to God's gospel. It is something that we may be tempted to take for granted, but in his view it is a factor that must assume a dominant influence.

Questions: How do I respond to God's gospel? Does faith as the response to it really vitalize my existence and my conduct? Am I ever ashamed of my faith in the Christian gospel? Have I ever reflected on God's uprightness or righteousness as exercised on my behalf? Do I really try to understand what it means to be acquitted of sinfulness in God's sight? Has my quest for salvation coped with the implications of what Paul makes known as God's gospel?

COLLOQUY: PSALM 96

> Sing to the LORD a new song;
> > sing to the LORD, all the earth.
> Sing to the LORD, bless his name;
> > announce his salvation day after day.
> Tell God's glory among the nations;
> > among all people, God's marvelous deeds.
> For great is the LORD and highly to be praised,
> > to be feared above all the gods.
> For the gods of the nations all do nothing,
> > but the LORD made the heavens.
> Splendor and power go before him;
> > power and grandeur are in his holy place.
> Give to the LORD, you families of nations,
> > give to the LORD glory and might;
> > give to the LORD the glory due his name!
> Bring gifts and enter his courts;
> > bow down to the LORD, splendid in holiness.

Tremble before God, all the earth;
 say among the nations: The LORD is king.
The world will surely stand fast, never to be moved.
 God rules the peoples with fairness.
Let the heavens be glad and the earth rejoice;
 let the sea and what fills it resound;
 let the plains be joyful and all that is in them.
Then let all the trees of the forest rejoice
 before the LORD who comes,
 who comes to govern the earth,
To govern the world with justice
 and the peoples with faithfulness.

See further *Romans*, 253-68, 105-7.

Pagan Humanity without the Gospel Is Subject to the Wrath of God (1:18-32)

[18] For God's wrath is being revealed from heaven against all the godlessness and wickedness of human beings who by such wickedness stifle the truth: [19] that what can be known about God is manifest to them. For God himself has made it evident for them. [20] Ever since the creation of the world his invisible qualities, his eternal power and divinity, have been perceived by reflection on what he has made. Consequently, such people are without excuse, [21] because, though they knew God, they did not glorify him as God or thank him. Instead, they were reduced to futile thinking, and their misguided minds were steeped in darkness. [22] Pretending to be wise, they became fools [23] and exchanged the glory of the immortal God for an image shaped like a mortal human being, like birds, four-footed creatures, or reptiles.

[24] For this reason God delivered them over to the craving of their hearts for impurity that their bodies might be degraded among them. [25] These people exchanged the truth about God for a lie and reverenced and worshiped the creature rather than the creator—blest be he forever! Amen. / [26] For this reason God delivered them over to disgraceful passions. Their women exchanged natural intercourse for that against nature; [27] and their men likewise abandoned natural relations with women and burned with lust for one another—males committing shameless acts with males and being paid in turn in their own persons the wage suited to their deviation.

²⁸ **As they did not see fit to acknowledge God, he delivered them over to a base mentality and to improper conduct.** ²⁹ **They became filled with every sort of wickedness, evil, greed, and malice; they were full of envy, murder, strife, craftiness, and spite. They became tale-bearers,** ³⁰ **slanderers, God-haters, insolent, haughty, and boastful; contrivers of evil, rebels against parents,** ³¹ **foolish, faithless, uncaring, and merciless.** ³² **Though they know full well God's requirement that those who do such things deserve to die, they not only do them but even give approval to those who so act.**

4.1 Paul begins to develop the thesis that he set forth in vv. 16-17, but he develops it first in a negative sense. He describes what happens to humanity when it is bereft of God's gospel. He will treat this negative approach in three ways before he sets out the positive development of his thesis. The first of these ways concerns pagans or heathens who are without the gospel; the second concerns the Jewish people, also without the gospel; and the third considers the wickedness of all human beings. Paul will maintain that all humanity without the gospel is subject to God's wrath. Whereas the gospel has revealed God's uprightness, divine wrath is manifested from heaven toward all godlessness. In effect, Paul is here coping with sin, even though it will be some time before he introduces the noun *hamartia* or the verb *hamartanein*, "sin." But he will eventually sum up the condition of all humanity without the gospel in this way, as sinful.

4.2 The exercitant will note in this passage of Romans certain elements that correspond to the Ignatian "Principle and Foundation" and to the initial meditations of the First Week of the *Spiritual Exercises*. Both Paul and Ignatius now confront sin in contrast to the purpose of human life; both also consider the role and purpose of other creatures in human existence. Whereas Paul sees other creatures becoming objects of idolatry, which degrades and leads to sin, Ignatius speaks of how human beings must make use of these other creatures to achieve the goal and purpose of human existence. By his presentation of the human condition without the gospel, Paul is in effect depicting what Ignatius does in the first exercise of the First Week, a meditation on three kinds of sin, that of the angels, that of Adam and Eve, and that of a person who has gone to hell after committing one mortal sin. The Ignatian threesome is not the same as Paul's, but both Ignatius and Paul seek to achieve the same end, to reflect on the sad plight of sinful creatures, of human beings in particular. Both seek to get their readers to "ask for shame and confusion" (§48), because of many grievous sins committed—in effect, because of their own sinful condition. We can reflect on the sinful condition of pagans or Jews, but that reflection touches home, when we realize that there but for the grace of God go I. We too must call to mind "the gravity and malice of sin against our Creator and Lord" (§52). Paul's vivid description of the degradation into which idolatry has reduced gospel-less pagan humanity vividly fills in the details of what Ignatius asks exercitants to ponder in the first prelude, where he counsels them to consider "my whole composite self as an exile in this valley [of tears]" (§47).

4.3 Paul speaks of God's reaction to humanity without the gospel. It is a manifestation of divine wrath: "God's wrath is being revealed from heaven against all the godlessness and wickedness of human beings" (1:18). Another divine attribute or quality is thus introduced, which stands in contrast to God's uprightness revealed by the gospel. The wrath, however, is not revealed by the gospel, but is manifested from heaven itself.

"The wrath of God" is another divine quality inherited from the Old Testament (Ps 78:31; Isa 13:13; 26:20). It expresses not an irresponsible or irrational outburst of rage, a capricious or arbitrary anger against human beings; nor is it to be associated with the Greek idea of angry deities that have to be appeased or placated. It denotes rather the divine reaction to human sin and evil, the justifiable reaction of a loving and faithful God to his disobedient people, prone to idolatry and evil conduct. For Paul it is not merely the wrath of the God of Israel, but that of the Creator.

This attribute has to be rightly understood. It is a good example of the protological thinking that Paul has inherited from the Old Testament. ("Protological" denotes a logical explanation of something given in a primitive form of thinking.) In the Old Testament God is often considered responsible for all that happens to his people or his creation, whether good or evil. Thus Second Isaiah depicts Yahweh saying, "I form light and I create darkness, I make peace and create evil; I, the Lord, do all these things" (45:7). Or, again, Amos says, "If evil comes upon a city, has not the Lord done it?" (3:6). The theological distinction between God's absolute will and his permissive will had not yet entered the history of ideas; it would have to wait until the time of Augustine. As a result Paul speaks of God's wrath being manifested from heaven. As J. A. T. Robinson has put it,

> 'Wrath' is the process of inevitable retribution which comes into operation when God's laws are broken. It contains the idea of what happens in the life of a man or society when moral control is loosened. It is what takes over if the situation is allowed to rip. Cf. 1.24, 26, 28, 'God gave them over', he leaves pagan society to stew in its own juice. The retribution which overtakes it, resulting in automatic moral degradation, is what 'comes on' almost like a thermostat when, as it were, the moral temperature drops below a certain point (*Wrestling with Romans*, 18).

The wrath of God is always something with which the sinner has to reckon, even though one finds in the Old Testament divine wrath linked at times with mercy and loving-kindness, when God is said to be "slow to anger, abounding in steadfast love" (Ps 103:8; Joel 2:13). This is the way Israel of old sought to temper its understanding of God's reaction to human sin and rebellion. But it is a reality that the sinner must never forget. For sinful human conduct calls forth the manifestation of such divine wrath.

4.4 In this first development Paul tells of God's wrath being manifested against *anthrōpoi*, "human beings" (1:18) and does not specify them as "Gentiles" or "Greeks." Yet it becomes clear from 2:1 on (or at least from 2:9 on, and especially at 2:17) that he has been thinking in this first subsection of non-Jewish humanity. Thus he implicitly returns to the division of humanity used in 1:16, "Jew and Greek," and by the latter he means pagans, heathens, or Gentiles. In 2:1–3:9 he will come to Jewish humanity.

4.5 For Paul the condition of pagan humanity results, first, from its failure to recognize God for what he is, to glorify him, and to thank him, when it could easily have done so, had it paid due attention to the traces of God and his qualities evident in the created world. The pagan condition thus stems from a suppression of the truth about God in their lives. As a result, their misguided minds have become steeped in idolatry. They have turned from the praise and glorification of the immortal God to the worship of images of mortal creatures, human or animal. Second, the pagan condition results from the moral degradation to which their idolatry has reduced them: to the craving of their hearts for impurity, moral perversion, sexual excess, and homosexual activity (1:26b-27). Third, the pagan condition is the result of every sort of improper conduct, and Paul catalogues their vices (1:29-30). Consequently, they are all in Paul's view "inexcusable." Paul's picture of pagan humanity owes much to pre-Christian Jewish thinking about heathenism. It depends much on Wisdom 13 and 14, which the exercitant would do well to read and ponder, as part of this exercise.

4.6 In the first part of this description of the pagan condition, Paul expresses the pagan's failure to achieve the proper goal of human existence. He formulates in his own way what Ignatius set forth in his "Principle and Foundation," when he wrote, "Human beings are created to praise, reverence, and serve God our Lord, and by this means to save their souls" (§23.2). Similarly for Paul, the be-all and end-all of human existence is to recognize God as Creator, to glorify him, and to thank him (1:19-21). Praise, reverence, and service is only another way of saying recognition, glorification, and thanksgiving.

God as Creator is an Old Testament teaching that Paul simply recalls. The psalmist sang, "What are mortals that you are mindful of them, mere mortals that you care for them? Yet you have made them little less than a god, crowned them with glory and honor. You have given them rule over the works of your hands" (Ps 8:5-7). For Paul, to recognize this status of God is a fundamental obligation of all human beings in this earthly life. Such recognition must lead them further to glorify and thank the Creator for the very being that is theirs. Thus we are being asked implicitly by Paul to acknowledge God as our maker, to glorify and praise the Source of our being, and to pour out our thanks to the One who has made us, the world in which we live, and all the created bounty with which we have been surrounded.

4.7 When Ignatius speaks of "the other things on the face of the earth" that have been "created for human beings to help them in the pursuit of the end for which they are created" (§23.3), of the need "to make ourselves indifferent to all created things" (§23.5), and of the obligation "to desire and choose only that which is more conducive to the end for which we are created" (§23.7), he is formulating philosophically what is similar to a conclusion that may be drawn from what Paul sees as the failure of the pagans to discern from the created things that surround them their position relative to them and to the very source of their being.

For Paul, such pagans, cultured and civilized though they may be, have not "perceived with reflection" that "since the creation of the world" God's "invisible qualities, his eternal power and divinity" have been manifest in all these things. They have not, therefore, recognized the purpose of "the other things on the face of the earth." Whereas Ignatius calls for indifference and proper use of all such created goods, Paul castigates the pagans for their stifling of the truth that these created goods make known. These two ways of reacting to the created universe are complementary; they teach us what should be the proper human reaction to the created universe in which we live. One can be tempted to ignore the traces of God in the universe and stifle the truth that they manifest; one can turn them into gods and adore them, in effect, "exchange the glory of the immortal God for images shaped like mortal human beings, birds, four-footed creatures, or reptiles" (1:23). To do this would be to misuse "the other things on the face of the earth," as Ignatius would put it. His call for indifference toward them is an implicit echo of Paul's warning about idolatry and its consequences, about making gods out of what are mere created things, and about failing to recognize one's proper relation to them. For all the other created things in this universe are destined to serve mankind and to lead human beings to a proper understanding of their place in the world and of their relation to their Creator. To become too attached to one or other of them is to make an idol of such created things; to develop the proper indifference toward them is to recognize them for what they are. There is the possibility of idolatry in the lives of all of us, and Paul's analysis of the effect of idolatry on the lives of pagans sounds a monitory note for everyone. We must not make gods out of mere created things.

4.8 Paul's description of the degrading condition of pagans should also give us pause. The craving for impurity, idolatry, homosexual activity, wickedness, evil, greed, malice, envy, murder, strife, craftiness, spite, tale-bearing, slander, insolence, haughtiness, boasting, rebellion, folly, infidelity, lack of care for others, mercilessness, even the God-hating attitude of some pagans is a description that can actually be true of all human beings. Paul's description of the pagans of his day may sound rhetorical, but some of the vices in this catalogue enter into the lives of all of us, even of the most faithful. They are sins against society, sins against one's neighbor. They stem from an incorrect understanding of God and human life. That Pauline catalogue can serve as the basis of examination of our own consciences.

4.9 Paul's verdict on such human activity: "those who do such things deserve to die" (1:32a), i.e. not just deserve to depart from this natural, earthly life, but rather deserve to experience total death, of which he speaks in Rom 5:12, 19, to be severed from association with God. That is described here by Paul as the lot of all pagans, but it is likewise the lot of all who sin. It amounts to exclusion from the kingdom of God (1 Cor 6:10; Gal 5:21), because "the wages of sin is death" (Rom 6:23). Even more telling is Paul's further comment: "they not only do them, but even give approval to those who so act" (1:32b). The failure of pagans to glorify and thank God leads not only to idolatry and sexual perversion, but to offenses against other human beings and even the approval of such offensive conduct in others. This description of the pagan human condition is food for thought for all who fail to heed God's gospel.

4.10 As we reflect on such a Pauline description of the pagan situation, we can rightly react to it in three ways: first, by a sincere act of praise of the Creator, as we strive to discern and acknowledge the traces that God has left in the good work of his hands on our behalf, which tell us about his divinity and eternal power; second, by a frank admission of our own failure to recognize, glorify, praise, and thank the Creator who has brought us into being and surrounded us with the bounty of his creation; and third, by a petition that we may learn better to use all "the other things on the face of the earth" with the proper indifference so that we may "desire and choose only that which is more conducive to the end for which we are created" (§23.7).

4.11 Questions. Does God's wrath against my sinful conduct ever enter my thinking? How often do I ever seek to find the traces of God's activity in the world about me? Am I too somehow "inexcusable" for failing to recognize my Creator and glorify or thank him? What is my attitude toward the other things on the face of this earth? Do I make gods of them and fail to realize the purpose for which God has put them here for my benefit? Am I sufficiently indifferent to all other things? Have I exchanged the truth about God for a lie and reverenced the creature rather than the Creator? Have I allowed myself to be morally degraded as a result of failing to use created things with indifference? Have I succumbed to moral degradation in the matter of sex or other improper conduct? Can I admit that the catalogue of vices that Paul uses has marked my existence? Am I really convinced that those who do such things "deserve to die"? Am I any better than an unenlightened pagan?

COLLOQUY: PSALM 14

> Fools say in their hearts,
> 　　"There is no God."
> Their deeds are loathsome and corrupt;
> 　　not one does what is right.
> The LORD looks down from heaven
> 　　upon the human race,
> To see if even one is wise,
> 　　if even one seeks God.
> All have gone astray;
> 　　all alike are perverse.
> No one does what is right,
> 　　not even one.
> Will these evildoers never learn?
> 　　They devour my people as they devour bread;
> 　　they do not call upon the LORD.
> They have good reason, then, to fear;
> 　　God is with the company of the just.
> They would crush the hopes of the poor,
> 　　but the poor have God as their refuge.

See further *Romans*, 269-90, 107-8, 135-36.

God's Judgment Manifested against Jews without the Gospel (2:1–3:9)

^{2:1} So you are without excuse, whoever you are who sit in judgment. In judging another, you condemn yourself, since you, the judge, do the same things. ² Yet we know that God's judgment falls in truth on all who do such things. ³ Do you really think that you will escape the judgment of God, you who sit in judgment on those who do such things and yet do them yourself? ⁴ Or do you make light of the abundance of his goodness, forbearance, and longsuffering? Do you not realize that what is good about God is meant to lead you to repentance? ⁵ With your stubborn and impenitent heart you are amassing wrath for yourself on the day of wrath, when God's just judgment will be revealed. ⁶ For *he will repay everyone according to his deeds:*[b] ⁷ eternal life for those who by patiently doing good strive for glory, honor, and immortality; ⁸ but wrath and fury for those who selfishly disobey the truth and are won over to wickedness. ⁹ There will be distress and anguish for every human being who does evil, for the Jew first and also for the Greek. ¹⁰ But there will be glory, honor, and peace for everyone who does good, for the Jew first and also for the Greek. ¹¹ For there is no partiality in God.

¹² All who have sinned apart from the law will also perish apart from the law, and all who have sinned under the law will be judged by the law. ¹³ For it is not those who listen to the law who are upright before God; rather, those who observe the law will be justified before him. ¹⁴ Thus whenever Gentiles who do not have the law observe by nature

precepts of the law, they are actually a law to themselves, though not having the law. [15] They show that what the law prescribes has been written on their hearts, as their conscience also bears witness and their thoughts either accuse or defend them—[16] on the day when, according to my gospel, God judges through Christ Jesus the secrets of human hearts.

[17] But suppose you call yourself a Jew, rely on the law, and boast of God, [18] knowing his will and scrutinizing the things that really matter, because you are instructed by the law, [19] and suppose you are persuaded that you yourself are a guide to the blind, a light to those in darkness, [20] a corrector of the foolish, a teacher of the immature, because you have in the law the embodiment of knowledge and truth–[21] then do you who would teach others fail to teach yourself? Do you who preach against stealing steal yourself? [22] Do you who forbid adultery commit it yourself? Do you who abominate idols rob temples? [23] As for you who boast of the law, you dishonor God by the transgression of the law. [24] As it stands written, *Because of you the name of God is blasphemed among the Gentiles.*[c]

[25] Circumcision, indeed, has value, if you observe the law. But if you are a transgressor of the law, your circumcision has become uncircumcision. [26] Again, if an uncircumcised man keeps the precepts of the law, will not his uncircumcision be reckoned as circumcision? [27] He who by nature is uncircumcised yet keeps the law will condemn you, with your written code and circumcision, as a transgressor of the law. [28] One is not a Jew outwardly only; nor is real circumcision external, in the flesh. [29] Rather, one is a Jew in secret, and real circumcision is of the heart, a thing of the spirit, not of the letter. His praise comes not from human beings, but from God.

[3:1] "Then what is the advantage of being a Jew, or what is the value of circumcision?" [2] Much in every way! First of all, Jews were entrusted with the oracles of God. [3] What then? Suppose some Jews were unfaithful? Will their infidelity nullify the fidelity of God? [4] Certainly not! God will be true, though every human being be a liar, as it stands written, *that you may be vindicated in your speech, and win out when you are being judged.*[d] [5] If our wickedness brings forth the uprightness of God, what are we to say? Is God unjust to bring wrath

upon us? (I am speaking, of course, in human terms.)
⁶ Certainly not! Otherwise how is God to judge the world?
⁷ Again, if through my untruthfulness the truthfulness of
God has overflowed to his glory, then why must I still be
condemned as a sinner? ⁸ And why should we not "do evil
that good may come of it"—as some people defame us with
the libelous charge that we so teach? (The condemnation of
such people is not unjust.) ⁹ What, then, is the situation? Are
we (Jews) at a disadvantage? Not at all! For we have already
charged that all, Jews and Greeks alike, are under the power
of sin.

   ᵇ Prov 24:12   ᶜ Isa 52:5
   ᵈ Ps 51:6

5.1 Paul's indictment of humanity without the gospel has not
yet come to an end, for he realizes that it not just the gospel-less
pagan that is the object of God's wrath, but even his gospel-less
former coreligionists, those whom he will eventually call "my
brothers, my kinsmen by race" (9:3). In this case, Paul describes a
de facto situation. He does not yet fault his fellow Jews for their
failure to react to God's gospel as he believes they should. Rather,
he criticizes them in their own existential situation as the people of
God. They are not pagans; they know what the will of God is on
their behalf, having the Mosaic law for their instruction. His
criticism is that they do not do what they should do; they do not
observe that law as they should. So they end up as much the object
of God's wrath as the pagans without the law. His argument
eventually implies that their situation too would be remedied by
faith in Christ Jesus and by the gospel of God's gracious salvation
coming through his Son.

5.2 For all its telling discussion of the law, this section of
Romans also includes other important Pauline teaching that
merits our reflection and meditation. Paul begins this section with
a consideration of the inevitable discernment with which all
human beings have to reckon and which is associated with God's
eschatological judgment of humanity (2:1-11). This epistle,
devoted mainly to the Pauline teaching of justification by grace
through faith, introduces the idea of God's judgment well before
the Apostle even mentions justification as an effect of the Christ-
event. In the thesis of the epistle (1:16-17) Paul spoke of God's

"salvation," not of the "justification" of sinners. Now he prepares for the discussion of the latter effect by recalling early on the basic Old Testament teaching about God's judgment of the conduct of all human beings. Paul does not mince words: "God's judgment falls in truth on all" who do evil (2:2); there will be a "day of wrath, when God's just judgment will be revealed" (2:5). In order to stress in the present context a teaching familiar to all his fellow Jews, Paul cites Prov 24:12, "God will repay everyone according to his deeds" (cf. Ps 62:13), and adds, "Eternal life for those who by patiently doing good strive for glory, honor, and immortality, but wrath and fury for those who selfishly disobey the truth and are won over to wickedness" (2:7-8). The pair "wrath and fury" appear often in the Greek Old Testament: Isa 13:9 (in a context that speaks of "the day of the Lord"); 30:30; Jer 7:20; 21:5. The evil conduct that enters all human life has to reckon with the divine judgment of which Paul speaks, a judgment that "falls in truth on all" (2:2), for "there is no partiality in God" (2:11). The importance of this teaching about God's eschatological judgment for Paul can be seen in the several references that he makes to it here and elsewhere (Rom 14:10; 1 Cor 3:13-17; 2 Cor 5:10; Phil 2:12).

5.3 A salutary aspect of divine judgment, however, is recalled, when Paul asks, "Do you make light of the abundance of God's goodness, forbearance, and longsuffering? Do you not realize that what is good about God is meant to lead you to repentance?" (2:4-5). In this context, we must recall how Paul has spoken of "God's wrath being revealed from heaven against all the godlessness and wickedness of human beings who by such wickedness stifle the truth" (1:18). In other words, God's wrath is already at work and manifests itself at times in the very earthly lives that some humans lead; for instance, in the pagan degradation that Paul has already described in chap. 1. Because it does not always so manifest itself in the case of others, that is a sign of divine forbearance. Rebellious human beings might be tempted to think that God does not care, or that he is always merciful, forbearing, and not judgmental. Yet Paul's words draw us up short, implicitly summoning us to repentance and penitence. He uses the word *metanoia*, "change of mind," which came in time to connote "remorse" and "repentance," a turning from sin and a turning to God. To such *metanoia* we are all summoned by Paul's reflective comment.

5.4 The unnamed person who applauds what Paul has said about pagan humanity and who thus sits in judgment of pagans is likewise said to be "without excuse": "whoever you are who sit in judgment" (2:1). From 2:17 it becomes clear that this imaginary interlocutor is a "Jew," and that is suggested even earlier in vv. 12-16 and 9-10, which build up to that identification. Paul's accusation against his fellow Jews is that they are no better than the pagans and are likewise the object of divine wrath, because in effect they "do the same things" (2:1). They are as much at fault as the rest of humanity without the gospel.

5.5 Paul insists, "All who have sinned under the law will be judged by the law" (2:12b). Paul is alluding to one of the prerogatives of Israel (see Rom 9:4, "the giving of the law"): the Jewish people have the Mosaic law, and through it they know God's will in their regard. Through the *tôrah*, which literally means "instruction," they know what God wants them to do; they know the "deeds of the law," i.e. the deeds prescribed by the instruction given through Moses. Despite this advantage they are, however, not saved from divine wrath, "For it is not those who listen to the law who are upright before God; rather, those who observe the law will be justified before him" (2:13). Paul thus admits that, in the context in which Judaism came into being, Jews have had a mode of achieving the status of uprightness or rectitude in God's sight. Although Paul admits this theoretically, his problem is that Jews do not keep the law. His indictment in vv. 17-24 is severe. His rhetorical diatribe sets forth Israel's boast in five assertions, then counters each of them with a query, and ends with a quotation of Isa 52:5, "Because of you the name of God is blasphemed among the Gentiles." Paul continues his diatribe, in effect answering a Jewish objection that they at least obey God's command about circumcision. Yet he adds, "Circumcision, indeed, has value, if you observe the law" (2:25). Paul repeats what he had written in Gal 6:13: "Even those who receive circumcision do not themselves keep the law." So runs Paul's indictment, and because this is the situation, the Jew is likewise subject to God's wrath. Paul's comments concern the Christian reader too, because what he levels against his fellow Jews, he can also level against fellow Christians. For they too have the advantage of knowing what God desires of them; they have their Christian Bible, given to the church, as a guide for their living and conduct. Therein they too find "oracles of God." But do they always follow its counsels in the conduct of their lives? Paul's conclusion is applicable to the Christian as well: "It is not those who listen to the law who are upright before God; rather, those who observe the law will be justified before him" (2:13).

Paul's comment has to be rightly understood. He is not contradicting what he will say in Rom 3:28 about justification not coming from "deeds of the law." He is rather commenting on the fact that the Jews might possibly pride themselves on having God's law for their instruction. His argument is: Possession of the law to which one listens is not enough; one has to observe it. He concedes that justification may come through the law, if one observes it; that he concedes for the sake of his argument.

5.6 Paul now compares the situation in which the Jewish people find themselves with that of the heathen Gentiles: "Whenever Gentiles who do not have the law observe by nature precepts of the law, they are actually a law to themselves, though not having the law. They show that what the law prescribes has been written on their hearts, as their conscience also bears witness and their thoughts either accuse or defend them" (2:14-16). To be noted here is that Paul says "whenever" and "Gentiles." He does *not* mean that Gentiles *always* know *all* that the Mosaic law teaches the Jewish people or that all Gentiles do "by nature" all the precepts of the law. He rather maintains that Gentiles on occasion know instinctively some of the precepts of the Mosaic law, e.g. some of the prohibitions of the Decalogue. The Gentile conscience tells them, "Thou shalt not steal," "Thou shalt not kill." Accordingly even Gentiles will be judged by God through Christ Jesus, when he reads "the secrets of human hearts" (2:16). In other words, there is no escape for either Jew or Gentile, when it comes to divine scrutiny, when God's judgment of human beings will be made. The Jew will be judged according to the Mosaic law (that will be the burden of the Jewish conscience): "all who have sinned under the law will be judged by the law" (2:12). The Gentile will be judged according to what he knows "by nature" or by his accusing or defending "thoughts" (that will be the burden of the Gentile conscience).

5.7 To the imaginary interlocutor's expostulation, "What, then? Are we (Jews) at a disadvantage?" (3:9ab), Paul replies: "Not at all! For we have already charged that all, Jews and Greeks alike, are under the power of sin" (3:9cd). Now for the first time in the epistle Paul mentions *hamartia*, "sin," even though his argument from 1:18 on has been dealing with the equivalent of the sins of pagans and the sins of Jews. Paul's conclusion is that all humanity, without the gospel, is under the domination of sin. Sin rules like a master, and human beings are enslaved to it. (Paul will come back on this again in chap. 7 and explain why this is so and what the answer to it is.)

5.8 Christians who read Paul's indictment of pagans and Jews cannot help but ask, "What about us?" A legitimate question, to which Paul will eventually give an answer. In fact, he begins a consideration of part of this question in 3:5, but does not fully answer it. For he asks,

> If our wickedness brings forth the uprightness of God, what are we to say? Is God unjust to bring wrath upon us? (I am speaking, of course, in human terms.) Certainly not! Otherwise how is God to judge the world? Again, if through my untruthfulness the truthfulness of God has overflowed to his glory, then why must I still be condemned as a sinner? And why should we not 'do evil that good may come of it'—as some people defame us with the libelous charge that we so teach? (3:5-8).

Directly, Paul is answering a charge that he has been advocating antinomianism, life without legal restraints. He realizes that his thesis about God revealing his uprightness and grace of acquittal to sinful humanity would make even Christians ask why they should not go on sinning and give God greater scope for his bounteous uprightness. Paul is carried away by his rhetoric and does not answer the objection here, but he will return to it in chap. 6. Meanwhile, Christians have to realize that sin is part of all human existence and that, normally speaking, they too can fall under the wrath of God, just as much as the gospel-less pagan or Jew.

5.9 As a Christian, the exercitant is also "under the power of sin," enslaved to such a master. Here we might borrow a few considerations from Ignatius' second exercise of the First Week, his meditation on our own sins. In the third point he counsels a reflection upon oneself in the use of examples that humble the sinner: "What am I when compared with all other human beings?" (§58.1). Am I any better than the pagan idolater or the pagan sinner whose life is marked by degradation and perversion? Am I any better than the Jew who does not observe God's law and does not take advantage of such divine guidance for the conduct of life? Again Ignatius reflects, "What is all of creation when compared with God? and then, I alone—what can I be?" (§58.3). Paul has invited the reader of his letter to consider the glory of God manifested in his created universe; in comparison with all that, what am I really? Ignatius outstrips Paul in his medieval description of the sinful human condition: "I will look at all the corruption and foulness of my body" (§58.4) and "I will look upon myself as a sore and abscess from which have issued such great sins and iniquities and such foul poison" (§58.5).

5.10 Questions. Do I realize that what is good about the forbearing God is meant to lead me too to repentance and remorse? Am I ready for such a turning? How often do I reflect on the divine judgment? That I too must appear before the divine tribunal to answer for my deeds in this life? Am I possibly amassing for myself wrath on the day when God's judgment will be revealed on my behalf? Am I in reality as bad as the gospel-less pagan that I might tend to criticize? Do I fail to listen to my conscience and my thoughts as they accuse or defend me? Do I listen to God's law written on my heart? Am I convinced that God through Christ Jesus will judge the secrets of human hearts? Do I take refuge in my Christian status as one who knows God's will and yet implicitly violates it? Is my heart really circumcised as it should be? Or am I only outwardly a Christian, and not one in the depths of my being? Do I sometimes act as though through doing evil good may come of it? Do I use evil means to achieve a good end? Do I reckon with the extent to which I am under the power of sin?

COLLOQUY: PSALM 78:1-11

Attend, my people, to my teaching;
    listen to the words of my mouth.
I will open my mouth in story,
    drawing lessons from of old.
We have heard them, we know them;
    our ancestors have recited them to us.
We do not keep them from our children;
    we recite them to the next generation,
The praiseworthy and mighty deeds of the LORD,
    the wonders that he performed.
God set up a decree in Jacob,
    established a law in Israel:
What he commanded our ancestors,
    they were to teach their children;
That the next generation might come to know,
    children yet to be born.
In turn they were to recite them to their children,
    that they too might put their trust in God,
And not forget the works of God,
    keeping his commandments.
They were not to be like their ancestors,
    a rebellious and defiant generation,
A generation whose heart was not constant,
    whose spirit was not faithful to God,
Like the ranks of Ephraimite archers,
    who retreated on the day of battle.
They did not keep God's covenant;
    they refused to walk by his law.
They forgot his works,
    the wondrous deeds he had shown them.

See further *Romans*, 296-331.

All Human Beings, Jews and Greeks Alike, Are Sinners (3:10-20)

[10] As it stands written,

> No one is upright, no, not one [e]
> [11] no one has understanding; [f]
> no one searches for God.
> [12] All have turned away, all have become depraved.
> No one does good, not even one.
> [13] Their throats are open graves [g]
> with their tongues they have practiced deceit;
> the poison of asps lies behind their lips. [h]
> [14] Their mouths are full of cursing and bitterness [i]
> [15] Swift are their feet to shed blood. [j]
> [16] Ruin and wretchedness strew their paths.
> [17] The path of peace they have not known.
> [18] Fear of God is not before their eyes. [k]

[19] Now we know that all that the law says is addressed to those who are under the law so that every mouth may be silenced and the whole world become accountable to God, [20] since *no human being will be justified before* [l] him through deeds prescribed by the law; for through the law comes the real knowledge of sin.

[e] Qoh 7:20   [f] Ps 14:1-3
[g] Ps 5:10   [h] Ps 140:4
[i] Ps 10:7   [j] Ps 59:7-8; Prov 1:16
[k] Ps 36:2   [l] Ps 143:2

6.1 This exercise is like a repetition in the Ignatian *Spiritual Exercises*, because Paul does not really advance his argument beyond what he has already set down in 3:9, that "all, Jews and

Greeks alike, are under the power of sin." But what he now considers is a fitting conclusion to his consideration of the sinfulness of all humanity. For he quotes the Hebrew Scriptures to bolster up his contention that all human beings are enslaved to sin. In so quoting the Old Testament, he is citing the testimony of "the oracles of God," of which he has just spoken. For he admitted earlier that this was one of the advantages of being a Jew; the Jews have been entrusted with "the oracles of God" (3:2). Now he strings together a catena of seven Old Testament passages that prove his point about the utter sinfulness of all human beings. The testimony comes from the Psalms, Proverbs, Isaiah, and Qoheleth. Although none of the quotations is drawn from the Pentateuch, Paul sums up the collection as the testimony of "the law" (3:19), and what "the law says is addressed to those who are under the law so that every mouth may be silenced and the whole world become accountable to God" (3:19). Jews have no complaint against the accusing God; their mouths are silenced, just as were those of the pagans who were the object of divine wrath in 1:18-32. Indeed, the "whole world" has become accountable to God, an echo of what Paul said in Rom 2:6, 11. All human beings must stand before God's tribunal as impious, godless, and sinful. A similar sentiment can be found in 2 Esdr 7:22-24: "But they [those who came into this world] were not obedient and spoke out against him; they concocted vain thoughts for themselves and proposed to themselves wicked frauds; they even declared that the Most High does not exist and ignored his ways! They scorned his law and denied his covenants; they have been unfaithful to his statutes and have not performed his works."

6.2 Noteworthy in the list is the catchword bonding of the quotations; they are strung together by the mention of different parts of the body: throat, tongue, lips, mouth, feet (on a path), and eyes. The connotation of such bonding is that all parts of human beings are involved in sin in God's sight; the whole individual has indulged in sin. The catena of texts declares that no human being is upright in God's sight and bases its declaration on the human failure to "search for God." All have turned away from God, and "no one does good, not even one" (3:12). In effect, the catena supplies the scriptural basis for Paul's indictment of pagans in

1:18-23. It likewise catalogues numerous human sins: deceit, cursing, bitterness, bloodshed, destruction. All these are the characteristics of sinful human conduct. What is striking is that, though Paul uses such a catena of Old Testament verses, it does not contain the word "sin," even though it is a telling description of sinful human conduct. It is all summed up, moreover, in the last citation, "Fear of God is not before their eyes" (3:18). In contrast, the Old Testament had taught that "the fear of the Lord is the beginning of knowledge" (Prov 1:7; cf. Ps 111:10).

6.3 This testimony from the Old Testament also gives an answer to the question asked above about Christians. What the Scriptures of old have said about Jews, Paul now echoes and applies to all human beings, as he prepares to introduce the positive development of the epistle's thesis, and he may be presumed to include Christians in his indictment.

6.4 The irony is that Paul seems to admit that somehow "the law" brings it about that human beings become sinful. At least one could so conclude, and many have so concluded. For he asserts that "through the law comes the real knowledge of sin" (3:20b). That assertion poses a problem, which Paul does not explain. He will eventually cope with it, especially in chap. 7 below, where it will become clear that "sin" has to be recognized as a transgression of God's will. Because it is that, the law brings the real knowledge of sin, making known to humanity what God has willed for it, and that sin is, in effect, a transgression of that divine will.

6.5 In 3:20a we encounter the *essential* Pauline affirmation about the human condition: "No human being will be justified before God through deeds prescribed by the law." He repeats what he wrote in Gal 3:11: "For it is clear that no one is justified before God through the law." In saying this, Paul sums up and enunciates his basic proposition about justification, which he will proceed to explain in 3:21-31. Now he alludes to Ps 143:2, which in the Greek Old Testament reads, *ou dikaiōthēsetai enōpion sou pas zōn*, "no living being will be justified before you," an almost exact reproduction of the Hebrew original. Paul slightly modifies the text, using "no flesh" instead of "no living being." Psalm 143 is a hymn of personal lament, in which the psalmist acknowledges his sinfulness and God's transcendent righteousness. The verse from it to which Paul alludes sums up well not only the Old Testament conviction about personal righteousness, but also Paul's position. Yet he not only uses this verse to stress that contrast between human sin and God but makes a striking addition to the psalm, by adding "through deeds of the law," i.e. through deeds prescribed by the law. That was hardly the Old Testament meaning of the psalm; it has now been given a distinctively Pauline twist. Cf. Gal 2:16, where Paul makes the same addition, alluding again to Ps 143:2.

We are thus brought face to face with Paul's basic affirmation: No one "will earn justification by...obedience to God's requirements" because "*erga nomou* in the sense of such a perfect obedience...are not forthcoming" (C. E. B. Cranfield, *Romans*, 198). Paul thus recognizes the reason for the basic Jewish failure to obey the Mosaic law, and that is why he sets forth this proposition. He has not yet explained why this is so. That will emerge in due time. In Gal 3:10 he was even more severe in his judgment, "All who rely on works of the law are under a curse; for it stands written, 'Cursed be everyone who does not abide by all the things that are written in the book of the law and do them'" (quoting from Deut 27:26 the curse that the law laid on those who were under obedience to it).

6.6 With such an affirmation Paul indicts all of us. We are all sinners in God's sight, sinners in what we think, plan, and plot; sinners in what we say, declare, and assert; sinners in what we do, carry out, and bring to pass; and sinners in what we omit, fail to do, and neglect. We might here borrow two final considerations from Ignatius' second exercise on sin: "I will consider who God is against whom I have sinned, by going through his attributes and comparing them with their opposites in myself: God's wisdom with my ignorance; God's omnipotence with my weakness; God's justice with my iniquity; God's goodness with my malice" (§59.1-2). I may make "an exclamation of wonder and surging emotion, uttered as I reflect on all creatures and wonder how they have allowed me to live and have preserved me in life.... How is it that [the saints] have interceded and prayed for me? Likewise, the heavens, the sun, the moon, the stars, and the elements; the fruits, birds, fishes, and animals. And the earth: How is it that it has not opened up and swallowed me, creating new hells for me to suffer in forever?" (§60.1,3-4).

With this universal indictment of gospel-less, sinful humanity Paul draws to a close the negative development of his thesis in Romans: humanity without the gospel ends up only in sin and has become the object of divine wrath. Christians too share in that wrath by their sinful conduct.

6.7 Questions. Has not my sin revealed that I too have failed to search for God? That I have become depraved? Have not I too sinned with my tongue, my lips, my mouth, my feet, even with my eyes? Has not this Pauline catena of Old Testament accusations indicted me as well? Have I come to realize what sin really is? Do I allow the biblical do's and don'ts to instruct me in the real knowledge of sin? Am I ready to confess my sinfulness before God, my Creator?

COLLOQUY: PSALM 51

> Have mercy on me, God, in your goodness;
> > in your abundant compassion blot out my offense.
> Wash away all my guilt;
> > from my sin cleanse me.
> For I know my offense;
> > my sin is always before me.
> Against you alone have I sinned;
> > I have done such evil in your sight
> That you are just in your sentence,
> > blameless when you condemn.
> True, I was born guilty,
> > a sinner, even as my mother conceived me.
> Still, you insist on sincerity of heart;
> > in my inmost being teach me wisdom.
> Cleanse me with hyssop, that I may be pure;
> > wash me, make me whiter than snow.
> Let me hear sounds of joy and gladness;
> > let the bones you have crushed rejoice.
> Turn away your face from my sins;
> > blot out all my guilt.
> A clean heart create for me, God;
> > renew in me a steadfast spirit.

Do not drive me from your presence,
    nor take from me your holy spirit.
Restore my joy in your salvation,
    sustain in me a willing spirit.
I will teach the wicked your ways,
    that sinners may return to you.
Rescue me from death, God, my saving God,
    that my tongue may praise your healing power.
LORD, open my lips;
    my mouth will proclaim your praise.
For you do not desire sacrifice;
    a burnt offering you would not accept.
My sacrifice, God, is a broken spirit;
    God, do not spurn a broken, humbled heart.
Make Zion prosper in your good pleasure;
    rebuild the walls of Jerusalem.
Then you will be pleased with proper sacrifice,
    burnt offerings and holocausts;
        then bullocks will be offered on your altar.

See further *Romans*, 333-39.

Since the foregoing exercise is relatively brief, the exercitant might want to fill it out by meditating on the fuller context of each of the Old Testament passages from which Paul has taken the verses that make up the catena that he has used.

At this point too the exercitant may well want to consider Ignatius' directives for the "general examination of conscience, to purify oneself, and to make a better confession" (§32-43).

God's Uprightness Is Manifested to All Sinners through Christ and Apprehended by Faith (3:21-31)

[21] But now, independently of the law, the uprightness of God has been disclosed, even though the law and the prophets bear witness to it, [22] the uprightness of God that comes through faith in Jesus Christ toward all who believe, toward all, without distinction. [23] For all alike have sinned and fall short of the glory of God; [24] yet all are justified freely by his grace through the redemption which comes in Christ Jesus. [25] God has presented him with his blood as a means of expiating sin for all who have faith. This was to be a manifestation of God's uprightness for the pardon of past sins committed [26] in the time of his forbearance, a manifestation of his uprightness also at the present time to show that he is upright and justifies the one who puts faith in Jesus. [27] Where, then, is there room for boasting? It is ruled out! On what principle? On the principle of deeds? No, but on the principle of faith. [28] For we maintain that a human being is justified by faith apart from deeds prescribed by the law. [29] But is God the God of Jews only? Is he not also the God of Gentiles? Yes, even of Gentiles. [30] For God who will justify both the circumcised in virtue of their faith and the uncircumcised through their faith is one. [31] Are we, then, nullifying the law by this faith? Certainly not! We are rather upholding the law.

7.1 Having shown that the void created in human existence

by the lack of the gospel is not filled by human effort, either by pagans following a law that is theirs "by nature" or by Jews following the prescriptions of the Mosaic law, Paul turns to the new era in human history that has emerged with the coming of Jesus Christ, whose mission was to make known in a new way God's upright activity whereby he now offers salvation to all humanity. For God has taken the initiative and has restored humanity to a right relationship with himself. The gospel proclaiming Jesus' ministry, passion, death, and resurrection and the effects of those events on humanity is thus the manifestation and revelation of "God's power (unleashed) for the salvation of everyone who believes" (1:16).

Verses 21-31 constitute the first of several important sections in the epistle to the Romans, in which Paul formulates significant aspects of his thesis about God's gospel. Now the essence of that gospel announces that justification for all human beings comes by grace through faith in Christ Jesus and in what he has done for humanity. These verses will explain how both Jew and Greek alike can now be justified and find salvation.

7.2 Since the prescript to the epistle and the following thanksgiving Paul has not mentioned Christ Jesus (see 1:1, 4, 6, 7, 8), apart from a fleeting reference in 2:16. Now he introduces Christ formally as the object of the good news that he proclaims. God's Son is the one sent forth to make manifest the new mode of justification that divine uprightness has devised for Jews and Gentiles, the new way of bringing it about that sinful human beings may stand acquitted before God's tribunal.

Here one can draw a parallel with the *Spiritual Exercises* of Ignatius. For neither in the "Principle and Foundation" nor in the "First Week" does Ignatius call upon the exercitant to meditate on what Jesus Christ has done or to contemplate any mystery of Christ. There is only a fleeting reference to Christ in the colloquy of the first exercise (§53.1-2).[5] For Ignatius the role of Christ begins with the exercise that he uses as the preface to the Second Week, "The Kingdom of Jesus Christ," and thereafter the exercitant will contemplate various "mysteries" of the life of Christ, beginning with his incarnation. In a somewhat similar way, Paul, having considered how humanity, both Jew and Greek, are "under

the power of sin," now introduces Christ Jesus and his role in the
realization and implementation of the Father's plan of salvation.
Whereas Ignatius uses the gospel "history" for exercises of the
second and following weeks, proposing Christ concretely as
someone to be known, loved, and imitated, Paul rather meditates
on the Christ-event as such and proposes various abstract effects of
what Christ Jesus has done for humanity. Thus both Paul and
Ignatius in different ways achieve similar results and motivate
exercitants to reflection and meditation on the role of Jesus Christ
in their spiritual lives.

7.3 Paul moves from the period of human history when
humanity was under the law to the new aeon or period when
humanity is under the gospel. For him it is the *eschaton*, "the last
age," inaugurated with Jesus Christ and his mission."The old age
has passed away; look, the new has come" (2 Cor 5:17). For this
reason Paul begins this section of the epistle significantly with the
so-called eschatological *nyn*, "But now." Yet he also insists that the
uprightness of God now made manifest through Christ Jesus was
already announced and prefigured in the law and the prophets, in
"the oracles of God" entrusted to Israel of old. God's salvific plan,
however, has begun now to be implemented and to work itself out
in a new dimension and a new aeon.

7.4 Paul repeats the background for God's initiative: "All
alike have sinned and fall short of the glory of God" (3:23). The
first part of that declaration recapitulates 1:18–3:20, about the
sinful plight of Greeks and Jews alike, but Paul's absolute
formulation broadens it so that it means "all individuals," in order
to stress the universality of human sin. Consequently, we too as
Christians have to consider ourselves as sharing in that plight.
Pantes hēmarton, "all have sinned," i.e. have engaged in activity or
conduct that denotes a moral failure. Greek *hamartia*, which we
usually translate as "sin," really means missing the mark or a
failure to attain a goal.

In the second part of the declaration, Paul exploits that
aspect of sin: they "fall short of the glory of God." He sees the goal
of human existence as a share in that glory of God, a share in the
status of God himself. This sinful humanity has failed to attain.

In the Greek Old Testament *doxa* translated Hebrew *kābôd*, "glory, splendor," the radiant external manifestation of Yahweh's presence (in the Tabernacle [Exod 40:34-35] or the Temple [1 Kgs 8:11]), i.e. the means by which the presence of Yahweh became known to his people Israel. It also came to mean a way of expressing the eschatological condition destined for human beings. It was thought of as something communicated to them the closer they drew to that presence of God (see Ps 3:4; Rom 5:2; 8:18, 21; 9:23; 1 Thess 2:12; 1 Cor 2:7). Estranged from the presence of God by sin, human beings are deprived of that enhancing quality, a share of which they should have had even in this life. Paul tells in 2 Corinthians about how we Christians gradually "are being transformed into the same image [of the risen Lord] from glory to glory" (3:18). In other words, a share in God's glory is precisely that for which humanity has been destined eschatologically. So Paul can assert that human beings because of their sin have fallen short of their goal. Their sinful conduct has made them miss the mark. This is the human predicament: humanity fails to attain the goal for which it has been destined.

7.5 *But now*—in the eschaton, in the new aeon—"all are justified freely by his grace through the redemption which comes in Christ Jesus" (3:24). This is the essence of Paul's gospel. This he proudly announces to us for our meditation and reflection. God's initiative on behalf of sinful humanity has now been made manifest gratuitously; and lest anyone fail to comprehend, Paul adds, "by his grace," i.e. by a manifestation of God's favor. It is thus a sheer gift of God to human beings. "When the fullness of time had come, God sent his Son, born of a woman, born under the law, to ransom" humanity (Gal 4:4-5). The eschatological "now" indicates the fullness of time in God's plan, i.e. the moment determined of old has now arrived. We who are Christians have been called to live in this new aeon, the era of God's favor and grace.

7.6 Paul uses four images to explain further the manifestation of this divine favor in Christ Jesus: justification and redemption (3:24), expiation and pardon of sins (3:25). The first, justification, means that God has graciously acquitted sinful human beings; the second, redemption, that God has bought them or ransomed them from bondage to sin; the third, expiation, that God has wiped away their sins; and the fourth, pardon, that he has remitted the debt of their sins. Such images are drawn from Paul's Jewish background and enable him to illustrate the various ways in which he has understood what Christ Jesus has done for humankind

The first favor, justification, is the direct manifestation of God's uprightness or righteousness, that quality in God in virtue of which he acquits in a just judgment the sinner who stands before the divine tribunal. The sinner hears the verdict, "Not guilty." As a result of God's powerful declaration of acquittal, the sinner achieves the status of uprightness, innocence, or rectitude in his sight. This is the very status that Israel of old sought to attain by observing deeds of the law. This God has graciously brought about "in Christ Jesus," for through him sinful humanity is "justified": God has applied Christ's uprightness to sinners who put faith in him. Because of Christ, not only is the sinner declared upright but is also "made upright" (5:19), for God's word effects what it announces (cf. Isa 55:10). This means that I, as a justified Christian, stand before God's tribunal and hear the verdict, "Not guilty," and through the merits of Christ I am made upright in God's sight. This tremendous grace God has granted me, the grace that makes me indebted to him for all that I now am. For he has not only created me, but he has justified me through Christ Jesus.

The second favor, redemption, expresses the same idea under a different figure or image, for God has graciously ransomed the sinner from bondage to sin (recall 3:9). Christ Jesus by his ministry, passion, death, and resurrection has acted as the kinsman *gô'ēl,* "ransomer," of old (as did Yahweh in Isa 41:14; 43:14; 44:6). Christ has bought me from slavery and bondage to sin and death. This too is another manifestation of the grace that God has extended to me in my life. He has not only created me and justified me, but he has bought me back and ransomed me from slavery to sin.

The third favor is expressed by yet another image, the expiation of human sin: "God has presented him [Christ] with his blood as a means of expiating sin for all who have faith" (3:25). Paul alludes to the crucifixion and death of Jesus, summarily expressed in the phrase, "with his blood." He also alludes to the ancient ritual of *Yôm Kippûr,* when the high priest entered the Holy of Holies once a year to sprinkle the *kappōret,* "lid" (of the ark of the covenant), with the blood of sacrificial goats in an act of expiation (Lev 16:13-16), i.e. to expiate or wipe away the sins of Israel committed during the past year. What the rite of old was to achieve for Israel, that the crucified Jesus has achieved for humanity, not only past but also present and future. In his famous translation of the Bible into German, Luther called that *kappōret* the *Gnadenstuel* (WAusg DB 7. 39) and the King James Version imitated his translation by rendering it in English as "mercy seat." Thus Christ Jesus, by shedding his own blood, has become the "mercy seat" of the new aeon. He has achieved for humanity once for all what the Day of Atonement ritual symbolized each year for Israel of old. This too is a sign of God's grace in my life, for God has not only created me, justified and redeemed me, but he has also expiated my sins.

The fourth favor, pardon of sins, expresses again the same idea under another figure, for God through Christ Jesus has remitted the debts incurred by my sinful conduct. I should have paid God his due praise and glory, but instead I have sinned and failed to give him his due. It is, however, still another manifestation of grace that God has granted me, for he has not only created, justified, and redeemed me, but he has graciously expiated my sins and pardoned my misdeeds and the debts of my sinful conduct.

This status of justification, redemption, expiation, and pardon is not something that we human beings could have attained on our own or by our own power. It is the "power" of God himself, associated with his "glory," that has wrought all this. In 6:4 Paul will recall that "Christ was raised from the dead by the Father's glory." In other words, he was given a share in the glorious presence of the Father. The gracious justification, redemption, expiation, and pardon of sinful human beings bring it about that I too can share in that glorious status of the risen Christ. "[God] is the source of your life in Christ Jesus, whom God made our wisdom, our uprightness, our sanctification, and our redemption" (1 Cor 1:30). Through him I thus attain the goal of human life, a share in the very glory that Christ enjoys in the presence of the Father.

7.7 Paul is more concerned in this paragraph to express that status in judicial or forensic terms, because of his recent dialogue with the imaginary Jewish interlocutor about "the law" and "the deeds of the law" (3:1-9). That is why he emphasizes justification by grace through faith. Paul actually makes use of at least ten different figures to express effects of the Christ-event (see *Romans*, 116-24), i.e. images derived from either his Jewish or his Hellenistic background, which enable him to show what Christ Jesus has done for humanity. Prime among them is "justification." This figure is not too familiar to Catholics, in part, because Luther made so much of it, and in part because Catholic theologians have often preferred to use other Pauline images, his more easily understood figures. Yet in the litigious society in which we live today, everyone understands what it means to be haled into court. The image itself was derived by Paul from his Old Testament and Jewish background, for the Jew of old knew what the status of righteousness or uprightness before God's tribunal meant. That is why Paul in Rom 3:20 even alluded to Ps 143:2, "no human being will be justified before" him through deeds of the law. So now Paul explains that Christ Jesus has brought it about that sinful human beings stand before the divine tribunal and hear the verdict of acquittal. Because of our sinfulness, we should hear from the divine judge the sentence, "Guilty; guilty on all scores." Yet because of Christ Jesus, we hear the sentence, "Not guilty." That status of acquittal or rectitude thus achieved in the sight of the divine judge is not really our own. As Martin Luther rightly called it, it is an "alien" righteousness (*iustitia aliena*), because it has been acquired for us through Christ. In effect, it is Christ's uprightness or righteousness that is attributed to us, that makes us upright. This is the "grace" of God that has been given to us. To the Philippians Paul had written: "For his [Christ's] sake I have suffered the loss of all things and count them as refuse so that I may gain Christ and be found in him, not having an uprightness of my own, based on law, but that which is through faith in Christ, the uprightness from God that depends on faith" (3:8-9).

Thus with four vivid images Paul describes what Christ Jesus has achieved for sinful humanity: he has justified sinners, he has redeemed them, he has expiated (or wiped away) their sins, and he has pardoned their sinful debts. All of this, Paul insists, has been done graciously by God "to show that he is upright and justifies the one who puts faith in Jesus" (3:26). Thus God has made manifest his uprightness, and his gospel has revealed it: "the uprightness of God has been disclosed" (3:21).

7.8 Now it emerges that the good news announced by the gospel as "the salvation of everyone who believes" (1:16) involves "faith in Jesus" (3:26). Thus Christ Jesus is the object of the faith that saves humanity. Finally, by way of summary, Paul reaffirms his basic thesis: "We maintain that a human being is justified by faith apart from deeds prescribed by the law" (3:28). So he repeats what he wrote in Gal 2:16: "We ourselves [Peter and Paul], who are Jews by birth and not Gentile sinners, know that a human being is not justified by deeds of the law but through faith in Christ Jesus; even we have believed in Christ Jesus in order to be justified by faith in Christ, and not by deeds of the law, because by deeds of the law no one shall be justified."

7.9 Questions. How aware am I of my destiny in God's glorious presence? To what extent do I allow that destiny to color my conduct? How can I become more and more aware of the deficient character of sinful conduct, which would make me miss the mark of all human existence? Am I sufficiently aware of how great is the grace of justification? Of the way that God has graciously covered up my sinfulness with the uprightness of Christ himself, thus making me upright in his sight? How does my faith measure up to what God expects of me as I seek to appropriate such effects of the Christ-event? If it is all due to God's grace, is my faith strong enough to exclude any boasting on my part? Is it strong enough to cooperate with the graces that will continue to come to me?

COLLOQUY: PSALM 143

> LORD, hear my prayer;
>> in your faithfulness listen to my pleading;
>> answer me in your justice.
> Do not enter into judgment with your servant;
>> before you no living being can be just.
> The enemy has pursued me;
>> they have crushed my life to the ground.

They have left me in darkness
    like those long dead.
My spirit is faint within me;
    my heart is dismayed.
I remember the days of old;
    I ponder all your deeds;
    the works of your hands I recall.
I stretch out my hands to you;
    I thirst for you like a parched land.
Hasten to answer me, LORD;
    for my spirit fails me.
Do not hide your face from me,
    lest I become like those descending to the pit.
At dawn let me hear of your kindness,
    for in you I trust.
Show me the path I should walk,
    for to you I entrust my life.
Rescue me, LORD, from my foes,
    for in you I hope.
Teach me to do your will,
    for you are my God.
May your kind spirit guide me
    on ground that is level
For your name's sake, LORD, give me life;
    in your justice lead me out of distress.

See further *Romans*, 341-67.

Abraham Was Justified by Faith, Not by Deeds (4:1-25)

4:1 What, then, shall we say that Abraham, our forefather according to the flesh, found? **2** If Abraham was justified by deeds, he has reason to boast, but not before God. **3** For what does Scripture say? *Abraham put his faith in God, and it was credited to him as uprightness.* " **4** Now when a person labors, wages are not credited to him as a favor, but as what is due. **5** But when one does not labor, yet puts faith in him who justifies the godless, his faith is credited as uprightness. **6** So too David utters a beatitude over the human being to whom God credits uprightness apart from deeds: **7** *Blessed are those whose iniquities have been forgiven, whose sins have been covered up;* **8** *blessed is the man whose sin the Lord does not credit.* "

9 Is this beatitude uttered, then, only over the circumcised, or over the uncircumcised too? We maintain that "faith was credited to Abraham as uprightness." **10** Under what circumstances, then, was it credited to him? When he was still uncircumcised and not yet circumcised? He was not circumcised, but uncircumcised. **11** He accepted the sign of circumcision as the seal of the uprightness, which came through faith while he was still uncircumcised. Thus he was to be the father of all who believe when uncircumcised so that uprightness might also be credited to them, **12** as well as the father of those circumcised who are not only such but who walk in his footsteps along the path of faith that Abraham our father once walked while he was still uncircumcised.

13 It was not through the law that the promise was made to

Abraham or to his posterity that he would inherit the world, but through the uprightness that came from faith. [14] For if the heirs are those who hold to the law, then faith has been emptied of its meaning and the promise nullified. [15] The law brings only wrath; but where there is no law, there is no transgression. [16] For this reason the promise depends on faith, that it might be a matter of grace so as to be valid for all Abraham's posterity, not only for those who adhere to the law, but for those who share his faith. For he is father of us all; [17] as it stands written, *I have made you the father of many nations.*[o] So he is in the sight of God in whom he put his faith, the God who gives life to the dead and calls into being things that exist not. [18] Hoping against hope, Abraham believed, so as to become the father of many nations according to what had been said to him, *So shall your posterity be.* [p] [19] He did not weaken in faith when he considered his own body as already as good as dead (being about a hundred years old) and the deadness of Sarah's womb. [20] /Yet he never wavered in disbelief about God's promise, but strengthened in faith, he gave glory to God, [21] fully convinced that God was capable indeed of doing what he had promised. [22] That is why Abraham's faith was credited to him as uprightness. [23] Those words "it was credited to him" were written not only for Abraham's sake, [24] but for ours too. It is also going to be credited to us who believe in him who raised from the dead Jesus our Lord, [25] who was handed over (to death) for our trespasses and raised for our justification.

[m] Gen 15:6	[n] Ps 32:1-2
[o] Gen 17:5	[p] Gen 15:5

8.1 Paul ended his discussion in the last section by maintaining that his teaching about justification by grace through faith in Christ Jesus was actually "upholding the law" (3:31), but he gave no explanation of how that was to be understood. He also said that "the uprightness of God" that now was disclosed in the coming of Christ Jesus had already been foreshadowed in "the law and the prophets," which "bore witness to it" (3:21). Now he will use the example of Abraham from the Old Testament to show that "the law" is upheld, because Abraham was the first real believer, and his story is told in the law of Moses or in the Pentateuch itself.

Before we meditate further on Paul's treatment of Abraham's faith in chap. 4 of Romans, it is important to realize that Paul follows resolutely the order of the chapters in the Abraham story in Genesis. Moreover, he departs from the interpretation of Abraham that was current among the Jewish people in the last pre-Christian centuries.

According to the Genesis story, Abram was a semi-nomad, wandering in the Syro-Arabian desert, with his base in Haran in Upper Mesopotamia. From there he was called by God to separate himself from his kin and travel to the land of Canaan, first to Shechem in the north, where God promised him, "To your descendants I shall give this land" (Gen 12:7). From Shechem Abram made his way to Bethel, Hebron, Gerar, and south to Beersheba. Because of a famine in Canaan, Abram descended with his wife Sarai to Egypt. On his return to Canaan he divided the land with Lot, his nephew. After the rescue of Lot and the defeat of the foreign kings, Abram wondered to what purpose he had amassed such wealth, seeing that he had no heir. Then God promised Abram a progeny as numerous as the stars of the heavens and the sands of the seashore, and Abram took God at his word: "Abram put his faith in God, and it was credited to him as uprightness" (Gen 15:6). From such belief and trust in God came forth the Hebrews, the offspring of Abram, who was the "forefather" par excellence. So runs the outline of the Genesis story about the call and the faith of Abram, the paragon of uprightness.

8.2 That story, however, was embellished in the later pre-Christian Jewish tradition. There Abraham was said to be "perfect *in all his deeds* before the Lord" and "pleasing in uprightness all the days of his life" (*Jubilees* 23:10). "None has been found like him in glory; he *kept the law* of the Most High" (Sir 44:19-20). This he did because God had implanted "the unwritten law" in his heart (*2 Apoc. Bar.* 57:2). For Paul's Jewish contemporaries Abraham, the forefather, had thus become an ideal figure, and they were his children, his offspring "according to the flesh." But among them Abraham's uprightness also came to be attributed to his observance of "the law of the Most High." Moreover, "when tested, he was found loyal" (Sir 44:19, 23). The "testing" refers to his having been asked to sacrifice his only son Isaac in spite of God's

promise of a numerous progeny (Gen 22:9-10). This became
explicit in 1 Macc 2:52: "Was not Abraham found faithful when he
was tried; and it was credited to him as uprightness." So Gen 15:6
was reinterpreted in terms of his fidelity when he was so tested (cf.
2 Apoc. Bar. 57:2). And this is found even in Jas 2:21 in the New
Testament. In other words, Abraham's *uprightness* or *righteousness*
was ascribed, not to his faith or trust in God, but to his being *tested*.

8.3 From such an interpretation of the Abraham story Paul
departs; instead he resolutely follows the Genesis story, and for
him Abraham becomes the paragon of faith. Hence Paul insists,
Abraham was not "justified by deeds." If he had acquired merit by
deeds, he would have reason to boast! Paul rejects this: "But not
before God"! Rather he cites Gen 15:6: "Abraham put his faith in
God, and it was credited to him as uprightness." This is the
cardinal verse in "the law" for Paul. Abraham took God at his
word, and that response to God's promise became the source of
his righteousness or uprightness in God's sight. Abraham's
reponse was "faith." That too is what is asked of us when we are
accosted by the Christian gospel.

The story of Abraham's faith and of his being accredited as
upright (Gen 15:6) precedes in the sequence of the Genesis story
the account of his being tested (Genesis 22), and this is all
important for Paul. Abraham did nothing to acquire merit before
God, and he was considered upright long before he was tested.
Abraham merely took God at his word, and that was sufficient for
his status of rectitude in God's sight.

8.4 Paul bolsters up his interpretation of the Genesis story of
Abraham by quoting the psalm in which David utters a beatitude
over the one to whom God credits uprightness: his iniquities are
forgiven, his sins covered up; "blessed is the man whose sin the
Lord does not credit" (Ps 32:1-2). That is the status of rectitude
that Abraham found in the sight of God because of his faith. He
accepted God as his word and never faltered. What a lesson there
is here for the Christian's faith and trust in God!

8.5 Paul goes on to maintain that this status of rectitude had
nothing to do with Abraham's obedience to God's command
about circumcision. Here again, the order of chapters in the
Genesis story of Abraham is operative. Abraham was accounted

upright because of his faith (chap. 15) *before* he entered into the
pact of circumcision with Yahweh (chap. 17). Hence Abraham's
justification came because of his faith, not in virtue of
circumcision or in virtue of his obedience to that which God
asked of him in this regard. This is supremely important for Paul,
because justification now comes to people of faith, and not only
to people of the circumcision. Thus the precedent of Abraham in
the "law" itself (the Pentateuch) confirms Paul's thesis, that
justification by grace through faith apart from deeds prescribed
by the law means that both Jew and Gentile stand on an equal
basis before an impartial God who judges them. So there is no
place for boasting, either in the case of the Jew or the Gentile. For
it all depends on God's grace.

In Galatians Paul had written about Abraham, "Thus
Abraham 'believed in God, and it was reckoned to him as uprightness.' So you see that it is people of faith who are the sons of
Abraham. And Scripture, foreseeing that God would justify the
Gentiles by faith, preached the gospel beforehand to Abraham,
saying, 'In you shall all the nations be blessed.' So then, those who
are people of faith are blessed with Abraham the believer" (3:6-9).

8.6 Paul also insists that, just as the promises of God were
made to Abraham, who was reckoned as upright because of his
faith and trust in those promises, so the divine promise continues
to come to the people of faith. Abraham may indeed be the
forefather of many Jewish people "according to the flesh," in the
sense that they are physically descended from him; but he is
actually "father of us all" (4:16d). "The promise depends on faith,
that it might be a matter of grace so as to be valid for all
Abraham's posterity, not only for those who adhere to the law, but
for those who share his faith" (4:16a-c).

8.7 Paul likewise stresses Abraham's hope: "Hoping against
hope, Abraham believed, so as to become the father of many
nations according to what had been said to him, *So shall your
posterity be*" (4:18). Thus Abraham becomes the paragon not only
of faith but also of hope.

8.8 From the story of Abraham in Genesis Paul draws an
important conclusion: "Those words 'it was credited to him' were
written not only for Abraham's sake, but for ours too. It is also

going to be credited to us who believe in him who raised from the dead Jesus our Lord, who was handed over (to death) for our trespasses and raised for our justification" (4:23-25). Only rarely does Paul make such an observation. What he is telling us is that the Old Testament story of Abraham bears an important lesson also for Christians. Everything depends on faith, faith in God who has brought about our justification through the death and resurrection of Christ Jesus. We are justified by God's grace, by the new initiative that God took to intervene in human history by sending his Son in the fullness of time. What Christ Jesus achieved for humanity by his death and resurrection is ascribed to us, if and when we live as persons of lively faith in him.

8.9 Here one must inject a word of caution. It may seem that Paul's emphasis on Abraham's faith, and not his deeds (his testing or his obedience in circumcision), undercuts the value of good deeds in human life. But one must remember that Paul stresses Abraham's faith because of the development thus far in the epistle. In the course of chap. 4 Paul has mentioned "deeds" (4:2), and in the context they refer to "deeds of the law," what the Jew was expected to perform in observance of the law. Yet because Paul speaks there only of "deeds," in his characteristic generalizing fashion, his teaching about justification by faith apart from deeds of the law was in time misunderstood and even caricatured. Evidence of that misunderstanding is seen in the Epistle of James (2:14-26), an important corrective that the New Testament also provides. When Paul's teaching is contrasted with James', one sees that there is a difference on three scores: First, for James "faith" is restricted to an intellectual assent of monotheism (2:19: "You believe that God is one, and you do well; even the demons believe that and tremble"). For Paul, however, "faith" has the full sense of a response to the gospel that results in a commitment, a dedication to God involving the whole person and all one's conduct. Second, for James the "deeds" are the "good deeds" of a Christian (2:17), those that manifest that faith is not dead, whereas for Paul "deeds" are Jewish deeds, those that are prescribed by the Mosaic law. Third, James interprets the justification of Abraham as did his Jewish contemporaries: "Was not Abraham our father justified by deeds, because he offered his son Isaac on the altar?" (2:21), whereas Paul interprets Gen 15:6 strictly and ascribes Abraham's justification to his faith. He says nothing about the testing of Abraham.

In all of this one must remember what Paul says about faith in Gal 5:6: "For in Christ Jesus neither circumcision nor uncircumcision amounts to anything, but rather faith working itself out through love." So the full concept of Pauline faith is one that results in conduct marked by love, by a concern for other human beings. When so understood, the Pauline concept of faith is not "dead" in the sense of James. The trouble is that this full concept of Pauline faith does not come to explicit formulation in the epistle to the Romans, even though it is implied in what Paul will teach in 13:8-10 about love as "the fulfillment of the law." Faith working itself out through love thus become the explanation of the "commitment of faith" (1:5), a faith that achieves for us as Christians what the observance of the law sought to achieve for the Jewish people of old.

8.10 The upshot of Paul's treatment is that Abraham has become the model of Christian faith, a model for our own Christian conduct and activity. Abraham accepted God's promise of a numerous progeny; he trusted God that Sarah would have a child in her old age. He trusted God, who eventually asked him to sacrifice his only-begotten offspring, realizing that somehow the divine promise of a numerous progeny would still be realized. Few human beings are confronted with such a challenge in their lives, as was Abraham. That is why he became for Paul the "father of us all" (4:16d). "So he is in the sight of God in whom he put his faith, the God who gives life to the dead and calls into being things that exist not. Hoping against hope, Abraham believed, so as to become the father of many nations according to what had been said to him, 'So shall your posterity be'" (4:17b-18).

Abraham is "the father of us all" because of his faith and trust in God. He is thus a great model for Christians who accept God's challenge in the gospel and respond to it with faith working itself out through love. This is how we are asked to respond to God's gospel in our daily lives. This is how we are to manifest God's justification of us through what Christ Jesus has achieved for us. Such faith working itself out through love is also the way in which we cooperate with God's prevenient grace. For just as Abraham was called to faith in God, so are we. This is why the new aeon is one of grace; it is not one that is brought about by our own "deeds" apart from grace.

8.11 Questions. Do I ever pray to father Abraham, asking him to obtain for me the grace that I might better imitate his faith and trust in God? Should I not beg God for the grace of cooperating better with his call, as did Abraham? Does my Christian faith work itself out in love? Do I really realize what such a commitment of faith should mean in my conduct, especially in my dealings with others? Is my Christian faith strong enough that it could be tested by God himself, as was Abraham's?

COLLOQUY: PSALM 105:1-15

> Give thanks to the LORD, invoke his name;
>> make known among the peoples his deeds!
> Sing praise, play music;
>> proclaim all his wondrous deeds!
> Glory in his holy name;
>> rejoice, O hearts that seek the LORD!
> Rely on the mighty LORD;
>> constantly seek his face.
> Recall the wondrous deeds he has done,
>> his signs and his words of judgment,
> You descendants of Abraham his servant,
>> offspring of Jacob, the chosen one!
> The LORD is our God
>> who rules the whole earth.
> He remembers forever his covenant,
>> the pact imposed for a thousand generations,
> Which was made with Abraham,
>> confirmed by oath to Isaac,
> And ratified as binding for Jacob,
>> an everlasting covenant for Israel:
> "To you I give the land of Canaan,
>> your own allotted heritage."
> When they were few in number,
>> a handful, and strangers there,
> Wandering from nation to nation,
>> from one kingdom to another,

He let no one oppress them;
>for their sake he rebuked kings:
"Do not touch my anointed,
>to my prophets do no harm."

See further *Romans*, 369-90.

The Lordship of Christ Jesus (4:24; 14:7-9)

^{4:24} It is going to be credited to us who believe in him who raised from the dead Jesus our Lord.

^{14:7} Yet none of us lives for himself, and none of us dies for himself. ⁸ If we live, we live for the Lord; and if we die, we die for the Lord. So whether we live or die, we belong to the Lord. ⁹ For this reason too Christ died and came to life again in order that he might exercise lordship over both the dead and the living.

9.1 Paul referred to Christ Jesus as *Kyrios,* "Lord," in the opening prescript of the epistle (1:4, 7), where he foreshadowed many of the themes and motifs of the epistle. Once he announced his thesis (1:16-17), however, and began the development of it (1:18–4:25), he never speaks of Christ Jesus with this title until the end of the episode on Abraham. Then, for the first time Paul so refers to Christ as Lord again, and from this point in the epistle he will use it more often. We pause at this juncture to meditate on what that title meant for Paul and what it should mean in Christian life.

The consideration of the lordship of Christ at this point in our meditations on the epistle to the Romans corresponds to Ignatius' "contemplation" of "the Kingdom of Jesus Christ." Though Paul on a few occasions mentions the "kingdom," it was not really an operative concept in his theology. So it is not surprising that Paul never speaks of Christ as king. Yet what Ignatius sought with his contemplation of the Kingdom is similarly sought by Paul and his idea of the lordship of Christ. Whereas

Ignatius derived his idea of the kingship of Christ from the medieval feudal society that he knew, Paul derives his idea of the lordship of Christ from his Jewish and Old Testament background.

9.2 *Kyrios* as a christological title reappears in Rom 5:1, 11, where it forms an important *inclusio,* unifying that paragraph; and again in 5:21; 6:23; 7:25; and 8:39, where it forms part of the ending of four significant chapters in the second doctrinal section of Romans. It is one of the markers of the unit that these chapters form in that section of the epistle. Paul also uses it strikingly of Jesus in 10:9 and 12. See also 12:11; 13:14; especially 14:8-9, 14; cf. 15:6, 30; 16:1, 8, 12bis, 13, 18, 20, 22.

9.3 *Kyrios* is no mean or idle title for Jesus. It did not originate with Paul, for it was already in pre-Pauline Christian usage. In fact, *Kyrios* had been used among Greek-speaking Jews as a title for *Yahweh.* Only fourth-century and later Christian copies of the Septuagint make use of it as a translation of *Yahweh,* whereas earlier manuscripts of the Greek Old Testament copied by Jews and for Jews normally inserted the tetragrammaton *YHWH* in Hebrew characters into the Greek text. Paul's quotation of Ps 32:2, however, in Rom 4:8 shows that he was following the custom of Greek-speaking Jews, who had already come to refer to Yahweh with that title. There he quotes it according to a Greek version that was already translating Hebrew *Yhwh* as *Kyrios.*[6] This use of *Kyrios* simply reflects the Palestinian Jewish custom of referring to Yahweh as *mārêh* or *māryā'* in Aramaic and as *'ādôn* in Hebrew. Despite what R. Bultmann and his followers have often said about the unmodified "Lord" or "the Lord" being "unthinkable" as a title for God in Jewish usage, Palestinian Jews clearly did so refer to Yahweh.[7] When used of Yahweh, "Lord" expressed the reverence and esteem the Jewish people had for God, whose proper name was for them unutterable. Rather than pronounce *YHWH,* they substituted for it *'ādônāy* or *mārêh.* This respect enhanced that name and gave it a sacred and awesome character. Among Greek-speaking Jews *Kyrios* functioned similarly.

9.4 Early Christians took over that august title of Yahweh and applied it to the risen Christ, proclaiming, "Jesus is Lord!" That part of the primitive kerygma was picked up by Paul in both Rom 10:9 and 1 Cor 12:3. Paul readily affirmed, "Even if there may be many so-called gods in heaven or on earth—as indeed there are many 'gods' and many 'lords'—yet for us there is one God, the Father, from whom are all things and for whom we exist, and one Lord, Jesus Christ, through whom are all things and through whom we exist" (1 Cor 8:5-6). Paul did much to popularize further that christological title, as did other New Testament writers. In using *Kyrios* of the risen Christ—for that is its christological usage par excellence—early Christians insinuated that for them he was on a level with Yahweh. That title did not mean *eo ipso* that Christ Jesus was regarded as divine, but it insinuated that he was on a par with Yahweh, the God of Israel, who was made known through the Hebrew Scriptures of old. It was a question of *Gleichsetzung*, "making equal," not of *Identifizierung*, "identification."

"Lord" was the name to which Paul referred, when in the hymn to Christ in Phil 2:9-11 he called it "the name which is above every name." At the mention of it "every knee in heaven, on earth, and under the earth shall bend," in adoration of Christ (thus extending the adoration given to Yahweh in Isa 45:23), and "every tongue shall confess that Jesus Christ is **LORD**."

For Paul, Jesus of Nazareth brought to realization or fruition the salvific plan of God, according to which he was to be recognized as "Lord," as "Jesus Christ our Lord." This is the role intended by the heavenly Father that the risen Christ was to play in our human lives. And it was the Father "who raised Jesus from the dead" precisely for this reason. We are being called on by God, as was Paul himself, to acknowledge the lordship of the risen Jesus Christ in our lives. In effect, Paul is asking his Christian readers what that lordship of Christ means in their lives.

9.5 At the end of chap. 4 Paul made use a bit of primitive Christian preaching when he affirmed about Christ Jesus, "that he was handed over (to death) for our trespasses and raised for our justification" (4:25). The resurrection of Jesus was not just a reward for his obedience to the Father in undergoing death (he will come back on this aspect in 5:19), but God raised him to become a vivifying force or "life-giving Spirit" (1 Cor 15:45), which gives us a share in his risen life, and a dynamic source of justification for us. In effect, by his being raised, Christ Jesus became the efficient cause of our justification and salvation. In the

Letter to the Philippians Paul explains, "May I know him and the power of his resurrection and share in his sufferings, becoming like him in his death, that if possible I may attain the resurrection from the dead" (Phil 3:10-11). So Paul understands the influence of the risen Lord in the salvation of each of us. In a work attributed to Ambrose of Milan we read: "For if he [Christ Jesus] did not rise for us, then he did not rise, since he had no personal reason for rising.... For himself, the resurrection was not necessary, since the bonds of death did not hold him captive; because, though as man he was dead, still in the city of death he was free!"

9.6 *Kyrios* fundamentally means "master," and this is one reason why Paul calls himself "a slave of Christ Jesus" (1:1). The title *doulos* thus denotes the Christian's relation to Christ Jesus as Lord and Master. Like us and all other Christians, Paul is a "slave" who serves his master, Christ Jesus the risen Lord. But the "Lord" is also one who protects his servants from harm and from enemies; he is the one who is faithful to them, as they are expected to be faithful to him and serve him. These are aspects of the lordship of Christ Jesus that we should never forget or lose sight of.

"Serve the Lord!" (12:11) is the Pauline motto, and it must become ours too. "None of us lives for himself, and none of us dies for himself. If we live, we live for the Lord; and if we die, we die for the Lord. So whether we live or die, we belong to the Lord. For this reason too Christ died and came to life again in order that he might exercise lordship over both the dead and the living" (14:7-9). The whole of Christian life must be led in service and obedience to the one Lord Jesus Christ. In so doing, we "live for God" (Gal 2:19). We must all ask ourselves what concretely that means in our lives, and what it must come to mean.

9.7 We may borrow the counsel of Ignatius and apply it to the lordship of Christ. He counsels each of us "to ask grace from our Lord that I may not be deaf to his call, but ready and diligent to accomplish his most holy will" (§91). For Christ as Lord addresses to us the words: "My will is to conquer the whole world and all my enemies, and thus to enter into the glory of my Father. Therefore, whoever wishes to come with me must labor with me, so that through following me in pain he or she may follow me also in glory" (§95.4-5). This is what the "commitment of faith" (1:5) must entail in the concrete when we consider our service of Christ as Lord.

It can also require more of us: "Those who desire to show greater devotion and to distinguish themselves in total service to their eternal King and universal Lord, will not only offer their persons for the labor, but will go further still. They will work against their carnal and worldly love, and they will make offerings of greater worth and moment..." (§97.1-2). Here Ignatius invites exercitants to more than mere indifference toward other things in this created world, but summons them to dedicate themselves wholly to the service of their Lord and even distinguish themselves in such service.

9.8 Questions. What does the lordship of Christ mean for me today? Is he the only one who exercises lordship in my life, who rules and guides my conduct? How vital is my faith in the risen Christ and how concretely does my conduct of life amount to a service of him as Lord? Am I ready to labor with the Lord and follow him in suffering or pain, so that I might also come to follow him in glory? Will this lordship of Christ Jesus summon me to distinguish myself still further in total service to the eternal King and universal Lord?

COLLOQUY (BORROWED FROM IGNATIUS):

"Eternal Lord of all things, I make my offering with your favor and help. I make it in the presence of your infinite Goodness, and of your glorious Mother, and of all the holy men and women in your heavenly court. I wish and desire, and it is my deliberate decision, provided only that it is for your greater service and praise, to imitate you in bearing all injuries and affronts, and any poverty, actual as well as spiritual, if your Most Holy Majesty desires to choose and receive me into such a life and state."

PSALM 24:1–8

> The earth is the LORD's and all it holds,
> the world and those who live there.
> For God founded it on the sea,
> established it over the rivers.

Who may go up the mountain of the LORD?
>Who can stand in his holy place?
"The clean of hand and pure of heart,
>who are not devoted to idols,
>who have not sworn falsely.
They will receive blessings from the LORD,
>and justice from their saving God.
Such are the people that love the LORD,
>that seek the face of the God of Jacob."
Lift up your heads, O gates;
>rise up, you ancient portals,
>that the king of glory may enter.
Who is this king of glory?
>The LORD, a mighty warrior,
>the LORD mighty in battle.

See further *Romans*, 112-13, 388-90, 691.

Justified Christians Are Reconciled to the God of Love: They Will Be Saved through Hope of a Share in the Risen Life (5:1-11)

⁵:¹ Therefore, now that we are justified through faith, we are at peace with God through our Lord Jesus Christ, ² through whom we have gained access in faith to this grace in which we now stand and boast of our hope for the glory of God. ³ Yet not only that, but let us also boast of our afflictions, since we know that affliction makes for endurance, ⁴ endurance makes for character, and character for hope. ⁵ Such hope does not disappoint, because God's love has been poured out into our hearts through the holy Spirit that has been given to us. ⁶ While we were still helpless, Christ died at the appointed time for the godless. ⁷ Rare, indeed, is it that one should lay down one's life for an upright person—though for a really good person one might conceivably have courage to die. ⁸ Yet God shows forth his own love for us in that, while we were still sinners, Christ died for us. ⁹ And so, since we are now justified by his blood, we shall all the more certainly be saved by him from the wrath to come. ¹⁰ For if, when we were God's enemies, we were reconciled to him through the death of his Son, now that we are reconciled, we shall all the more certainly be saved by his life. ¹¹ Yet not only that—but we boast of God

through our Lord Jesus Christ, through whom we have now received reconciliation.

10.1 We have come to the end of the first development in the doctrinal section of the epistle to the Romans. Paul has set forth his thesis about God's gospel and explained his understanding of justification by grace through faith in Christ Jesus. The divine attribute that dominated that first development was "the uprightness of God" (1:17). The task of the gospel was to reveal that divine quality and show how it has been operative through the Christ-event. Now Paul's focus shifts a bit as he begins to speak rather of "the love of God." This will be the attribute that dominates chapters 5 to 8. This shift will enable us to meditate in the coming chapters on another all-important aspect of God. For Paul now presents us with a less juridical consideration of God, with the God of love. For God has taken the initiative and expresses his outgoing concern for us who are sinners. We learn now about an outpouring of that love, with which God has even filled our hearts.

10.2 In the crucial discussion of 3:21-31 Paul mentioned four effects of the Christ-event, justification, redemption, expiation, and pardon of sins. Now he will develop two more, reconciliation and salvation. The latter had been mentioned in the statement of Paul's thesis in 1:16; he returns to it and gives it greater prominence. We learn that the divine initiative manifests itself in reconciling humanity to God and bringing about its eschatological salvation, and all of this is an expression of the love of God, made manifest to us through the death of his Son.

What one meets in this second part of the doctrinal section of the epistle is the consequence of faith in Christ Jesus. Whereas humanity left to itself without the gospel came only under the wrath of God, through the gospel and through the grace of God that it proclaims humanity has found justification, redemption, expiation, and pardon of sins. All these different images express the one reality: what God's love has moved him to do for us. In effect, because of God's gospel about his Son and the bounty that it announces, human beings can now be at peace with God, and divine love is further manifested toward them in reconciliation and salvation.

10.3 Noteworthy is the way Paul now casts the discussion of this paragraph in the first plural; he speaks of an experience that justified Christians should recognize, for it is our common lot. He moves from justification to a discussion of the Christian experience in itself, analyzing how reconciliation and salvation are assured and even experienced by the Christian. For the justified Christian is, in fact, reconciled to God and experiences a peace that the distressing troubles of human existence in this world cannot disturb or upset. The reason for this, our existential experience, is that God's love has been poured into the hearts of us who have been justified, through the holy Spirit that is given to us.

10.4 Paul has often stressed the significance of the death of Jesus for us: "Christ died for our sins in accordance with the Scriptures" (1 Cor 15:3); "he died indeed for all that those who live might live no more for themselves but for him who for their sakes died and was raised" (2 Cor 5:15). That death is foremost in Paul's mind as he develops this paragraph: "(Christ) died" (5:6, 8); "by his blood" (5:9); "through the death of his Son" (5:10). Yet, as 4:25 shows, the resurrection of Christ is not far from Paul's vision: "he was handed over (to death) for our trespasses and raised for our justification." The death and resurrection of Christ Jesus in reality form a unit, but Jesus' vicarious suffering is now given slightly greater emphasis, for through it Christ Jesus has reconciled us to God and put us at peace with God. In this regard Paul sees us enjoying three things: we are at peace with God; we can boast of our hope of the glory of God; and we are reconciled to him.

10.5 First, through the death of Christ Jesus "we are at peace with God" (5:1). This does not mean merely peace of mind, or peace of conscience about sins committed and forgiven, or only (negatively) an experience of the absence of war (as in Deut 20:12; 1 Sam 7:14). Rather (positively) it is an experience of the Old Testament *šālôm*, the fullness of a right relationship with God, implied in justification itself, and of other bounties that flow from it and are associated with it. "The effect of uprightness will be peace, and the result of uprightness, quiet and trust forever" (Isa 32:17). Once we enjoy such a right relationship with God, our condition may be one of inner calm and quiet composure, or undisturbed conscience; but the essential element is the experience of a proper relationship with God, of a God-given integrity and wholeness that marks our Christian existence. Those who are now at peace with God are no longer objects of wrath. For them Christ Jesus has removed all wrath, and peace comes from God himself through the mediation of "our Lord Jesus Christ."

Paul expresses this peace in still another way: Through Christ "we have gained access in faith" (5:2). We have been introduced into the sphere of divine favor by Christ, who has, as it were, escorted us into the royal audience-chamber of God's presence. The implication is that we are no longer estranged from God as sinners and excluded from his presence, because our relations with God have been altered through what Christ Jesus has done for us. Christians bask in God's regal presence because of "this grace in which we now stand" (5:2b). It is not something that we have achieved by our own powers; it is a "grace in which we now stand," and yet it is ours because of our faith: "we have gained access in faith," through putting our faith in God and in what his Son has done for us.

10.6 Second, through Christ Jesus we can "boast of our hope for the glory of God" (5:2c), i.e. the hope of eschatological salvation. Whereas because of our sins we had fallen short of the glory of God (3:23), had missed the mark, and failed to attain the goal and destiny of all human life, now we are assured of it. A share in God's glorious presence is our destiny once again, because of the death of Christ Jesus. With the resurrection of Christ the aeon of "risen life" has proleptically begun, and justified Christians may expect a share in it. In other words, we Christians hope for the "glory" of God that is to be communicated to us, a glory still to be attained indeed, when we come to salvation, even though we have already been introduced into the sphere of "grace."

In this verse Paul makes use of "grace" and "glory" in an interesting way, which will prove to be the basis of a famous theological distinction of later centuries (about grace leading to glory).

Such hope enables us to weather the hardships and afflictions of human life. Paul even says that we can, as a result of Christian hope, "boast of our afflictions" (5:3), because they make for endurance, which produces character, which in turn builds up the hope that does not disappoint. At the root of this conviction is Paul's keen awareness of God's grace that enables us to stand up against the storms, hardships, and afflictions of our earthly existence. In effect, he is inviting us to reflect on the vivifying role of divine grace in our lives and the vitalizing and strengthening role that it can play in the afflictions that beset us.

10.7 That "grace" is now expressed in terms of "God's love (that) has been poured into our hearts through the holy Spirit that has been given to us" (5:5). This explains why Christian hope does not disappoint. The certainty of God's love is the basis and guarantee of Christian hope. At issue here is not "our love of God," as many older commentators who followed Augustine once understood it, but "God's love for us," as modern commentators generally understand it, a subjective genitive. "God's love" is a Pauline way of expressing the divine energy and power manifesting itself in an overwhelming embrace of once godless creatures who are smothered with his openness and concern for them. It is not simply that we become aware that God loves us, but in the very experience we receive an assurance of that love, which becomes the central motivating force of our moral beings. That force is nothing other than the holy Spirit. Paul does not now say how this works, but he will later explain it in chap. 8. In 2 Corinthians Paul had written: "It is God who establishes us with you in Christ and has commissioned us; he has put his seal upon us and given us his Spirit in our hearts as a guarantee" (2 Cor 1:21-22).

10.8 This love is experienced because God's Spirit has been given to us. As for Old Testament writers, so too for Paul, the "Spirit" is a way of expressing the presence of God to his world or his creatures. Here it denotes God's presence to the justified Christian. It is "the firstfruits" (8:23) of the glorious destiny of Christians. God "has put his Spirit into our hearts as a guarantee" (2 Cor 1:22), i.e. the first installment of eschatological glory, the first installment of salvation itself.

10.9 Third, we have been reconciled to God: "For if, when we were God's enemies, we were reconciled to him through the death of his Son, now that we are reconciled, we shall all the more certainly be saved by his life" (5:10). Paul recognizes that our human condition was one of "weakness," "godlessness," and "sinfulness" (5:6, 8), a condition that made us enemies of God, hostile to him, and alienated from him. But now, because of the death (and resurrection) of Christ Jesus, we are "reconciled" to God (see 2 Cor 5:18; cf. Col 1:21-22), i.e. we are restored to friendship and intimacy with God. "Reconciliation" is an image drawn from the world of social relations, in effect, only another way of saying "peace." It is a figure drawn from Paul's Greco-Roman background to express yet another effect of the Christ-event. *Katallassein*, "reconcile," means to change the relationship between individuals, groups, or nations in a social or political sense. It would denote a change from anger, hostility, and aliena-tion to love, friendship, and intimacy. (Feelings may accompany such a change of relations, but they are not essential). In this change, the initiative again lies with God, who through the death and resurrection of Christ Jesus, his Son, has brought it about that human sinners are now friends of God, at peace with him. One should beware of reading into this Pauline concept cultic or sacrificial nuances; the image is not derived from such a background. It is a social or political image, used by Paul to stress how the effect of justification results in a Christian's share in an aspect of the risen life of Christ, in other words in a share of the salvation to come. Though justification and reconciliation are now experienced, we still await the full term of that experience, salvation in the eschatological sense. That is why Paul expresses it in the future: "we shall all the more certainly be saved by his life" (5:10).

10.10 Paul ends his discussion with the significant decla-ration: "We boast of God through our Lord Jesus Christ, through whom we have now received reconciliation" (5:11). Because we have been justified by Christ, we can "boast of God" (see 1 Cor 1:31). For in him our salvation is now guaranteed, whereas in our sin we stood in fear of his wrath. Having experienced God's love in what Christ has done for us, we can now exult in and boast of the very thought of God and his love for us.

10.11 Questions. Do I realize what it means to be at peace with God? Should I not thank Christ our Lord for such peace and reconciliation? For the basis of my genuine hope of salvation? Does this not give new meaning to the hardships and afflictions that we experience in this life? If it is rare that a person would lay down his or her life for a good person, how great should be my gratitude for the love of God manifested in his Son's death for me, a sinful wretch! If I were indeed an enemy of God because of my sins and am now reconciled, how can I pour out my gratitude to him for what he has done for me? Christ died vicariously for me. Do I really understand what that means? Do I grasp sufficiently the meaning of "the love of God" that has been poured out for me?

COLLOQUY: PSALM 85

> You once favored, LORD, your land,
> > restored the good fortune of Jacob.
> You forgave the guilt of your people,
> > pardoned all their sins.
> You withdrew all your wrath,
> > turned back your burning anger.
> Restore us once more, God our savior;
> > abandon your wrath against us.
> Will you be angry with us forever,
> > drag out your anger for all generations?
> Please give us life again,
> > that your people may rejoice in you.
> Show us, LORD, your love;
> > grant us your salvation.
> I will listen for the word of God;
> > surely the LORD will proclaim peace
> To his people, to the faithful,
> > to those who trust in him.
> Near indeed is salvation for the loyal;
> > prosperity will fill our land.
> Love and truth will meet;
> > justice and peace will kiss.
> Truth will spring from the earth;
> > justice will look down from heaven.
> The LORD will surely grant abundance;
> > our land will yield its increase.
> Prosperity will march before the LORD,
> > and good fortune will follow behind.

See further *Romans*, 393-402.

Christian Life Brings Freedom from Sin and Death (5:12-21)

¹² Therefore, just as   one
man, and through sin   all
human beings, with the   p to
the time of the law sin   n is
not accounted, when th   way
from Adam until Moses   ned
in a way similar to Ada   e of
the one who was to come. ¹⁵ But the gift is not like the
trespass. For if many have died because of the trespass of
one man, how much more have the grace of God and his gift
overflowed to the many because of the grace of one man,
Jesus Christ. ¹⁶ Moreover, the gift is not like the result of one
man's sin; for judgment resulting from one trespass became
condemnation, whereas the gift following upon many
trespasses brought justification. ¹⁷ If by the trespass of one
man death came to hold sway through that one man, how
much more will those who receive the abundance of God's
grace and his gift of uprightness reign in life through the
one man, Jesus Christ. ¹⁸ So, just as through one trespass
condemnation came upon all, through one act of uprightness justification and life came to all human beings. ¹⁹ Just
as through the disobedience of one man many were made
sinners, so through the obedience of one many will be made
upright. ²⁰ The law slipped in that trespass might increase;
but where sin increased, grace has abounded all the more, ²¹
so that, just as sin held sway in death, grace too might reign

through uprightness to bring eternal life through Jesus Christ our Lord.

11.1 Paul now probes further into the experience of the justified Christian. He does not immediately continue the discussion begun in 5:1-11; rather he takes up the status of humanity before Christ's coming and shows how it was affected by various well-known problems, sin and death, selfishness, and the law, problems which now find a resolution in what Christ Jesus has done for humanity. Before he continues the discussion of the influence of the Spirit in Christian life, he considers it important to note how Christ has set humanity free from such problems. This, in effect, is the burden of the rest of this chapter; it will be continued in the first part of chap. 6 and will be carried over into the whole of chap. 7. In chap. 8 Paul will pick up again the discussion of 5:1-11.

11.2 The problem of sin and death has afflicted humanity ever since Adam. Mankind has had to live with the baneful effects of Adam's sin. Paul develops the theme of Adam's sin, by comparing him, the first parent of the human race, with Christ, the head of humanity in the new aeon. Although he does not say so here, Paul is alluding to the image of Christ as the Adam of the *eschaton* (used in 1 Cor 15:22, 45-48). He does not depict Christ as *Adam redivivus*, but rather sets up Christ in antithetic parallelism and in contrast with Adam. He uses the contrast to get across his major concern about the new life that has come in Christ. As through the one man, Adam, sin and death came upon Adamic humanity, so through the one man, Jesus Christ, came uprightness and eternal life upon Christic humanity. "Adam is the head of the old aeon, the age of *death*; Christ is the head of the new aeon, the age of *life*" (A. Nygren, *Romans*, 210).

Unfortunately, the comparison of Adam and Christ is not perfectly formulated. It would have been clearer, if Paul had written:

> Just as sin came into the world through Adam (and with it death, which affects all human beings), so through Christ came uprightness (and with it eternal life).

But instead Paul wrote:

Just as sin entered the world through one man, and through
sin death, and so death passed to all human beings, with the
result that all have sinned—[13] up to the time of the law sin was
in the world, even though sin is not accounted, when there is
no law; [14] yet death held sway from Adam until Moses, even
over those who had not sinned in a way similar to Adam's
transgression—who is a type of the one who was to come.

Paul felt the need to explain his novel teaching about the influence
of Adam's sin, and so he broke the parallelism to stress that it was
Adam's *sin* that affected all humanity. In 1 Cor 15:22 Paul had
attributed to Adam the *death* of all humanity. That was in line with
contemporary Jewish thinking about the effect of the sin of Adam
and Eve. But here he attributes to Adam not only death, but also
sin. This was a theological novelty. Because of this break in the
parallelism, anacoluthon appears at the end of 5:12 (hence the
dash in the translation), and Paul's real conclusion is expressed
only indirectly in 5:14, when he says that Adam was the type of the
one who was to come. The antithesis, however, is reformulated in
5:15-17, where Paul stresses the surpassing quality of what Christ
has done, when it is compared with Adam's influence. Paul argues
a minori ad maius: Christ, the Adam of the eschaton and head of
humanity in the new aeon, was incomparably more beneficent
toward humanity than Adam was maleficent. This idea is repeated
again in 5:18-19, and the last verse is an echo of 5:12.

11.3 In this paragraph Paul alludes to the Yahwist account of
the creation of Adam and Eve in Gen 2:4b–3:24, especially to their
transgression of the command that Yahweh had laid on them (Gen
3:3, 17). He speaks of Adam's "trespass" (5:15, 17) and his
"disobedience" (5:19), but prescinds from the dramatic details of
the story to concentrate on the theological truth of the consequent
enslavement of human beings to sin and death that Adamic
humanity has incurred. The unmistakably etiological character of
that Genesis story insinuates that the sin of Adam was the cause of
universal mortality, misery, and sin. That story in Genesis sought
to explain the origin of sin and death, which affects all human
beings. Its message is: Sin and death have been around as long as
humanity has; they did not come from God, but find their origin
in humanity itself (symbolically called "Adam" in Genesis). Paul

picks up on the etiology and makes of "Adam" a historical figure as he ascribes to him a baleful influence, one that has affected all human beings and made them mortal sinners.

This teaching about Adam and his influence, however, is secondary in this paragraph, for Paul is concerned much more to affirm the superabundant life-giving effect of the Christ-event. Although Paul ascribes to Adam a causality for the sin of humanity, he does not explain how that baneful effect of Adam took place; he makes no mention of sin's hereditary character, as Augustine would later explain it in his controversy with Pelagius ("This is [said] of propagation, not of imitation").

11.4 Paul is aware, however, that our mortal condition is not owing to Adam alone. This he makes clear in 5:12d: "with the result that all have sinned," echoing what he had said in 3:9 and 3:23. In effect, Paul thus attributes the mortal condition of humanity to a dual causality, to Adam and to the sins of individual human beings. We are all sinners, not only because of Adam, but also because of our own wicked conduct. This means that our sinful human life has a dual polarity. On the one hand, we are part of sin-prone humanity; we inherit an Adamic condition. We are what the psalmist of old said, "True, I was born guilty, a sinner, even as my mother conceived me" (Ps 51:7). Sin has marked my life ever since I came into being, as a member of sinful humanity. On the other hand, we are actively sinners, persons who in the conduct of our lives miss the mark, because of what we do and fail to do. So we are responsible for the sinful character of our existence. We cannot blame it all on Adam.

11.5 In his *Exercises* Ignatius asks us to meditate on the sin of Adam and Eve in the first exercise of the First Week. Though his use of the Genesis story is quite different, he too noted "the enormous corruption it brought to the human race, with so many people going to hell" (§51.2). Yet both Ignatius and Paul are asking us to meditate on what came to be called in Christian theology "Original Sin," a term that betrays its western Latin formulation, *peccatum originale*. Both of them trace human sinfulness to Adam, Ignatius in following the tradition of the church that grew out of the Augustinian teaching, and Paul who formulated an interpretation of Adam's sin, which gave rise to that traditional teaching. Ignatius emphasizes more than Paul the sinful effects of Adam's corruption of the human race, whereas Paul uses Adam more in the sense of a foil to Christ Jesus. Adam is what Paul calls the "type," whereas Christ Jesus is the "antitype," the one who corresponds to the type, but in a different sense. For now Christ Jesus has enabled us to transcend that sin-prone Adamic condition. We are now part of Christic humanity, having been justified and redeemed by the passion, death, and resurrection of Christ Jesus.

11.6 "The gift is not like the trespass" (5:15). There is no comparison between what Christ has graciously done for us and what Adam did. Adam may well have been in Paul's view "the type of the one who was to come" (5:14), but Christ, the antitype, has far surpassed Adam's influence, for in him "the grace of God and his gift have overflowed to the many" (5:15). What Paul thus affirms is something that we can never forget. What Christ Jesus has done for us is a manifestation of God's favor and grace, without which we could not be justified, reconciled, or saved. For all our striving and effort to be reconciled with God, we cannot do it on our own; we can only cooperate with God's prevenient grace. God has taken the initative in leading and enticing us to the conduct of good lives; he draws us on by this grace which surpasses all that we can accomplish by our own feeble efforts.

11.7 The contrast between Adam and Christ that Paul spells out in vv. 15-19 merely reiterates what he has been saying since the beginning of this paragraph. It is important to note what Paul says in v. 19: "Just as through the disobedience of one man many were made sinners, so through the obedience of one many will be made upright." This is the climax of the antithetic parallelism: Adam made us sinners, but Christ has made us upright. The influence of the "one man" is crucial in Paul's affirmation. The one man, Adam, has had a detrimental influence on our lives, but the influence of the one man, Christ Jesus, has also had an influence for good, and in a superabundant way, far surpassing the influence of Adam.

Paul briefly recapitulates his doctrine of justification. If there has been some hesitation about the meaning of the verb *dikaioun*, whether it means "declare righteous/upright" or "make righteous/upright" (as it has been debated ever since the sixteenth century), Paul states in this verse that through Christ Jesus "many will be *made* upright." He use *katastathēsontai*, which leaves little doubt about its meaning. What is operative here is the performative aspect of God's declaration. Because of the Christ-event God declares that sinful human beings are upright in his sight. As a result of that declarative acquittal, they become such— literally, "are made" to be such. Recall Isa 55:10-11: "For, as the rain and the snow come down from the sky and do not return before having watered the earth, fertilizing it and making it germinate to provide seed for the sower and food to eat, so it is with the word that goes from my mouth: it will not return to me unfulfilled or before having carried out my good pleasure and having achieved what it was sent to do."

11.8 "Just as sin held sway in death, grace too might reign through uprightness to bring eternal life through Jesus Christ our Lord" (5:21). So Paul expresses the goal of the Christ-event. Christ Jesus came to save us, and through the grace that comes from his death and resurrection we become upright in God's sight and so come to share in his risen life, which is nothing else but "eternal life."

11.9 Questions. How much aware am I of my Adamic condition? Not just my mortality, but my sinful heritage? Even if I have never dishonored God by transgressing his laws in imitation of Adam's violation of the command laid on him, am I nonetheless aware of my share in sinful humanity? How much more so, if I have indeed transgressed? By contrast, do I fully comprehend the immense gift of uprightness that has come to me in Christ Jesus? Do I thank God for the grace bestowed in Christ Jesus that will bring me one day to life eternal?

COLLOQUY: READ PRAYERFULLY LUKE 15.

See further *Romans*, 405-22, 135-36.

Freedom from Sin and Self through Baptism (6:1-23)

[handwritten note: Thur 6:19-23]

6:1 What, then, shall we say? that grace may abound"? **2** C have died to sin go on living those of us who were b baptized into his death? **4** Thro we were indeed buried with him so that, from the dead by the Father's glory, we too m ourselves in a new way of life. **5** For if we have grown to union with him through a death like his, we shall also be united with him through a resurrection like his. **6** This we know, that our old self has been crucified with him so that the sinful body might be rendered powerless and we might no longer be slaves to sin. **7** For the one who has died has been acquitted of sin. **8** But if we have died with Christ, we believe that we shall also come to live with him, **9** since we know that Christ has been raised from the dead and dies no more; death no longer has sway over him. **10** For in dying as he did, he died to sin once and for all; and in living as he does, he lives to God. **11** So you too are to consider yourselves dead to sin, but alive to God in Christ Jesus.

12 Do not, then, let sin hold sway over your mortal body so that you obey its lusts. **13** Do not put your members at sin's disposal as weapons of wickedness, but instead put yourselves at God's disposal as those who have come to life from death and offer your members to God as weapons of uprightness. **14** Sin is not to have sway over you, for you are not under law but under grace. **15** What, then, does this mean? Should we sin because we are not under law, but under grace? Certainly not! [16] Do you not know that, if you put yourselves at anyone's disposal in obedience, you become slaves of the one you obey—whether of sin, which leads to death, or of real obedience, which leads to uprightness. [17] But thanks be to God, you who were once slaves of sin have wholeheartedly become obedient to the standard of teaching to which you have been entrusted. [18] Freed then from sin, you have become slaves of uprightness. [19] I am putting this in human terms because of your weak human nature: just as you used to put your members slavishly at the disposal of impurity and iniquity, which led to anarchy, so now put them slavishly at the disposal of uprightness, which leads to holiness. [20] When you were slaves of sin, you were free from uprightness. [21] But what benefit did you then have—save things of which you are now ashamed? Things that result in death! [22] But now that you have been freed from sin and have become slaves of God, the benefit you have leads to holiness, which results in life eternal. [23] For the wages of sin is death, but the gift of God is eternal life in Christ Jesus our Lord.

12.1 Paul continues his treatment of the freedoms achieved in Christ Jesus, moving from his consideration of sin and death to another dimension, freedom from sin and self. Whereas his foregoing discussion centered on the Adamic sin-prone condition that besets all of human life, he now moves to a consideration of personal actual sin.

The question asked in 3:5-8 comes once again into focus. The question was: Why not do evil so that good may come of it? If God brings about the justification and salvation of sinners gratuitously through Christ, then why should one not go on sinning? What difference, then, does it really make? If my sinning elicits from God a manifestation of his uprightness, then why should I not give God greater scope for such a manifestation? Just as Christian readers of the epistle might have been inclined to ask about themselves, when Paul described the plight of pagans and Jews without the gospel, their question ("Let us persist in sinning so that grace may abound") now gets a Pauline answer.

The answer is a *reductio ad absurdum* (6:2, 4c, 11, 12, 14). Once you realize what it means to be in Christ or to live in Christ, how can you even think of sinning? "Certainly not! How shall we who have died to sin go on living in it?" (6:2).

12.2 In effect, Paul is rephrasing what he taught in Gal 2:19-20, where he was describing Christian life: "For through the law I died to the law, that I might live to God. I have been crucified *with* Christ; it is no longer I who live, but Christ who lives in me. The very natural life that I now live, I live by faith in the Son of God who loved me and gave himself over for me." Those verses in the Letter to the Galatians not only provide the basis of Paul's answer here in Romans, but they also express the principle of an integrated Christian life. Such a life is lived when the ontological reality (Christ is in me) has surfaced to the psychological level (I am aware that Christ lives in me). Now Paul recasts that principle of integrated Christian life and contrasts the indicative (you are a Christian!) with the imperative (become the Christian that you have been enabled to be!). You have been co-crucified with Christ; you have died with him to sin! So put off sin; put off the old self! You have been raised to a new life in Christ; so live that new life in him. Thus, the very physical existence that a justified and reconciled Christian leads has to be lived out consciously in faith. For such a Christian, sin cannot enter his or her ken.

It is clear that we, even as justified Christians, can sin. Once justified and reconciled with the Father, the Christian can still be allured, tempted, and even seduced by the attraction of sin. But Paul seeks to give such a person a perspective from which one can cope with such allurement, temptation, and seduction.

12.3 Back in 4:7-8 Paul uttered a beatitude over the one who has been justified like Abraham, quoting Ps 32:1-2, "Blessed are those whose iniquities have been forgiven." Medieval theologians interpreted those "iniquities" as the *fomes peccati*, "the tinder of sin," or as "concupiscence," the law of one's members, the consequence of original sin (Peter Lombard). For them, it was part of the inherited Adamic condition. One can still succumb to the allurement of sinful conduct. That medieval teaching goes beyond what Paul affirms, but it helps us to understand what the perspective is that Paul seeks to instill in the justified and reconciled Christian. You are in Christ; so you cannot think any more of sinning. You have died with Christ crucified; so you have died to sin. That means that you must say no to the allurement of sin. That is Paul's answer to the specious questions that his imaginary interlocutor posed to him.

12.4 As part of his answer, however, Paul introduces a secondary, but important, consideration, drawn from Christian baptism, which further explains what he really means. If Paul's argument thus far in Romans has hinged on the "faith" that a person must have in Christ Jesus in order to be justified and saved by the grace of God (see 1:16-17; 3:25-26), he now relates baptism to that faith. He simply takes it for granted that the person who believes in Christ Jesus is baptized. (Certainly, for Paul baptism is not a "deed," something legally prescribed that the person must carry out in order to obtain salvation.) In his view baptism is not a mere supplement to faith, for in baptism the risen *Kyrios* begins to exercise dominion over Christians who by their faith recognize his lordship and live their lives in union with him as a consequence of that faith, acknowledging thereby their obedience to him as *Kyrios*. "You were washed, you were sanctified, you were justified in the name of the *Lord* Jesus Christ" (1 Cor 6:11).

12.5 Paul undoubtedly derived the relation of baptism to faith from the primitive Christian tradition that existed before him, but he is the earliest Christian theologian to give us an elaborate teaching about its meaning. The Acts of the Apostles reveals how Peter's response to the Jews who accepted the challenge of the gospel that he preached to them on the first Christian Pentecost was one about baptism: "Repent, and be baptized in the name of Jesus Christ" (Acts 2:38). Such a tradition would also have recalled the way Jesus himself had referred to his own death as a baptism (Mark 10:38-39; Luke 12:50). From such traditional ideas and from the primitive Christian awareness that all believers were bonded together by the experience of grace and the holy Spirit, it was not difficult for Paul to deduce his idea that "through one Spirit we have all been baptized into one body" (1 Cor 12:13). "Now that faith has come, we are no longer subject to a disciplinarian, for in Christ Jesus we are all children of God through faith. As many of us as were baptized into Christ have been clothed with Christ" (Gal 3:25-27). So Paul now appeals to that experience of baptism, which has incorporated us into the body of Christ, to explain further his answer why we as Christians cannot even think of sinning.

12.6 In this regard the first important Pauline assertion is that we "were baptized into Christ" (6:3a), i.e. we have been incorporated into the body of Christ. We live by a kind of symbiosis with him, by a close bond that unites us with the risen Christ, with the Christ of glory. Here we must recall the full Pauline sense of "faith" as a commitment of the whole self to God in Christ, who has become the Lord in our new lives. Significantly, Paul uses the preposition *eis*, "into," not only with the verb *pisteuein*, "believe," but now also with *baptizein*, "baptize." In the latter case, it may suggest immersion, but it may also be a cryptic bookkeeping expression, equaling the fuller phrase *eis to onoma Christou*, "into the name of Christ," i.e. we have been booked to the account of Christ, inscribed in the ledger of life under his name. The latter would mean that we belong to Christ. But in any case the preposition *eis*, used either of faith or of baptism, expresses the initial movement of introduction or incorporation by which we are born to life "in Christ." As a result of faith and baptism we as Christians have to realize that we now live our lives "in Christ." Christ is "the power of God" (1 Cor 1:23), and he must be recognized as the dynamic force that activates our existence. That is the ontological reality of Christian existence, but it has to surface to the level of psychological consciousness so that we become aware that we are indeed "in Christ." If we so live "in Christ," then there can be no question of continuing in sin.

12.7 To show that the Christian has died to sin, Paul goes on to affirm that we "were baptized into his death" (6:3b), "indeed (were) buried with him" (6:4a), "so that, as Christ was raised from the dead by the Father's glory, we too might conduct ourselves in a new way of life" (6:4bc). Thus baptism symbolically represents the death, burial, and resurrection of Christ. We Christians descend into the baptismal bath, are covered with its waters, as if we were buried with Christ, and emerge from that condition to a new life, going through the experience of Christ Jesus' death, burial, and resurrection. As a result, "we have grown into union with him" (6:5), literally, "we have become grown-together with him." Paul makes use of a bold image derived from grafting; a young branch grafted onto a tree grows together with it in an organic unity and is nourished by its life-giving sap. So Paul envisages the communication of the risen life of Christ to us who are justified and reconciled Christians. As a result, we live in symbiosis with him. For baptism is not only a "likeness of his death," but also a "likeness of his resurrection." The consequence is that "our old self has been crucified with him" (6:6), the "old man," or the self that we once were, the self that belongs to the old aeon, the self dominated by sin, has died with him. "I have been co-crucified with Christ" (Gal 2:19). The result: "that the sinful body might be rendered powerless and we might no longer be slaves to sin" (6:6b). Hence we must consider ourselves "dead to sin" (6:11). This is the Pauline answer to the question that he posed back in chap. 3 and again at the beginning of this chapter.

12.8 It is an exalted view of Christian life that Paul puts before us and all his Christian readers. He does not mince words. If our Christian destiny is "to be always with the Lord" (1 Thess 4:17), then that means that we must live our earthly lives "in Christ," i.e. in a close relationship with him so that, when this earthly life comes to an end, we shall be worthy to "be always with the Lord," i.e. to share his risen life in the glory of the Father. But living "in Christ" means that we shall be cooperating with the graces that come through him from the Father, who has called us and destined us for that glory. "For all of us, with unveiled faces and beholding the glory of the Lord, are being changed into his likeness from one degree of glory to another; for this comes from the Lord who is the Spirit" (2 Cor 3:18). This is what is meant by cooperating with the grace of God. It is nothing less than a synergism, a collaboration which effects the gradual transformation of our earthly lives into the glorious life of the resurrection, our destiny as Christians. "God raised the Lord and will also raise us up by his power" (1 Cor 6:14).

12.9 In the remainder of chap. 6 Paul exhorts his readers to a fuller understanding of this new life in Christ. In the course of it he seeks to explain how this freedom from sin and self, which has been won through faith and baptism, is actually a freedom for commitment (6:12-23). This part of chap. 6 sounds like a baptismal exhortation, laden with hortatory language. (The exercitant should reread these verses.)

Paul seems to be answering a question: In what sense are we Christians to consider ourselves slaves who owe obedience? In his answer he plays on the idea that one who is a slave (*doulos*) is owned by a master (*kyrios*), to whom the slave is expected to render obedient service. In other words, he seeks to answer whether we as baptized Christians can be slaves to sin or to uprightness, and in what sense we are to be regarded as slaves to the God who has acquitted us. To give his answer Paul makes use of diverse images in order to "show how, despite the setting aside of the law and setting up of faith as the sole salvific principle, ethical conduct is not an *adiaphoron* [an indifferent matter], but the necessary, indispensable attestation of the new Christian condition" (H. Lietzmann, *An die Römer*, 71).

12.10 As part of his exhortation Paul urges the baptized Christian not to "let sin hold sway over your mortal body" (6:12), i.e. let it not continue to reign in you. Because the "new life" (6:4) that you now live "in Christ Jesus" is beginning, you may not let sin reign in you. Christians, who are in Christ Jesus, are still "in the sinful body" (6:6) and may find themselves enticed by "its cravings." The "body of sin" denotes a state in which even baptized Christians can find themselves; with such a body they too can still be subject to sin. Certainly Paul does not mean that they have become sinless or incapable of sin through faith and baptism. They are still human beings and bear in themselves the effects of the Adamic condition. Sin, personified here, can still reign over them. Hence Paul's urging.

What Paul calls "sin" in 6:12 came to be understood in the Augustinian tradition as "concupiscence" or *fomes peccati*, "the tinder of sin" (*Contra duas epistolas Pelagianorum* 1.13.27; CSEL 60. 445). The Council of Trent, in speaking of concupiscence, said that "the apostle sometimes calls [it] sin" and refers to Rom 6:12. It explained, however, that concupiscence itself is not sin, but "comes from sin and tends toward sin" (DS 1515). Though that is an exact theological transposition, it is a precision not yet found in the Pauline text. We have to reflect on that facet of human life. Concupiscence is always with us and we have to school ourselves, with God's grace, to thwart this tendency to sin. We are still children of Adam, prone to sinful conduct, even though we have been justified, reconciled to God, and live "in Christ Jesus." This we must always remember, and Paul will later, in chap. 8, explain how the Spirit of God that has been poured into our hearts will enable us to deal with the enticement of "sin that dwells in me" (7:17), or of concupiscence.

12.11 What Paul has been describing in this hortatory section of Romans 6 is only another way of putting what Ignatius in the Second Week of the *Exercises* called the Two Standards, the one of Christ and the other of Lucifer, the mortal enemy of our human nature. When Christians obey sin and not uprightness, they line themselves up under the standard of Lucifer and succumb to his successive allurements of riches, honor, and pride, and thus go from one stage of bondage to another. But if they obey uprightness, they choose to align themselves with the apostles and disciples under the standard of Christ the Lord and rather accept with him the successive roles of poverty, contempt, and humility in their lives.

12.12 Questions. Do I really grasp what it means to have died to sin in Christ Jesus? What it means to live "in Christ"? As a baptized Christian, do I allow that identification with Christ to surface to my consciousness, to the level of my conscious activity? Do I ask myself: Is this the way a Christian, baptized into Christ, would act? If I really belong to Christ, should that status not enable me to resist the allurements of sin? How do I cope with concupiscence, with this "sinful body"? If Christ is indeed my Lord and Master, do I rightly seek to serve him? Do I align myself under his standard and choose with him poverty, contempt, and humility?

COLLOQUY: PSALM 121

> I raise my eyes toward the mountains.
> > From where will my help come?
> My help comes from the LORD,
> > the maker of heaven and earth.
> God will not allow your foot to slip;
> > your guardian does not sleep.

> Truly, the guardian of Israel
>> never slumbers or sleeps,
> The LORD is your guardian;
>> the LORD is your shade
>> at your right hand.
> By day the sun cannot harm you,
>> nor the moon by night.
> The LORD will guard you from all evil,
>> will always guard your life.
> The LORD will guard your coming and going
>> both now and forever.

See further *Romans*, 429-39, 443-52.

EXERCISE 13

Freedom from the Law by the Death of Christ (7:1-6)

⁷:¹ Or are you unaware, brothers—for I am speaking to those who know what law is—that the law has authority over a human being only as long as one is alive? ² Thus a married woman is bound by law to her husband while he is alive. But if the husband dies, she is released from the law regarding her husband. ³ Accordingly, she will be called an adulteress, if she gives herself to another man, while her husband is still alive. But if her husband dies, she is free of that law and does not become an adulteress, if she gives herself to another man. ⁴ So you too, my brothers, have died to the law through the body of Christ that you might give yourselves to another, to him who has been raised from the dead, so as to bear fruit for God. ⁵ For when we were living merely natural lives, sinful passions aroused by the law were at work in our members, so as to bear fruit for death. ⁶ But now, by dying to what we were once held captive, we have been released from the law so that we might serve God in a new way of the Spirit and not in the old way of a written code.

13.1 Paul now turns to the third freedom won through Christ Jesus, freedom from the law. This is another of the important chapters in the epistle, but one that is not easy to understand. The problem that confronts Paul here is that the law of Moses, given to Israel for its guidance and the conduct of its life, was actually a gift of God. How then could it have created problems in Jewish life? Was it sinful? Was it not something good? Earlier in the

epistle (2:1–3:9) Paul had written that the Jew under the law was
an object of God's wrath. What role did the law still play in human
life? How can the law be a minister of death and condemnation (2
Cor 3:7, 9)? What is the Christian's relation to the law? Now Paul
finally comes to grips with these and other questions about the
law.

This is the famous chapter in Romans wherein Paul
describes the human predicament, wherein the Ego realizes that
it does what it does not want to do and has to cope with indwelling
sin. The consideration of this topic seems to interrupt the flow of
Pauline thought because it introduces sin once again, albeit from
a different perspective. Similarly, in the Ignatian *Spiritual Exercises*
the contemplations on the mysteries of Christ's life in the Second
Week are interrupted by the "Election" and the "Consideration of
the States of Life." In the course of the latter Ignatius asks the
exercitant to "observe the intention of Christ our Lord and, in
contrast, that of the enemy of human nature" (§135), as one
prepares for the meditation on the Two Standards, the standard
of Satan and the standard of Christ. Ignatius' meditation deals in
its own way with the struggle between good and evil that
characterizes chap. 7 of Romans. Under whose standard do I
align myself, under that of Satan or of the Lord, under that of sin
or of Christ?

Paul's treatment in this chapter will be meditated on in three
sections. The first (7:1-6) explains in what sense the death of
Christ has resulted in a liberation of humanity from the law. In
the second and the third sections (7:7-13 and 7:14-25), the
paragraphs will deal with the relation of the law to God and to sin.

13.2 Most of what Paul teaches about the law is found in this
chapter, but one has also to consult Rom 8:1-7; 9:31; 10:4-5; 13:8-
10; Gal 2:16–6:13; 1 Cor 9:20; 15:56, where some important
details are mentioned. Of what law does Paul speak? It has been
said by some commentators to mean "law" in general, or "the
legal system." Some others understand it of Roman law, because
Paul is writing to Romans, who because of their famous law would
know what he was talking about. Most commentators, however,
understand it as the Mosaic law, because the immediate context
(vv. 2, 3, 4b), as well as 5:20 and 6:14, seems so to suggest. It

certainly does not refer to the so-called natural law or even to the command laid on Adam in Gen 3:13, as some patristic and modern writers have tried to interpret it because of 7:13. Paul is envisaging the law given to Israel by Moses, for this has been on his mind all through the epistle up to this point (see 2:13, 23; 3:20, 28, 31).

13.3 In the first six verses Paul interweaves two arguments, which call for our careful meditation. The first is that law binds or has authority over only the living (7:1, 4a). Paul thinks of the law as a *kyrios*, a master that lords it over human beings who must obey it as long as they are alive. After 6:9 and 6:14 where the same idea was used of sin and death, law now joins them as a threesome that tyrannizes human existence.

Consequently, Christians who have died "through the body of Christ" are no longer bound to observe the law, for Christ has died to the law. It is not that the law itself has died, but that human beings who have put their faith in Christ have died with him and so are no longer in the life of the old aeon, under law. It is the Christian who has died to the law together with the crucified Christ. "I have died to the law that I might live for God; I have been crucified with Christ" (Gal 2:19). Thus Paul speaks of a co-crucifixion with Christ Jesus.

13.4 The second argument is that a wife is freed by the death of her husband from the specific prescription of the Mosaic law binding her to him. In v. 1b Paul had spoken simply of *anthrōpos*, "human being," in relation to the Mosaic law, but now he uses a more specific example of a human being, a married woman, for whom the Mosaic law contained definite regulations. In the Old Testament the wife was considered the chattel or property of the husband, who had rights over her that could be violated by her or by another man (see Gen 20:3). Hence every extramarital sexual act of hers was regarded as adultery (Exod 20:14, 17; 21:22; Lev 20:10; Num 30:10-16). From that condition the Jewish wife was freed when her husband died. "A wife is bound to her husband as long as he lives; if the husband dies, she is freed to be married to whomever she wishes, only in the Lord" (1 Cor 7:39). Now Christians are like the Jewish wife whose husband has died. As she is freed from "the law of the husband" through death, so

Christians have died to the law "through the body of Christ," and they are freed from the law (7:2, 3, 4b).

The second argument is supposed to be an illustration of the first, but it is not perfect. It is useless to try to work out the details of the comparison. The point Paul is trying to make is that Christians who "have died" with Christ are no longer people who have to worry about specific dictates of the Mosaic law; they are freed of obligation to it.

The problem is to explain how they are so freed "through the body of Christ." Because Paul in his writings uses the expression "body of Christ" in different senses, commentators debate the sense in which it is to be understood here. For it can mean the crucified body of Christ, or the eucharistic body of Christ (1 Cor 11:24), or the ecclesiastical body of Christ (1 Cor 12:27). In this context, however, it hardly refers to either the eucharistic or ecclesiastical body, even though some commentators have at times tried so to argue. It is rather the first meaning, the physical, crucified body of the Jesus of history, as Origen proposed long ago (PG 14. 1073-74). For in Gal 2:19-20 Paul said that Christians have died to the law's condemnation by having been co-crucified with Christ. He died to the law, and in that death all humanity shared by God's decision (see 2 Cor 5:14-15: When Jesus died for all "in the likeness of sinful flesh" [Rom 8:3], then all died). This, however, does not make Paul an antinomian, someone who preaches license to do what one pleases and to disregard all law. Later in this epistle Paul will spell out obligations of Christian life, and not a few of them will echo obligations imposed on the Jews of old by the Mosaic law. For such details we must be patient.

13.5 The purpose of being freed from the law is "that you might give yourselves to another" (7:4b), the conclusion that Paul draws from his second comparison. The Jewish wife was freed from "the law of the husband" by his death and could give herself as wife to another man, without incurring the charge of adultery. Now Paul argues that that "other" is he "who has been raised from the dead," i.e. the glorified Christ, who as *Kyrios* becomes a sort of "second husband" and is the Lord of the Christian henceforth. This is but another way in which Paul reiterates the lordship of Christ.

Christians must not think of themselves as lorded over or tyrannized by legal prescriptions in life. "For freedom Christ has set us free; so stand fast and do not submit again to the yoke of slavery" (Gal 5:1), i.e. slavery to the law. Rather "serve the Lord" (12:11).

13.6 This obligation to the risen, glorified Christ has its own purpose: in order that we may "bear fruit for God" (7:4c). The union of the risen Christ and the Christian has been depicted in terms of marriage. Paul continues the figure: such a union is expected to produce the "fruit" of a life dedicated to God. That is the reform of life that the apostle now calls for. "I have died to the law that I might live for God" (Gal 2:19).

13.7 Paul recalls by way of contrast that, before Christians came to live "in Christ," they were still conducting themselves *en sarki*, "in the flesh," i.e. living merely natural lives, lives dominated by that aspect of themselves that is earth-oriented and not open to God. In that situation "sinful passions aroused by the law were at work in our members, so as to bear fruit for death" (7:5). Our propensity to sin was excited by such "cravings" of the mortal body of flesh (see 6:12). It is well to consider such a contrast, because, even though we may now be justified and reconciled Christians, we too can still be lured by "the flesh" and be tempted by what the law forbids, by forbidden fruit.

13.8 Now, however, in the new aeon of the Christian dispensation, we have died to what once held us in bondage, to the legal prescriptions that tyrannized. In other words, we have been released from the law so that we might serve God in a new way, in the way of the Spirit. This service of God through the Spirit will be explained more fully in chap. 8, but here Paul introduces only the contrast of the Spirit and the written code: the *pneuma*, "Spirit," must now dominate our Christian lives, and not the *gramma*, "letter" (of the law), which sought to dominate the life of everyone under it. The Spirit must become the dynamic principle of our Christian lives. Paul called himself the minister of a new covenant, "not of the letter, but of the Spirit. For the letter brings death, whereas the Spirit gives life" (2 Cor 3:6). The "letter" is only another way of referring to the Mosaic law. He claims that it "brings death," because as a legal code it uttered a curse on all those who did not observe what it prescribed. "All who depend on deeds of the law are under a curse; as it stands written, 'Cursed be everyone who does not persevere in doing all that is written in the book of the law'" (Gal 3:10, where Paul quotes Deut 27:26a). Such a curse meant "death," and Paul even called the law of old "a ministry of death, carved in letters on stone" (2 Cor 3:7). Christians will always be tempted to look for security to legal prescriptions to guide their lives, instead of listening to the prompting of the Spirit, and this aspect of human existence is called in question by the consideration that Paul proposes to us here. "I do not nullify God's grace; for if justification came through the law, then Christ died to no purpose" (Gal 2:21).

13.9 Questions. Under whose standard do I align myself, under that of Satan or of the Lord, under that of sin or of Christ? How do I react to law in my life? Do I treat it as a taskmaster that I must obey? Or do I allow the freedom that comes in Christ Jesus to enhance that facet of life? Do I lead my life, even under the restraints of various regulations with which I must reckon, as a life dedicated to God? Does my attitude toward law entice me with forbidden fruit because I am still "in the flesh"?

COLLOQUY: PSALM 86:1-12

> Hear me, LORD, and answer me,
> > for I am poor and oppressed.
> Preserve my life, for I am loyal;
> > save your servant who trusts in you.
> You are my God; pity me, LORD;
> > to you I call all the day.
> Gladden the soul of your servant;
> > to you, LORD, I lift up my soul.
> LORD, you are kind and forgiving,
> > most loving to all who call on you.
> LORD, hear my prayer;
> > listen to my cry for help.
> In this time of trouble I call,
> > for you will answer me.
> None among the gods can equal you, O LORD;
> > nor can their deeds compare to yours.

For you are great and do wondrous deeds;
    and you alone are God.
Teach me, LORD, your way
        that I may walk in your truth,
        single-hearted and revering your name.
I will praise you with all my heart,
        glorify your name forever, LORD my God.

See further *Romans*, 454-62.

The Role of the Law in Human Life (7:7-13)

[7] What then can we say? Is the law sin? Certainly not! Yet I would not have known sin, if it were not for the law. I would not have known what it was to covet, if the law had not said, *"You shall not covet."* [q] [8] But sin, using the commandment, seized the opportunity and produced in me every sort of covetousness. Now in the absence of law sin is as good as dead. [9] Indeed, I once lived in the absence of law, but when the commandment came, sin sprang to life, [10] and I died. The commandment that was meant for life was found to be death for me. [11] For sin, using the commandment, seized the opportunity and deceived me; through it sin killed me. [12] Yet the law is holy, and the commandment is holy, upright, and good. [13] Did, then, what was good become death for me? Certainly not! Rather, sin, that it might be unmasked as sin, produced death in me by using what was good so that through the commandment it might become sinful beyond all measure.

[q] Exod 20:17; Deut 5:21

14.1 Finally, Paul comes to grips with the problem of the law. He began the consideration of it in the preceding exercise, where he addresses his readers in the second plural (7:4) and eventually identifies himself with them, using the first plural (7:5-6). Thus he speaks to all of us. His message was: We have been freed from the law through the body of the crucified Christ. Now he speaks as a Christian, as a Christian so liberated by Christ Jesus, but one who cannot forget his Jewish past. This makes him debate the role of

107

law in all human life. His message, then, becomes one that is crucial for all of Christian existence. We have to live with do's and dont's. How should the justified and reconciled Christian react to them? What is their place in Christian life?

Paul begins to speak rhetorically in the first singular. He might have spoken about the human predicament that we all recognize, using simply "we," or *anthrōpos*, "human being," or *tis*, "someone," but he chooses to speak rather of *egō*, as he does elsewhere at times (cf. 1 Cor 8:13; 13:1-3, 11-12; 14:6-19; Gal 2:18-21).

The identification of the Ego has been a problem for centuries. Because he uses the first singular, one might be tempted to think that he is speaking autobiographically, reflecting on his own youthful experience as he grew up and was confronted with the demands of the Mosaic law. That interpretation, which has often been used, however, contradicts what Paul says about himself in Phil 3:6, where he speaks as a Christian looking back on his Jewish past and says, "as for righteousness based on the law I was blameless"; cf. Gal 1:13-14. So Paul is scarcely speaking only of himself. It has also been understood as Adam, father of the human race, confronted with the commandment of Gen 2:16-17. But that is to import into this complicated chapter a figure, who is not mentioned or otherwise clearly envisaged. The Ego has also been understood of a Christian believer faced with obligations of this new mode of existence. Yet that introduces too specific an identification for the generic scope of the discussion. (Christians who read this passage today have to understand the basic Pauline position, even though they find a certain existential resonance in it.) It is best understood in a cosmic-historical dimension, i.e. as a rhetorical device to dramatize the experience common to all unregenerate human beings faced with law and relying on their own resources to meet its demands. In other words, Paul looks at unregenerate humanity with Jewish spectacles and depicts it faced with the Mosaic law and striving to achieve the status of righteousness by observing such a law. Under his own quasi-person Paul treats of the general issue that confronts humankind.

The trouble with most of the interpretations of the Ego that have been proposed is that they tend to trivialize Paul's insight. The confrontation of the Ego with sin and law is not considered by

Paul on an individual, psychological level, but from a historical and corporate point of view. Paul views humanity as it was known to him through Jewish-Christian eyes, without Christ and in Christ. Some of his generalizing statements in this passage are susceptible of application to experiences beyond his own immediate perspective. Hence what he says in vv. 7-25 is undoubtedly the experience of many Christians faced with divine, ecclesiastical, or civil law or with the regulations of society or family. When these verses are read in such a context, few persons will fail to appreciate their significance. For Paul asks the questions that bother all human beings confronted with obligations that they have to carry out. Hence it is important that all of us take to heart what Paul says in rest of this chapter.

14.2 In 3:20 Paul had acknowledged that "through the law comes the real knowledge of sin," and in 4:15, that "the law brings only wrath," and again in 5:20, that "the law made its entrance so that the trespass (of it) might increase." Such comments were meant to bring out aspects of the Mosaic law: that one of its functions was to reveal the character of evil conduct as a transgression of God's law. This is, indeed, the "real knowledge of sin." Through it we come to know how evil conduct subjects us to divine wrath and how we are seduced by forbidden fruit. But one might conclude from such assertions that the law itself was somehow sinful, leading human beings to sin, or aiding their own propensity to it. And yet, did the law not come from God? Was it not given to Moses and Israel for a good purpose? Was it not meant to bring them life (Lev 18:5)? This is the anomaly of the law, and with this problem Paul now tries to cope. We too can ask similarly: Are not all the obligations in life, with which we have to live, meant for a good purpose, even though they might entice us to violate and transgress them? Verses 7-13 are a confession, in which the Ego recognizes its deception by sin, which makes a tool or henchman of the law, using the law to its own purpose.

14.3 "What then can we say? Is the law sin?" The question may be rhetorical, but it expresses a realistic reaction of human beings to what Paul has been saying. The identification of the law with sin Paul resolutely rejects, because it is a power opposed to sin, even though he has to recognize that "if it were not for the law, I would not have known sin! I would not have known what it was to covet, if the law had not said, 'You shall not covet'" (7:7). This is the famous story of "forbidden fruit," a story that has been around as long as humanity has. It is told in Genesis 2–3 itself: If God had not told Adam and Eve that they were not to eat of the tree of life, the tempter's enticement would never have come. We have seen it exemplified in the lives not only of small children and the cookie jar, but of adults who run the red lights and scoff at penal laws.

When Paul says that "if it were not for the law, I would not have known sin," what he really means is that the law brings it about that evil conduct and sin are unmasked as a transgression of the will of God. For a human being knows the difference between good and evil, even before he or she recognizes it as "sin" or as a transgression even of a legal code.

The example that Paul uses, "You shall not covet," comes from the Decalogue (Exod 20:17 or Deut 5:21): You shall not covet your neighbor's wife, house, field, manservant, maidservant, ox, ass, or anything he has. The prohibition seeks to teach human beings that they are not be distracted by created things as their natural desires lead them to have created goods, which are not their ultimate good, God the Creator. Through the commandment, which formulates the prohibition, the sluggish human conscience should be educated and properly formed, but it is instead often enticed and seduced by that very prohibition.

14.4 "Sin, using the commandment, seized the opportunity and produced in me every sort of covetousness" (7:8). Paul personifies sin and law, making Sin (with a capital S) the master of unregenerate human earthly life, which uses Law as its henchman to achieve its own purpose of enslaving the Ego. It has made an ally of what should have been its mortal enemy. Sin and the Law thus become actors on the stage of human history. The "commandment" may sound like an allusion to Gen 2:16, to the command laid on Adam. This is the reason why some commentators have understood the Ego as Adam, but Paul's perspective here in chap. 7 is not that of 5:12-14. It is rather a specific "commandment" of the law that entices the Ego. The actor Sin has used Law with its list of do's and dont's to stir up in the Ego every sort of covetousness, the desire for every sort of thing that the Ego should not have or do.

14.5 "In the absence of law sin is as good as dead," i.e. it is lifeless. The actor Sin is like a corpse, powerless to make the evildoing of humanity a flagrant revolt against God's will. When there was no Law, human beings in their wickedness were not conscious of being necessarily in open rebellion against God.

To understand this Pauline view of human wickedness and Sin, one has to recall his view of human history. He looks at it with Jewish spectacles and thinks of it as having three stages or periods: From Adam to Moses, from Moses to the Messiah, and the period of the Messiah (Christ). In the first period, from Adam to Moses, people did evil, but they did not violate precepts of a law, as did Adam who disobeyed the commandment (recall Rom 5:14). In the second period, when the Law "was added" (Gal 3:19), their evil deeds became violations of that Law. In the third period Christ has freed humanity from Sin and the Law. So from Adam to Moses Sin was corpselike.

In itself the actor Law was "holy, upright, and good" (7:12) and was "meant for life" (7:10), because it basically came from God and was given for a good purpose. But it has been used by Sin to become "the power of sin" (1 Cor 15:56) in human life, because it provided the *aphormē*, the "jump start," the opportunity or occasion for formal violations of its commandments. As a result in the second period, from Moses to the Messiah, when the Law was introduced and added to human experience, the evil that people did became recognized as a violation of law. People consciously sinned, i.e. they transgressed the Mosaic law; they violated its commandments. In the final period, that of the Messiah, Christ has freed humanity from Sin (5:12-21), enabling them to live without the restraints of do's and dont's (just how will be explained in chap. 8). Here Paul is concentrating on the first and second periods, when the Ego "once lived in the absence of law" (7:9), i.e. from Adam to Moses, when Sin was "as good as dead" (7:8), when humanity lived in ignorance of the real nature of its evil conduct.

14.6 "When the commandment came, sin sprang to life, and I died" (7:9-10). With the addition of the Mosaic law to human existence, Sin became formally known as a violation of God's will, and desiring became "coveting." The result was that the Ego died, for "the wages of sin is death" (6:23). Here "death" means not just the end of natural, earthly life, but total death, the opposite of eternal life, a status of existence without God and apart from his glorious presence. Because of the relationship of Sin to death in this sense, one realizes how the Ego has missed the mark and has fallen short of the glory of God, the destiny of which Paul spoke in 3:23.

14:7 Now Paul gives utterance to the anomaly that the Law has introduced into human existence: "the commandment that was meant for life was found to be death for me" (7:10). The Mosaic law promised "life" to those who would obey its prescriptions: "by the observance of which one shall find life" (Lev 18:5, quoted by Paul in Gal 3:12; Rom 10:5); cf. also Deut 4:1; 6:24. Although the regulations of the Mosaic law were meant to oppose Sin and teach human beings about it, that "the whole world might become accountable to God" (3:19), the Law became instead, through being used by Sin as a tool, a means to deliver them to death. How did it do this? The actor Law became an "occasion" for sin (7:5, 11), a moral informer (7:7), and indeed leveled a condemnation to death on the one who did not obey it (Deut 27:26). This is the paradox of Sin and the Law. The desire and coveting that Sin produces in the Ego reveals that the Ego is deceived and becomes a child of death.

14.8 "Sin, using the commandment, seized the opportunity and deceived me" (7:11). This assertion is merely a repetition of what Paul had said in 7:8a. Paul does not mean that Sin deceived the Ego through the Law, but rather that Sin seized the occasion that the Law with its prescriptions and prohibitions provided in order to deceive the Ego, to seduce it, to lead it astray. The seducer is Sin, not the Law. As God's commandment gave the tempting serpent the opportunity to deceive Eve, and through her Adam too, so Sin used the opportunity of the Law to deceive the Ego thus confronted and entice it to go after forbidden fruit. In saying this, Paul is undoubtedly alluding to Gen 3:13, where "deceived me" is also found, used by Eve in her answer to God, who asked her why she did such a thing.

14.9 "Yet the law is holy, and the commandment is holy, upright, and good" (7:12). This is Paul's explanation of the answer that he gave to the question in v. 7, whether the law was sin. He resolutely rejected such a conclusion there, and now one sees why.

In v. 22 he will frankly call it "God's law," and that is the reason for its sanctity; it comes from God and is related to God. In itself, then, the Law cannot be sinful or lead to sin. But good though it is, it can be used by Sin as a tool, as an occasion to entice the Ego to do what is unlawful. Through the Law with its precept Sin entices the Ego with forbidden fruit, and that creates the anomaly of the Law. "Did, then, what was good become death for me?" (7:13a). Another suggestion that Paul rejects. "Sin, that it might be unmasked as sin, produced death in me by using what was good so that through the commandment it might become sinful beyond all measure" (7.13bc). *Nomos* did not cause the "death" of the Ego, but it proved to be the occasion of death, playing a secondary role, quite accidentally. The real culprit was indwelling Sin, whose true colors are thereby revealed, disclosed by Law.

Sin dwells in me; that is the Pauline explanation of the human predicament. In commenting on Rom 6:12 (see 12.10 above), I mentioned that the Council of Trent adopted the Augustinian explanation of this indwelling Sin as "concupiscence," a precision that Paul himself does not make, but that is a valid interpretation of his idea. For even the justified and reconciled Christian experiences concupiscence or the "tinder of sin," which in itself is not sin, but comes from sin and can lead to sin. It is the result of the Adamic condition. When Sin is thus understood, the Pauline explanation of the role of Law becomes intelligible even in Christian life.

14.10 Questions. Do I not find in this passage a description of my own existential condition? How often have I sensed the temptation of "forbidden fruit"? Even within the past year? To what extent am I aware of Sin dwelling within me and luring me with its enticements? Am I willing to recognize that divine, ecclesiastical, and even civil laws are good? Do I reckon with the possibility that the evil that I may do in violation of such regulations can actually be a violation of God's law?

COLLOQUY: PSALM 69:1–15

> Save me, O God,
>> for the waters have reached my neck.
> I have sunk into the mire of the deep,
>> where there is no foothold.

I have gone down to the watery depths;
    the flood overwhelms me.
I am weary with crying out;
    my throat is parched.
My eyes have failed,
    looking for my God.
More numerous than the hairs of my head
    are those who hate me without cause.
Too many for my strength
    are my treacherous enemies.
Must I now restore
    what I did not steal?
God, you know my folly;
    my faults are not hidden from you.
Let those who wait for you, LORD of hosts,
    be not shamed through me.
Let those who seek you, God of Israel,
    not be disgraced through me.
For your sake I bear insult,
    shame covers my face.
I have become an outcast to my kin,
    a stranger to my mother's children.
Because zeal for your house consumes me,
    I am scorned by those who scorn you.
I have wept and fasted,
    but this led only to scorn.
I clothed myself in sackcloth;
    I became a byword for them.
They who sit at the gate gossip about me;
    drunkards make me the butt of their songs.
But I pray to you, LORD,
    for the time of your favor.
God, in your great kindness answer me
    with your constant help.
Rescue me from the mire;
    do not let me sink.

See further *Romans*, 462-72.

Complaint and Cry of Human Beings Enslaved by the Law (7:14-25)

[14] **Now we know t**   I am of
flesh, sold in bonda   **what I
do. For I do not do w**   **at I do.**
[16] **Yet if I do what I d**   **s good.**
[17] **But as it is, it is no**   **wells in
me.** [18] **I know that nc**   **flesh. I
can desire what is g**   **For I do
not do the good I d**   **desire.**
[20] **Yet if I do what I d**   **o it, but
sin that dwells in n**   **at work:
When I want to do right, evil is ready at hand.** [22] **For in my
inmost self I delight in God's law;** [23] **but I see another law in
my members battling against the law that my mind
acknowledges and making me captive to the law of sin that is
in my members.** [24] **Wretch that I am, who will rescue me from
this doomed body?** [25] **Thanks be to God—(it is done) through
Jesus Christ our Lord! So then I myself in my mind am a
slave to God's law, but in my flesh a slave to the law of sin.**

15.1 Paul finishes off his discussion of the role of law in human life by continuing to analyze a crucial aspect of human existence; for it is beset by weakness because of the component that is flesh, and Sin dwells within and dominates that weak flesh. In effect, he carries on his discussion of the role of the actor Law, recognizing that the difficulty is not *per se* with Law, but with human beings themselves, who are carnal, creatures of flesh that is weak, and prone to succumb to attacks of Sin, which dwells within them (as a result of Adam's effect on them). Because of that indwelling Sin, human beings fail to achieve what God desires of them. Yet not all in human beings is sinful; there is also the mind (*nous*) that recognizes God's law and acknowledges what that law asks of humanity. But that mind cannot of itself resist the seductions of Sin.

If vv. 7-13 were a confession in which the Ego recognized its deception by Sin that was making use of the Law, vv. 14-25 are rather an apology for Law itself. It is almost a philosophical discussion of the makeup of human beings, as Paul describes the moral experience of the Ego faced with Law. It is described as a battle between the Ego of flesh dominated by Sin and the spiritual Law of God.

15.2 "We know that the law is spiritual" (7:14). Because of its God-given origin and its purpose of leading human beings to "life," the Mosaic law belongs to the realm of the Spirit. It does not belong to the world of earthbound, natural humanity. It is *pneumatikos*, "spiritual," and not *sarkinos*, "carnal," which is the way Paul describes a human being in its Adamic condition, turned from God and disoriented. That condition results from human bondage to Sin, to the condition inherited from Adam. Paul will now describe the resulting human predicament.

15.3 "I do not understand what I do" (7:15). As one sold under Sin, the Ego is a mystery to itself. It stems from a conflict in the inmost depths of a human being, the cleavage between reason-dominated desire and actual performance. So imperious is indwelling Sin that the Ego acts without realizing what it is doing. "I do not do what I want to." The Ego's moral aspirations and its performance are not integrated. Even the pagan Roman poet Ovid acknowledged the same, *Video meliora proboque, deteriora sequor*, "I perceive what is better and approve of it, but I pursue what is worse" (*Metamorphoses* 7.20-21). So runs the universal formulation of the human predicament.

15.4 "If I do what I do not want, I agree that the law is good" (7:16). For the reason-dominated desire to do what is right involves an implicit recognition of the goodness of what the Law prescribes. As far as willing is concerned, the Ego is at one with the Law. To carry it out, however, is another problem. For "as it is, it is no longer I who do it, but sin that dwells in me" (7:17). Indwelling Sin dominates the Ego in its existence as flesh. It may seem that Paul is absolving human beings of their sinful conduct by ascribing it to indwelling Sin, but it is still the sin of the Ego, for in 5:12 Paul traced the sinful condition not only to Adam, but also to individual human acts. For Sin is still human sin, the evil that the individual does. "I can desire what is good, but I cannot carry it out," because of the weak condition of the flesh that I am. Paul merely repeats what he had said above. Everyone who reads this Pauline description of sinful human nature immediately recognizes its pertinence.

15.5 "I know that no good dwells in me, that is, in my flesh" (7:18). The added qualification is important, because Paul finds the root of the predicament in the human self, considered as *sarx*, "flesh," to be the source of all that is opposed to God and his desires for humanity. From the Ego as flesh dominated by Sin proceeds all the evil that one does.

15.6 "If I do what I do not want, it is no longer I who do it, but sin that dwells in me" (7:20). Paul repeats what he has already said in vv. 17-18. In the battle between God's will set forth in the Law and evil conduct, the Ego wants to stand on the side of God, yet it realizes that indwelling Sin is the source of its wickedness.

15.7 "In my inmost self I delight in God's law" (7:22), lit., "according to the inner man." Though dominated by Sin, when it is considered as "flesh," the Ego still experiences that it desires what God desires; the mind or reason recognizes the ideal proposed by the Law given by God. That reaction to God's law is not just a merely rational assent, but one that the Ego even relishes, simply because of what it is, a guiding directive coming from God himself to assist the Ego in its conduct of life.

15.8 The trouble is that the Ego realizes that there is something more within it than just an awareness or even a delight in what God desires of it. "I see another law in my members battling against the law that my mind acknowledges" (7:23). Paul is playing on the word *nomos*, which has normally meant the Mosaic law, but is now used in the sense of a "principle," which concretely refers now to indwelling Sin. It should not be confused with the "law" to which Paul referred in 2:14, when he admitted that at times Gentiles are a "law" to themselves. Because indwelling Sin rather uses Law like a tool or a henchman, Paul freely transfers the term *nomos* even to Sin. That is why he speaks in the next sentence of "the law of sin," by which he means Law as used by Sin, which makes me a captive. Because he has rejected the idea that "the law is sin" (7:7), one sees that he is here using *nomos* of Sin in a figurative sense. Thus the Ego has to be fully aware of the seduction of this other *nomos*, which is nothing else but indwelling Sin. This teaching has to be extended for the Christian to concupiscence, the effect of the Adamic condition that remains in the baptized. This is Paul's explanation of why the Christian can still sin and why Christians too must be on their guard against what he here calls indwelling Sin.

15.9 The miserable condition in which the Ego finds itself finally gives utterance to an exclamation: "Wretch that I am! Who will rescue me from this doomed body?" (7:24). Paul describes the Ego's condition as existence in a "body of death," one destined for total death, for separation from God and the glorious divine presence. This is the agonizing cry of the Ego weighted down with the sinful burden and prevented from attaining its goal. So Paul expresses the tension between existence in Adam and existence in Christ. His answer: "Thanks be to God! (It is done) through Jesus Christ our Lord!" (7:25). The Ego's gratitude to God is thus formulated, as it realizes what has been achieved for it in Christ Jesus.

Verse 25 may, however, be simply a doxological expression, "Thanks be to God through Jesus Christ our Lord!" Then it would express thanks to God for the recognition of the wretched condition in which the Ego finds itself. The answer to the question would then come in 8:1-4. But the cry seems to call for some answer, and to interpret the verse merely as a doxology seems less appropriate after the exclamation. Even if one takes it as it is first translated, as an elliptical expression, then the fuller explanation of that brief answer, "(It is done) through Jesus Christ," is given in 8:1-4. In either case, the Ego expresses its thanks to God as it realizes what has been done for it and all humanity through Christ Jesus.

15.10 The last verse is merely a concluding summation to the discussion in chap. 7: "I myself in my mind am a slave to God's law, but in my flesh a slave to the law of sin" (7:15cd). So Paul formulates again the contrast between what the mind recognizes and what the Ego actually does.

15.11 Questions. How readily do I recognize that I am carnal and sold in bondage to Sin? How often have I succumbed to the human predicament? Do I really recognize that God's law is something good for me? Should I not frankly admit that I am captive to Sin that dwells in me? To the allurements of concupiscence? What can I do in the future to improve this situation?

COLLOQUY: PSALM 13

> How long, LORD? Will you utterly forget me?
>> How long will you hide your face from me?
> How long must I carry sorrow in my soul,
>> grief in my heart day after day?
>> How long will my enemy triumph over me?
> Look upon me, answer me, LORD, my God!
>> Give light to my eyes lest I sleep in death,
> Lest my enemy say, "I have prevailed,"
>> lest my foes rejoice at my downfall.
> I trust in your faithfulness.
>> Grant my heart joy in your help,
> That I may sing of the LORD,
>> "How good our God has been to me!"

See further *Romans*, 472-77.

EXERCISE 16

Through the Spirit the Christian Becomes a Child of God, Destined for Glory (8:1-17)

¹ Now then there is no condemnation for those who are in Christ Jesus. ² For in Christ Jesus the law of the Spirit of life has set you free from the law of sin and death. ³ What the law, weakened by the flesh, was powerless to do, God has done: by sending his own Son in a form like that of sinful flesh and for the sake of sin, he condemned sin in the flesh, ⁴ so that the requirement of the law might be fully met in us who conduct ourselves not according to the flesh, but according to the Spirit. ⁵ Those who live according to the flesh develop an outlook for the things of the flesh, whereas those who live according to the Spirit develop an outlook for the things of the Spirit. ⁶ Now the outlook of the flesh is death, whereas the outlook of the Spirit is life and peace. ⁷ Since the outlook of the flesh is hostility toward God, it is not submissive to God's law; nor can it be. ⁸ So those who live by the flesh cannot please God. ⁹ Yet you are not in the flesh; you are in the Spirit, since God's Spirit dwells in you. If one does not have Christ's Spirit, he does not belong to Christ. ¹⁰ But if Christ is in you, though the body be dead because of sin, the spirit has life because of uprightness. ¹¹ And if the Spirit of him who raised Jesus from the dead is dwelling in you, he who raised Christ from the dead will give life even to your mortal bodies through his Spirit that is dwelling in you. ¹² So then, brothers, we are not indebted to the flesh, to have to live according to it. ¹³ If you live indeed according to

**the flesh, you will die; but if through the Spirit you put to
death the deeds of the body, you will live.**

**[14] For all those who are led by God's Spirit are children of
God. [15] You did not receive a spirit enslaving you again to
fear, but you received a Spirit of sonship, one in which we
cry, "*Abba,* Father!" [16] The Spirit itself bears witness with
our spirit: We are children of God! [17] If children, then heirs
too, heirs of God and coheirs of Christ, if we now suffer with
him in order also to be glorified with him.**

16.1 We come now to another of the important parts of the
epistle. In fact, it is the most important chapter in Romans from
the standpoint of what Paul teaches in it about the holy Spirit and
its role in Christian life. Three meditations will be devoted to the
influence of the Spirit as treated in this chapter.

This is the counterpart of Paul's discussion in chaps. 5–7,
where he developed in a negative way the secondary theme
announced in 5:1-11, by explaining the freedoms that have come
in Christ Jesus: freedom from sin and death (5:12-21); freedom
from sin and self (6:1-23); and freedom from the law (7:1-25).
Those who have put faith in Christ Jesus and have been baptized
into his death, burial, and resurrection have become justified
Christians, not only liberated from such evils, but also empowered
to live a new life as a result of God's love manifested in such freeing
acts of Christ Jesus. They are thus able to live this new life "for
God," whose love has been poured out through the dynamic
source of such life, the Spirit of God. Chapter 8 is a literary unit
that develops positively the secondary theme thus announced in
5:1-11.

16.2 Paul has mentioned the Spirit so far only three times
(indirectly in 1:4; more directly in 5:5 [announcing the theme]; and
in 7:6). Now he will mention it nineteen times in the course of this
chapter alone. He thus takes up the topic explicitly. If one realizes
the importance that Paul attributes to the Spirit's role in Christian
life, one has to note by contrast that Ignatius in his *Spiritual
Exercises* gives relatively little scope to such a factor, apart from his
treatment in the discernment of spirits (which we tend today to
read in terms of the holy Spirit). This is perhaps surprising, but

then his treatment of this factor of Christian spiritual life is a relic of the kind of medieval spirituality that he inherited in his day.

16.3 In speaking of *to pneuma*, "the Spirit," Paul tends to treat it as it appears in the Old Testament (compare Ezek 36:26, "I will give you a new heart and place a new Spirit within you, taking from your bodies a heart of stone and giving you a heart of flesh," or Isa 44:3: "I shall pour water on the thirsty ground, streams upon the dried up land; I shall pour out my Spirit upon your offspring, my blessing upon your descendants"). There, it is a mode of expressing God's outgoing activity and presence to the world and his people in a creative, prophetic, quickening, or renovative fashion. See further such passages as Gen 1:2; Pss 51:11; 139:7; Isa 11:2; Ezek 37:1-14. This basic Old Testament understanding Paul attributes to *to (hagion) pneuma*, "the holy Spirit," which is not yet understood by him as a person, distinct from the Father and the Son, as it would become in later Christian trinitarian theology of the patristic period. There it is clearly seen as the third person of the Trinity, a logical development beyond Paul's way of thinking and speaking. He may, indeed, personify the Spirit, i.e. personify the activity and presence of the Old Testament sense, but it has not yet come to be conceived as a person in his theology. Rather, it is for him a way of expressing the dynamic influence of God's presence to justified Christians, the manifestation of God's love for them, and the powerful source of their new life in Christ. It is the vivifying power of the risen Christ himself (1 Cor 15:45: "the last Adam became a life-giving Spirit"; cf. 2 Cor 3:18, "the Lord who is the Spirit"). Thus "God's Spirit" has also become for Paul "Christ's Spirit." (To be noted in such passages is the lack of a clear distinction between the risen Lord and the Spirit. That stands in contrast to the triadic description of the Three in 2 Cor 13:13.) The dominance of the Spirit's activity is the sign of the new aeon inaugurated with the coming of Jesus of Nazareth, and it manifests how God's love is now poured out, which is the counterpart of God's uprightness, the object of Pauline emphasis in Romans 1-4.

16.4 "Now then" (8:1), again Paul begins with the eschatological "now," because he is speaking of the new aeon (see p. 56). The aeon of sin, death, and law has come to an end. It is rather the aeon of the Spirit.

"There is no condemnation for those who are in Christ Jesus" (8:1). This is Paul's victory cry: through Christ Jesus baptized Christians, who live by faith in him, have vanquished all the forces that tyrannized their carnal existence, especially the force of law in human life. "Condemnation" is no longer leveled by the law against those not observing its specific prescriptions; nor is there the "condemnation" that comes from sin (5:16, 18), from the sin stemming from Adam. *Katakrima,* "condemnation," which occurs in the New Testament only here and in 5:16, 18, means the same as "the curse" of Gal 3:10, which was derived from the law itself: "Cursed be the one who fails to fulfill the provisions of this law" (Deut 27:26; cf. Deut 28:58-61). For the actor Law also acted as a judge of human conduct and passed judgment on those who violated its precepts. Its verdict clung to human beings in their Adamic condition, and the result was their being torn in two, as Paul has described in chap. 7. But now "in Christ Jesus" this is no longer true; those who live "in" him are freed of that condemnation, freed of that "curse of the law."

16.5 "For in Christ Jesus the law of the Spirit of life has set you free from the law of sin and death" (8:2). So Paul continues his victory cry in this chapter, expressing it as an oxymoron: "the law of the Spirit of life." For the "Spirit" is hardly a "law"; it is anything but a law. Yet in applying *nomos* to the "Spirit of life," or "the Spirit of God" (8:9a, 14), or the "Spirit of Christ" (8:9b), he is underlining the ruling function of the Spirit in the sphere of Christ. It is now the dynamic "principle" (as *nomos* should again be understood) of the new life "in Christ," creating vitality and severing humans from the tyranny of Sin and Death. Indeed, the Spirit supplies the very vitality that the Mosaic law itself could not give, because it was a mere list of do's and don'ts, which supplied no power or force to observe them. The life-giving Spirit of God, which "dwells" in the justified Christian (8:9), now becomes the principle of new Christian life. Paul's assertion in this verse directly alludes to 7:23, where he spoke of "the law of sin that is in my members." In contrast, the Spirit actively dominates the Christian who now lives in union with Christ. See Gal 2:20; 5:25.

16.6 "What the law, weakened by the flesh, was powerless to do, God has done" (8:3). What was impossible for the law was precisely its inability to supply human beings with the power to obey its prescriptions. After all, it was a list of regulations posted, as it were, outside of human beings, who were themselves creatures of "flesh," i.e. made of all that pulls human life down and makes it earth-oriented, closed in on itself, and not open to God. Paul has already described that weak flesh as inhabited by Sin (7:22-23). As a result, the actor Law was incapable of putting human beings in a status of rectitude in God's sight. But now God, who has taken the initiative, has remedied that situation. God has put sinful humanity in a status of rectitude before his tribunal through what Christ Jesus has done. For through him God has poured out the Spirit into Christian hearts as the energizer of new life.

In other words, God has graced us with his Spirit as a dynamic force that enables us, who were sinners, to live righteous and upright lives in his sight. Theologians of a later date would call this a divine "grace" granted to us, which sanctifies us. It is well to reflect on the relation of the gift of the Spirit to such grace. For those theologians often made an important distinction between God's uncreated grace and his created grace, meaning the Spirit by the former and sanctifying grace by the latter. That is how the concept of "sanctifying grace" entered the Christian tradition, because the term as such does not appear in Scripture. When one looks for the basis of it there, one has to appeal to Pauline teaching about the Spirit. The two aspects, created and uncreated grace, are important, because we have already noted how *charis* normally denotes for Paul, not "grace" in the sense of sanctifying grace, but God's "favor," i.e. that aspect of God by which he freely and graciously bestows bounty on the world and his people. The two aspects, as distinguished by later theologians, can be illustrated thus. The Spirit and sanctifying grace are like the head that lies upon a pillow, making a dent in it. The dent is not the head, nor is it the pillow itself. It is a modification of the pillow caused by the head. The Spirit is like the head, and sanctifying grace is like the dent, a modification of the pillow. Similarly, the Spirit is not the Christian disciple, but by its indwelling the Spirit modifies (activates or energizes) the Christian. That is why one can speak of the pillow's obediential potency. The pillow has the capacity of receiving not only the head, but also the dent. So too Christians have the capacity of being affected by the Spirit, being energized by the Spirit; but also the capacity of being modified by sanctifying grace, which the Spirit creates.

The Spirit has thus become the divine energizer of the spiritual life of Christians in the new aeon. To use a modern illustration, God has put the Spirit within Christians as a cardiac surgeon inserts a pacemaker into a person with a faulty heart condition. The Spirit enables Christians still subject to the Adamic condition to function as they should, to lead a life "in Christ."

16.7 "By sending his own Son in a form like that of sinful flesh and for the sake of sin, he condemned sin in the flesh" (8:3b-c). By sending "his own Son," God has made known the initiative that he has taken. The origin of the new Christian life has to be traced back to God the Father, whose love for humanity is thus manifested. God has sent his Son to be one of us: "in a form like that of sinful flesh." So Paul enunciates the soteriological taking on of the human condition by God's Son; this is the closest that he ever comes to expressing what Johannine theology expresses as the incarnation. Paul's mode of expression here might seem docetic ("in the likeness of the flesh of sin"), but elsewhere he clearly asserts the full humanity of Christ Jesus: He was sent as a man, born of a woman, born under the law (Gal 4:4). Jesus was also sent "for the sake of sin," i.e. either to deal with sin (C. E. B. Cranfield), or to conquer sin (E. J. Goodspeed), or to expiate sin (BAGD). So Paul enunciates the purpose of the coming of Jesus Christ; his assuming human form was for a soteriological purpose. The Son even entered the realm of sinful humanity to bring God's judgment against Sin. In this way, "(God) condemned sin in the flesh," issuing the decisive verdict against the actor Sin in the very realm in which Sin itself had reigned and dominated human life. Through the death of Christ Jesus, his Son, on the cross God carried out the sentencing of Sin, which could touch him only as human. In saying this, Paul is, in effect, personifying Sin, as he has personified the Law and Death, those powers that dominated humanity in the old aeon. The gift of the Spirit is thus intimately linked with the sending of God's own Son. "When the fullness of time had come, God sent forth his Son, born of a woman, born under the law, so that we might receive adoptive sonship. Because you are sons, God sent the Spirit of his Son into your hearts" (Gal 4:4-6).

Commentators have debated the meaning of "in the flesh." For some, following Augustine, it could mean "by the (innocent, sinless) flesh" (of Christ). Others, following some Greek Fathers, have understood it of the incarnation, when the Father, by sending the Son "in the flesh," implicitly passed sentence on Sin: it was, then, a condemnation in principle. Still others, following Origen and other Greek Fathers, have interpreted it of the crucified "flesh" of Christ: the Father passed definitive judgment against Sin in that the death that Christ died on the cross "in the flesh" sentenced to impotence Sin that had reigned in human flesh. Almost any of these meanings is possible; but the last mentioned seems preferable. The important thing is to realize what Christ Jesus in his mortal status has achieved for us.

16.8 "So that the requirement of the law might be fully met in us who conduct ourselves not according to the flesh, but according to the Spirit" (8:4). This noteworthy statement has to be rightly understood. Paul is saying that what the Mosaic law required of human beings subject to it was that they become upright in God's sight and thus achieve a status of moral rectitude before him by obeying it. That was the be-all and end-all of the Mosaic law imposed on Israel of old. Yet that was not achieved. Israel failed in this regard and missed its mark; it fell short of the glory that it was destined to attain. But now, in the new aeon, God himself has brought it about that that requirement is met. "The requirement of the law" indeed "is fulfilled." That is a theological passive; it is fulfilled by God. "The fulfillment spoken of here is in no sense something achieved by Christians themselves; it is something which God, the author of all, works in us through the Spirit as a consequence of the Christ-event. There is a fulfillment of the moral demand...[but this] righteousness is entirely the creation of God operating through the Spirit" (B. Byrne, *CBQ* 43 [1981] 569). It is not that Christians through the Spirit can now observe the specific commands of the Mosaic law, i.e. by their deeds thus fulfill its detailed requirements and so attain the status of uprightness before God that was asked of Israel of old. The goal of the Law is rather achieved for Christians, who in the new aeon conduct themselves according to the Spirit. For the Spirit enables justified Christians to surmount the seductions of the flesh and arrive at the goal of uprightness or rectitude that the Law had proposed long ago. Christians are no longer under Law, but under Grace (now personified too). The uprightness that Christians now achieve in the sight of God is one that is not their own, achieved by their own deeds or merits, but one that is attributed to them because of what Christ Jesus has done for them. Paul uses a Greek participle with the negative *mē*, which has a proviso or conditional sense, "provided we walk not according to the flesh."

16.9 Paul introduces an important contrast that he will develop in the rest of this paragraph, the contrast between "the Spirit" and "the flesh." What is striking is the Pauline implication that Christians might still go on living according to "the flesh." Paul, however, insists that those who put their faith in Christ Jesus, are baptized, and are open to the promptings of the Spirit manifest in their lives "the fruits of the Spirit" (Gal 5:22-23): "love, joy, peace, patience, kindness, goodness, faithfulness, gentleness, self-control; against such there is no law." Because Christ lives in Christians, they live no longer motivated by the things of the flesh. They are rather energized by his Spirit.

In the latter part of this paragraph (especially vv. 9-13) the reality of the Christian experience is expressed in different ways that should be noted: Christians are said to be "in the Spirit" (8:9b); or "the Spirit dwells in you" (8:9c); or one "has the Spirit of Christ" (8:9d); or one "belongs to him [Christ]" (8:9b); or "Christ is in you" (8:10a) or "the Spirit of him who raised Christ...dwells in you" (8:11); and "through his Spirit dwelling in you" (8:13). When one first meets such diverse modes of expression, they seem confusing, and one might ask, "Who is in whom?" Yet by them Paul forestalls an overfacile interpretation of how the Christian is united with Christ in the service of God. He is trying to describe the indescribable symbiotic union of Christ and the Christian. Lastly, to be noted is the triadic character of the text, which serves as the basis for the patristic theological teaching about the indwelling of the three persons of the Trinity in the Christian. For Christians, indeed, are related not only to Christ, but to the Father and the Spirit as well. "Do you not know that your body is the temple of the holy Spirit within you, which you have from God? You are not your own; you were bought with a price. So glorify God in your body" (1 Cor 6:19-20).

16.10 Paul proceeds a step further in his explanation of the theme announced in 5:1-11. It is not just that God's Spirit enables us to accomplish in our earthly lives what was the goal of the law of old, "the requirement of the law" (8:4). Nor is new Christian life simply the mortification of deeds of the body (mentioned in 8:13), which does not really constitute that life, even though it may be requisite for the living of it. Rather, as the gift of our heavenly Father, the Spirit makes us children of God: "In one Spirit we have all been baptized into one body, whether Jews or Greeks, slave or free, and we have all been given to drink of one Spirit" (1 Cor 12:13). In different ways, then, Paul strives to explain what the new life of baptized Christians is, when influenced by God's Spirit.

First of all, Paul understands the Spirit as "leading" us, showing us the proper paths on which we are to walk or conduct our lives. "If we live by the Spirit, let us also walk by the Spirit" (Gal 5:25). This leading of the Spirit is Paul's way of expressing what later theologians would call prevenient grace, the initiative that God takes in guiding Christian life by the Spirit. When we are led by the Spirit, we conduct ourselves by "the law of the Spirit of life in Christ Jesus" (8:2). So we are led to "live with Christ" (6:8) and live "in Christ." Of this reality we have to become gradually more and more aware, on the psychological level.

Second, Paul thinks of Christians "drinking" of the "one Spirit." We were not only washed in baptismal waters "in one Spirit," but we derive the nourishment of our spiritual lives directly from the Spirit. We "drink of one Spirit," and thus experience the solidarity of Christian life. Together as Christians we share one fountain, the "one Spirit," just as "we all partake of the one loaf" (1 Cor 10:17), when we share together the Lord's supper. All of this explains why we are "children of God," for our Christian lives are thus fed by the risen Christ and his Spirit. Just as Christ now "lives for God" (Rom 6:10), so in our "newness of life" (6:4), derived from his risen life and his Spirit, we too live in a new relationship to God. We are no longer "enemies" (5:10), but because of the reconciliation brought about for us by Christ Jesus, we have become "children of God."

Third, Paul says that we have become literally "sons" of God. Such guidance of the Spirit makes it plain that we are now "children of God," that we have been begotten anew by God through Christ Jesus, and that we live new lives in filial relation to God. This is the ontological reality of Christian existence. In vv. 16-17 he will speak of us as "children" (*tekna*), but he also uses the word "sons," because he will eventually relate it to "heirs." That is why he first expresses it as masculine. Moreover, into the hearts of such "sons" God has sent "the Spirit of *his* Son" (Gal 4:6) to establish that intimate relationship with himself. This status is initiated through faith and baptism. "In Christ Jesus you are all sons of God through faith. For as many of you as have been baptized into Christ have put on Christ" (Gal 3:26-27). That status is activated and realized through the indwelling Spirit (8:14), which is the guarantee of eschatological filiation (8:19, 23).

16.11 This is further explained, when Paul says, "You did not receive a spirit enslaving you again to fear; you received a Spirit of sonship" (8:15). This is a reformulation of what he said in 8:14. Paul now plays on the two senses of *pneuma*, "spirit" (as an aspect of a human being) and "Spirit" (as the divine presence). God did not instill in us a cringing mentality or the obsequious or servile disposition such as a slave might have, which might make us stand before him in fear, as if he were a stern taskmaster, requiring our obedience and our toeing of the line. On the contrary, we have received a liberating "Spirit of sonship," or possibly a liberating "spirit of sonship." Because Paul has been playing on the sense of *pneuma*, it is hard to say which nuance he intends here, "spirit" or "Spirit." In any case, the Spirit is what brings about the sonship that is ours. *Huiothesia* is a compound term that Paul has derived from his Greco-Roman background, where it was used to express "adoptive sonship." It is not found in the Septuagint, because the custom of adopting children was practically unknown in ancient Judaism. In the Greco-Roman world it was known and denoted the taking of a person into the *familia*, to whom even family rights, inheritance, and legal status were given as a member in that form of society. For Paul the word denotes the special status that the

Christian has because of faith and baptism. Such persons have been taken into God's family and have come under the *patria potestas*, "paternal authority," of God and have a legitimate status in such a family, not just as slaves, who also belonged in a sense to it, but as "sons." Paul exploits this nuance of sonship. "Sonship is the expression for the freedom of the baptized person, who needs to recognize no other tie but the will of God, for the understanding that God has committed himself to humanity, and for the trust that grows out of this fatherhood" (O. Michel, *Der Brief an die Römer*, 260). The attitude, then, of Christians should correspond to this filial status that they enjoy.

16.12 "One in which we cry, 'Abba, Father'" (8:15b). The Spirit empowers Christians to cry "Abba" to their heavenly Father. The verb *krazein* can mean "cry out" in prayer (as in Exod 22:22; Ps 3:5) or in proclamation (Rom 9:27). Later in this chapter Paul will explain how the Spirit enables Christians to pray properly, and this may be the nuance intended here. Through the Spirit Christians are enabled to address God as Father. If it has the other sense, then it would mean that through the Spirit Christians are enabled to proclaim that God is their Father. Cf. Gal 4:6, where Paul says that God has sent the Spirit of his Son into our hearts, which itself cries "Abba, Father." The upshot of this is that Christians cry, "Abba, Father," because the Spirit so enables them and cries with them.

Paul has retained as the model Christian prayer an Aramaic word often regarded as the term with which Jesus addressed his heavenly Father (cf. Mark 14:36). The early church recalled his way of addressing God and retained it as the essential expression of the relationship of Christians to God. In Aramaic the word for "father" is *'ab*, but the emphatic form (with the article) is *'abbā'*, "the father." Because the Aramaic language has no vocative form, the emphatic was used to address someone as "Father!" (see Dan 2:4, 29, 31 [*malkā'*, "O King"]). Jesus himself would not have used both Aramaic and Greek. When the Aramaic form was retained in use among Greek-speaking Christians, it was literally translated *ho patēr*, "the Father." From this comes the inherited double form of address, "Abba, Father," both here and in Gal 4:6. For Paul it has become the noteworthy way that Christians should address God— as Jesus himself did. For we are adoptive children of God, children taken by him into his family, and children who gratefully express our relation to God in this vital way, and implicitly that we are brothers of Christ Jesus, his real Son.

16.13 "The Spirit itself bears witness with our spirit: We are children of God!" Paul uses a compound verb *symmartyrein*, which can mean either "testifies along with" or simply "testifies, certifies." If the latter sense is used, it would mean that the Spirit "testifies to our spirit," i.e. makes us aware of our adoptive sonship, that we are children of God. But the former sense exploits the preposition *syn-*. Paul would not mean, then, that persons in their Adamic condition, without the aid of the Spirit, could come to the knowledge of adoptive sonship, so that the Spirit would merely concur with the human spirit becoming aware of such a relationship. The preceding context makes it clear that the vital dynamism given by the Spirit constitutes the sonship itself and bestows the power to recognize such a status. So Paul is going further and emphasizes that the Spirit concurs with Christians as they acknowledge in prayer or proclamation this special relation to God, the Father. The Christian cry is thus likewise the cry of the Spirit. The inspired *Abba*-cry proclaims that Christians are indeed children of God and destined for glory.

16.14 "If children, then heirs too, heirs of God and coheirs of Christ" (8:17ab). We have been adopted into the *familia* of God through what Christ Jesus has done for us. "For in one Spirit we were all baptized into one body, whether Jews or Greeks, slaves or free, and we were all given to drink of one Spirit" (1 Cor 12:13). "Now you are Christ's body, individually parts of it" (1 Cor 12:27). This status implies, however, still another: a status in society based on descent from a father in a household. In this case, the status is analogical, because though God is considered to be Father, we are only adopted children. Yet the adoptive sonship assures us of a heritage in that family. Christians are not only admitted into God's family, but are granted by that gratuitous adoption a right to share in the inheritance of the Father's estate, i.e. in glory. Though we have no natural right to it, we acquire this status through Christ Jesus and his Spirit, which constitutes the adoptive sonship. This is why the Spirit has been poured into our hearts, as a manifestation of God's love for us. "So through God you are no longer a slave but a son, and if a son then an heir" (Gal 4:7; cf. Gal 3:29). We could not ask for more.

We become coheirs with Christ himself, destined to share with him the glorious status that he already has acquired in the presence of the Father as of his resurrection. Christ Jesus is the unique Son, the heir in the first and proper sense; he has already received his share of the Father's estate (glory, Rom 8:21). Now Christians are destined to share in that glorious estate as coheirs. Paul sometimes also speaks of that heritage as *aphtharsia*, "incorruption" (1 Cor 15:50), or as *basileia theou*, "kingdom of God" (1 Cor 6:9, 10; 15:50), or as "eternal life" (Rom 5:21).

16.15 "If we now suffer with him" (8:17c). Christian existence has to reckon with suffering, for the pain and affliction that are encountered in human life become a share and a way of participating in what Christ suffered in his life here on earth. We are still mortal creatures, subject to the ills and misfortunes of earthly life. But that suffering takes on a new meaning in Christian existence, for Paul understands it as a suffering with Christ. In such problems, we share with him, with the important phase of his existence that we usually call his "passion." In order to make the transit from his earthly life to the glorious presence of the Father, Christ Jesus had to suffer and die. His passion and death bestow a meaning on the fragile and suffering existence of Christians. For it is a form of co-passion, a form of suffering with Christ. What he suffered in his passion was meant to suffuse and give meaning to the sufferings of Christians in this life. That suffering can be of many sorts; it can be physical or psychic; it can be grief and mourning over the suffering or loss of loved ones. It can take many forms. Through his suffering and death Christ Jesus achieved for us justification, salvation, and redemption, and the Christian is thus seen by Paul as sharing in the sufferings of Christ. Not that we somehow merit thereby our salvation. Rather we are identified with him, the suffering Jesus, who did achieve it for us.

16.16 "In order also to be glorified with him" (8:17d). The purpose of such human suffering is a share in the glorious status of the risen Christ himself. The glorification of the Christian is still another effect of the Christ-event. Without him we should never be able to attain that glorious destiny, which is one that we Christians now share with the risen Christ because of what he has achieved for us. The Spirit that empowers our lives as Christians is the firstfruits of that glory, the guarantee of our destiny.

16.17 Questions. How conscious am I of the influence of the indwelling Holy Spirit in my life and activity? Have I let the Spirit and its outlook dominate the instincts of the flesh (its hostility to God, selfishness)? Do I really want to be led more by Christ's Spirit? How can I intensify my awareness of the Spirit's guidance? Am I really convinced that I am a child of God, adopted through what Christ Jesus did for me? Have I ever prayed, "Abba, Father"? Do I comprehend what it means to be a coheir with Christ? To suffer with him that I may be glorified with him?

COLLOQUY: VENI, SANCTE SPIRITUS

> Come, Holy Spirit, come!
>> And from thy heavenly home
>> send a ray of light divine!
> Come, Thou Patron of the poor!
>> Come, thou source of all our good;
>> come and shine within our hearts!
> Thou, of comforters the best;
>> thou, the soul's most welcome guest,
>> sweet refreshment here below!
> In our labor, rest most sweet;
>> grateful coolness in the heat,
>> solace in the midst of woe.
> O most blessed Light divine,
>> shine within these hearts of thine;
>> fill our inmost being full!
> Where thou art not, one hath naught,
>> nothing good in deed or thought,
>> nothing free from taint of ill.
> Wash our wounds, our strength renew;
>> on our dryness pour thy dew;
>> take the stains of guilt away.
> Bend the stubborn heart and will;
>> melt the frozen, warm the chill;
>> guide the steps that falter still.
> On thy faithful, who adore

and confess thee, evermore
in thy sevenfold gift descend.
Give them virtue's sure reward;
    give them thy salvation, LORD;
    give them joys that never end. Amen.

See further *Romans*, 479-504, 124-26.

Three Things Testify to This New Life: Creation Groaning in Travail, the Fact of Christian Hope, and the Spirit Itself (8:18-27)

[18] I consider the sufferings that we now endure not worth comparing with the glory that is going to be revealed in us. [19] Indeed, creation itself is waiting with anxious expectation for the revelation of the children of God. [20] For creation has been subjected to frustration, not of its own choice, but by him who subjected it—with hope—[21] because creation itself too will eventually be freed from its bondage to decay and brought to the glorious freedom of the children of God. [22] Yes, we realize that all creation has been groaning and laboring in pain up to the present time. [23] Not only that, but we ourselves, though we have the Spirit as the firstfruits, are groaning inwardly as we wait for the redemption of our bodies. [24] For in hope we have been saved. But a hope that is seen is no hope at all. Who hopes for what he sees? [25] But if we hope for what we do not see, we wait for it with endurance. [26] Similarly, the Spirit too comes to the aid of our weakness, for we do not know for what we should pray. But the Spirit itself intercedes for us with ineffable sighs. [27] Yet he who searches our hearts knows what the mind of the Spirit is, because it intercedes for God's dedicated people in accordance with his will.

17.1 Paul has brought to an end his description of new

Christian life empowered by the Spirit, but he is not content to set forth that the Christian is destined for a share in such glory, a share in the risen life of Christ. He now lists three things that testify to this status, three things that assure Christians that what he has just described is indeed a reality. The first is the groaning of all creation, particularly of subhuman material creation, as it awaits that status to be revealed to us. The second is the fact of hope in Christian life, and the third is the Spirit itself. All of these support his view of Christian life in the Spirit and its destiny. Paul wants the justified and reconciled Christian to become better aware of the ontological reality that is Christian existence, of the life of one who lives in Christ and has a destiny to be with the risen Christ in the glorious presence of the Father.

17.2 At the end of the preceding paragraph Paul had mentioned suffering, the suffering with Christ that is part of Christian existence: "if we now suffer with him," we shall one day "be glorified with him" (8:17). He now reflects further on the meaning of those sufferings. They can loom large in human existence; they can preoccupy us for a long time. But even so Paul counsels us about their meaning. They have a place in Christian life, because we are fragile, mortal human beings. They are, however, nothing when compared with the destiny that awaits the Christian. "I consider the sufferings that we now endure not worth comparing with the glory that is going to be revealed in us" (8:18). It is not that Paul wants to play down human sufferings or treat them as insignificant in this life. He seeks rather to put them in proper perspective and wants us to realize that, though they must be endured as part of our earthly condition, they are insignificant in comparison with the glory awaiting us. In the long run, his concern is much more an assurance of what Christian destiny holds for us.

17.3 Paul sees such human suffering as part of the groaning of all creation that has been subjected to frustration. "Creation itself is waiting in anxious expectation for the revelation of the children of God" (8:19). The "creation" of which Paul speaks is subhuman, material or physical creation, distinct from human beings, as 8:23 makes clear. At the end of that verse Paul will again mention "redemption," an effect of the Christ-event. But now it becomes evident that even that subhuman, material creation has also been affected by the Christ-event. In this case, the effect is not only anthropological (affecting human beings), but also cosmic (affecting all creation too). Paul personifies creation and depicts it as "waiting in anxious expectation" for the arrival of what will transform "the children of God." The problem is that creation "has been subjected to frustration, not of its own choice." It was not so created by God, in a condition of frustration, futility, or purposelessness, and it did not bring this situation about on its own. The suffering of human beings, of which Paul spoke in v. 17, is now seen to be only a part of the frustrated condition of all creation.

17.4 Whence comes this frustration of all creation? It results from "him who subjected it—with hope" (8:20cd). So Paul alludes to the Genesis story of Adam again (Gen 3:17-19; 5:29), where the earth has been cursed as a result of Adam's sinful transgression. Commentators have debated who is meant by "him" in the masculine participle *hypotaxanta*. Adam, sinful man, God, Christ, or Satan? It cannot be Adam, sinful man, or Satan, because none of these could have "subjected it—with hope." So Paul is thinking of God and his curse of the earth in Gen 3:17. But he makes a bold addition to the story itself. In Genesis there is no mention of "hope" associated with the cursing of the earth. This is the way that Paul reads Genesis. He understands the Genesis story in the light of the Christ-event and reads into the story of Adam's transgression and punishment a message of hope. This "hope" is introduced to give Christians assurance about their glorious destiny. Paul's thinking is undoubtedly tributary also to the Old Testament apocalyptic teaching and promise of "a new heaven and a new earth," such as one finds in Trito-Isaiah (Isa 65:17; 66:22). In later intertestamental literature such a promise was transferred to the messianic age: *1 Enoch* 45:4-5 (the earth will be transformed for the righteous ones along with the Chosen One, the Messiah). Similarly in *Jubilees* 4:26; *2 Apocalypse of Baruch* 31:5–32:6. Such thinking made it possible for Paul to conceive of frustrated creation as liberated by Christ Jesus, the Messiah of Christians. Though God cursed the ground because of Adam's sin, he still gave it a hope of sharing in human redemption and liberation. This notion of hope thus gives frustrated creation the basis for its "anxious expectation," as it awaits the revelation of the children of God, i.e. as it waits for the manifestation of what those children will become, the manifestation of their glorious destiny. (The "hope" should not be facilely identified with Gen 3:15, which expresses not victory, but lasting enmity between the serpent and its offspring and the woman and her offspring.)

17.5 "Creation itself too will eventually be freed from its bondage to decay and brought to the glorious freedom of the children of God" (8:21). Paul sees the frustration of creation as a "bondage to decay." This is the state of subhuman creation, enslaved to corruption and decay, which he sees as an indirect result of Adam's sin. It is not just moral corruption, but the reign of dissolution and death found in material, subhuman creation. Because Adam transgressed the command laid on him, God cursed the earth, and that curse resulted in perishability and putrefaction. Yet that same creation is not just to be a spectator of the glorification of the children of God; it is to share in it as well. When the children of God are definitively liberated by the Christ-event from their mortal condition to share in eternal glory, so too will subhuman creation share in that liberation and in the glory that is to attend them. The freedom is not yet a possession of Christians; it is the characteristic of the status of eschatological glory, that awaited in the *eschaton*.

17.6 "We realize that all creation has been groaning and laboring in pain up to the present time" (8:22), literally, "groans with (us) and labors in travail with (us)." Paul uses verbs compounded with *syn-*, to express the harmony of the groaning of creation together with that of humanity in its longing for its glorious destiny. He seems to be borrowing from Greek philosophical writers the image of the vernal rebirth of nature compared with a woman's travail as she gives birth. Thus Heraclitus the Stoic, "When [after the winter's cold] the groaning earth gives birth in travail to what has been formed within her" (*Quaestiones homericae* 39 [58.9]). In the groaning and travail of creation Paul sees the eschatological expectation of material creation, awaiting its share in the destiny of Christian humanity. This cosmic dimension of the redemption and freedom of

Christians is thus also an effect of the Christ-event. It teaches us something about our ennobled destiny, how all of material creation is striving along with us to attain a glorious goal.

17.7 "We ourselves, though we have the Spirit as the firstfruits, are groaning inwardly" (8:23ab). The "firstfruits" of the Spirit have already been given to us as justified and reconciled Christians, which is the foretaste of glory. Paul uses *aparchē*, "firstfruits," like those of the harvest, which, when consecrated to God, were considered dedicated and holy and betokened the consecration of the whole harvest to him. But this word was often used also in the sense of Greek *arrabōn*, "earnest money, a guarantee of what was still to be paid, of what was to come." The Spirit has been given to us as a down-payment that guarantees that the rest will come in due course, i.e. glory in the presence of the Father. Yet Paul maintains that, in spite of this down payment, we are still creatures that groan within ourselves, as we await the fulfillment of our destiny. For, as Augustine once put it, "Restless is our heart until it rests in you, (O God)" (*Confessions* 1.1.1).

17.8 "As we wait for the redemption of our bodies" (8:23c). The liberation that comes from the Christ-event will affect us in our very selves, releasing us to share in the risen life of Christ himself. Some manuscripts read at this point: "as we wait for adoption, the redemption of our bodies." In this case, Paul would mean that the full status of our adoptive sonship has not yet been attained, and that we are still awaiting its full dimension. Material creation, which is waiting along with us, would likewise share in that expected destiny in order to be freed of its bondage.

17.9 Hope is also a sign that the new life of Christians empowered by the Spirit of God is a reality. Paul cited in vv. 18-23 the groaning of all material creation in expectation of the glorious destiny of Christians. Now he appeals to the fact that Christians are people of hope (8:24-25). It may seem like a peculiar argument, but what Paul is trying to say is that we, as Christians, are people whose earthly lives are lived in hope, in hope of eternal salvation that has already been achieved for us in Christ Jesus. This aspect of Christian life on this earth is something that cannot be ignored. That fact that Christians hope, then, assures us of the life that Paul has described, a life lived in the power of the Spirit of God. In 1 Thess 4:13c Paul spoke of those "who have no hope," i.e. pagans whose whole orientation was to this world. This hope-less situation is well illustrated in an ancient Greek papyrus letter found at Oxyrhynchus in Egypt (2d cent. A.D.), in which an Egyptian woman, Irene, writes to a family in mourning: "Irene to Taonnophris and Philo, good comfort! I was sorry and wept over the departed one as I wept for Didymas. And all things, whatsoever were fitting, I did, and all mine, Epaphroditus, Thermution, Philion, Apollonius, and Plantas. Nevertheless against such things one can do nothing. So comfort one another. Farewell!" For this Irene the situation was hopeless. But Paul sees it differently; Christians live in hope. Hence to this fact he now appeals to bolster up his description of the new life that they lead.

17.10 "For in hope we have been saved" (8:24). Normally Paul speaks of "salvation" as something eschatological, something awaited in the future, something still to be attained (see Rom 5:9, 10; 9:27; 10:1, 9, 10, 13; 11:11, 14, 26; 13:11; 1 Thess 2:16). Here he understands salvation as something already achieved for us through Christ Jesus. Significantly, however, he adds, "in hope," meaning thereby that we still have not attained the full dimension of it. That too is why he says in Phil 2:12, "Work out your salvation in fear and trembling." In both instances, whether he states it as an object of "hope" or something yet to be attained "in fear and trembling," he knows that we do not attain it all on our own. For in Phil 2:13 he immediately adds, "For God is the one who, for his good purpose, works in you both to desire and to work." That working of God within us is thus the basis of the hope in which we have been saved. It is a matter, once again, of our cooperation with his prevenient grace. Grace leads to glory, and that is the basis of Christian hope. That prevenient grace is none other than the indwelling Spirit of God which leads us on.

17.11 "A hope that is seen is no hope at all. Who hopes for what he sees? But if we hope for what we do not see, we wait for it with endurance" (8:24b-25). Our destiny as Christians is not yet before our eyes. We know of it not by sight, but by faith—by the eyes of faith! Paul argues now from the very nature of hope. In 2 Cor 4:18 Paul wrote, "We look not for the things that are seen, but for things that are unseen," and again in 2 Cor 5:2, "We walk by faith, not by sight." In other words, Christians who are motivated by faith, which works itself out in love, are aiming at an unseen goal, the object of their hope. Hence, faith, love, and hope—in that order—sum up the new Christian life. In Gal 5:5 Paul wrote, "Through the Spirit, by faith, we wait for the hope of uprightness," i.e. the definitive status of rectitude in the sight of God our judge. Hope, then, also enables Christians to bear with "the sufferings" they now endure (8:18). It also makes them witnesses to the world of a lively faith in the resurrection (1 Cor 2:9).

17.12 "Similarly, the Spirit too comes to the aid of our weakness" (8:26a). The third testimony borne to the new life of the Christian as Paul has described it is the Spirit itself. It makes known to us our status in God's sight, i.e. that we are human beings empowered by God, who is present to us, that we are adoptive children of God. It remedies our weak human condition. What we could not know on our own, that the Spirit manifests to us, that we are children of God, adoptive sons. But it even goes further: "for we do not know for what we should pray" (8:26b). Paul's statement does not mean that we "do not know how to pray as we ought" (as the RSV, NRSV, NAB put it). Rather it is the object of prayer that he stresses. The human condition vis-à-vis God the Creator and Father of all is recognized by Paul: human beings do not acknowledge his eternal power and divinity; nor do they honor and thank him as they should (1:20-21). This inadequacy is now remedied by the Spirit. Christians might be inclined to ask of God only what is good for them and thus fail to pray for what they should. This the Spirit now teaches them.

17.13 "The Spirit itself intercedes for us with ineffable sighs" (8:26c). Paul acknowledges the further assistance of the "in-dwelling Spirit" (8:11) as being that of intercession with the Father on behalf of weak and feeble Christians. It pleads our cause with the Father, helping us to formulate properly our prayer. Paul recognizes the "ineffable sighs" of the Spirit as the source of all genuine Christian prayer. Such assistance is not limited to the prayer of petition, but would include all manner of communing with God, be it doxology, blessing, praise, thanksgiving, penitent confession, supplication, or, above all, recognition of God as

Father (8:15) and Jesus as Lord (1 Cor 12:3b). For Paul, genuine Christian prayer is addressed to God the Father, through Christ his Son, and in the holy Spirit.

The idea of "intercession" attributed by Paul to the Spirit is found only here in the New Testament. It is based on an Old Testament idea of praying for others, such as the intercession of Abraham for Sodom (Gen 18:23-33), Moses for the Hebrews and against Pharaoh's Egypt (Exod 8:8, 12, 26-28), priests (Lev 15:21-22), kings (2 Sam 12:16), angels (Tob 12:12), and upright persons in the after-life (2 Macc 15:12-16). But this attribution of such an intercessory function to the holy Spirit is a Pauline novelty.

Such assistance of the Spirit is granted to all of "us," i.e. to all Christians, not just to the so-called charismatics, but to the eggheads as well. No partiality is shown.

17.14 "He who searches our hearts knows what the mind of the Spirit is" (8:27a). So Paul refers to God, as in 1 Sam 16:7; 1 Kgs 8:39. For only God, and no human being, understands the ineffable sighs of the Spirit. "Because it intercedes for God's dedicated people in accordance with his will" (8:27b). By its intercession the Spirit of God overcomes the weakness of praying Christians, those who are in God's sight "saints," i.e. persons dedicated to him and to his service and worship. This the Spirit does in accordance with God's will. In other words, it was part of the divine plan of salvation that the Spirit should play one day such a dynamic role in the aspirations and prayers of Christians and in their longing for glory. That plan will be briefly described in the following verses.

17.15 Questions. Have I ever tried to understand my sufferings as part of the groaning of all creation in expectation of the glorious destiny of Christians? Would not such an understanding of trouble and suffering in my life invest them with a proper, and perhaps missing, dimension? How can I let the consideration of my destiny color such problems in life in the future? To what extent to I ever reflect on the role of hope in my earthly life? Do I let the Spirit lead me in prayer so that I pray for what I as a Christian should pray? Do I ask the Spirit to pray along with me to God our Father? Do I ask the Spirit to intercede for me in accordance with God's will?

COLLOQUY: PSALM 103

Bless the LORD, my soul;
    all my being, bless his holy name!
Bless the LORD, my soul;
    do not forget all the gifts of God,
Who pardons all your sins,
    heals all your ills,
Delivers your life from the pit,
    surrounds you with love and compassion,
Fills your days with good things;
    your youth is renewed like the eagle's.
The LORD does righteous deeds,
    brings justice to all the oppressed.
His ways were revealed to Moses,
    mighty deeds to the people of Israel.
Merciful and gracious is the LORD,
    slow to anger, abounding in kindness.
God does not always rebuke,
    nurses no lasting anger,
Has not dealt with us as our sins merit,
    nor requited us as our deeds deserve.
As the heavens tower over the earth,
    so God's love towers over the faithful.
As far as the east is from the west,
    so far have our sins been removed from us.
As a father has compassion on his children,
    so the LORD has compassion on the faithful.
For he knows how we are formed,
    remembers that we are dust.
Our days are like the grass;
    like flowers of the field we blossom.
The wind sweeps over us and we are gone;
    our place knows us no more.
But the LORD's kindness is forever,
    toward the faithful from age to age.
He favors the children's children
    of those who keep his covenant,
    who take care to fulfill its precepts.
The LORD's throne is established in heaven,
    God's royal power rules over all.

Bless the LORD, all you angels,
>   mighty in strength and attentive,
>   obedient to every command.
Bless the LORD, all you hosts,
>   ministers who do God's will.
Bless the LORD, all creatures,
>   everywhere in God's domain.
Bless the LORD, my soul!

See further *Romans*, 504-21.

The Christian Called and Destined to Glory; Hymn to the Love of God Made Manifest in Christ Jesus (8:28-39)

[28] We realize that all things work together for the good of those who love God, for those who are called according to his purpose. [29] Those whom he foreknew, he also predestined to be conformed to the image of his Son that he might be the firstborn among many brothers. [30] Those whom he predestined, he also called; those whom he called, he also justified; and those whom he justified, he also glorified.

[31] What then shall we say about this? If God is for us, who can be against us? [32] He who did not spare his own Son, but handed him over for all of us—how will he not give us everything else along with him? [33] Who will bring a charge against God's chosen ones? God himself, who justifies? [34] Who will condemn them? Christ Jesus, who died, or rather who was raised, who is at God's right hand and even intercedes for us? [35] Who will separate us from the love of Christ? Will distress or anguish or persecution or famine or nakedness or danger or the sword? [36] As it stands written, *"For your sake we are being put to death all day long; we are considered as sheep to be slaughtered."* [r] [37] Yet in all this we are more than victors because of him who loved us. [38] For I am convinced that neither death nor life, neither angels nor principalities, neither the present nor the future, nor any

powers, [39] **neither height nor depth, nor any other creature will be able to separate us from the love of God, which is in Christ Jesus our Lord.**
    [r] Ps 43:23

18.1 Having set forth the reasons why the new Christian life empowered by the Spirit is what it is, Paul sums up his exposé by reiterating his basic thesis about the call and destiny of Christians. God not only listens to the ineffable sighs of the Spirit, which assists the prayer of Christians and intercedes for them, but he also listens to them as they pray. Moreover, God sees to it that their very lives, their aspirations, their sufferings, their joys, and all that they do contribute to the good of those who pray in this way. Paul now introduces a formal affirmation of Christian destiny, the basis of the hope discussed in vv. 17-27. In 3:23 he had said that without the gospel all human beings have fallen short of the glory of God, but now through the gospel God has not only manifested his uprightness and salvific power in Christ Jesus, but even reveals how the divine purpose, the plan of salvation, has destined all justified and reconciled Christians for a share of glory in his presence. All are called in accord with this divine plan, and as it works itself out in reality, it orders all things in conformity with it.

Paul may have finished his discussion about the role of the Spirit in Christian life (8:27) and may be moving on to the place that Christians now play in that plan conceived of old. Verse 28 is problematic; it may be transitional, forming a bridge to the discussion in vv. 29-30. The problem is partly text-critical, because the text has not been uniformly transmitted in all the Greek manuscripts.

18.2 "We realize that all things work together for the good of those who love God" (8:28). "All things" probably refers to all the items just mentioned in vv. 18-27: sufferings, destiny in glory, the groaning of creation, Christian hope, and perhaps even the Spirit (depending on how the verse is translated). The sense of Paul's statement would be: All such factors in Christian life are brought into harmony for those who love God, because they are all elements in the implementation and execution of the divine plan of salvation. In 5:5, 8 Paul spoke of God's "love" for justified and reconciled human beings, and he will speak of it again in 8:39.

Now he speaks of their love of God, using the same verb *agapan* (as in 1 Cor 2:9; 8:3). In effect, "those who love God" becomes for him a definition of the Christian. When he so speaks, he scarcely means that Christians can rest their confidence in themselves in loving God, assured that all that happens to them will work for good. Rather, the reason that all things work for good is not found in Christians themselves, but in God, who takes the initiative and sees that all things will work for good. Compare *Pss. Solomon* 14:1: "Faithful is the Lord to those who love him."

"To love God" is an Old Testament idea, first enunciated in the Decalogue itself (Exod 20:6; Deut 5:10), and often thereafter (e.g. Deut 6:5; 7:9; 10:12; Pss 31:24; 97:10; Sir 1:10; 2:15-16). "The love of God, which is commanded in Scripture, is nothing less than the response of a man in the totality of his being to the prior love of God. It thus includes the whole of true religion" (J. Calvin, quoted in Cranfield, *Romans*, 424-25).

18.3 Four different ways of translating v. 28 have been proposed, depending on the text-critical problem. The best Greek manuscripts, however, omit *ho theos*, "God"; and in them *panta*, "all things," is taken as the subject of intransitive *synergei*: "all things work together for the good of those who love God." That is, God's plan is behind all that happens to Christians; he is in control of human history and their lot. God's transcendent power governs those who love God. His power and influence are such that all things, even what is done against his will, subserve the guidance that comes from him. All that happens to us, all that we experience and suffer, is a manifestation of God's love and protection, a divine answer to the love that we show to him. Thus God's governance is triumphantly effective. Cf. *Pss. Solomon* 4:25, "May your mercy, Lord, be upon all those who love you."

18.4 Here the exercitant might well pause to reflect on what "all things" might mean in his or her life. It might be good to consider the points of Ignatius' "Contemplation to Attain Love" as a means to such reflection: (a) By calling to mind "the gifts I have received—my creation, redemption, and other gifts particular to myself. I will ponder with deep affection how much God our Lord has done for me, and how much he has given me of what he possesses." (b) By considering "how God dwells in creatures; in the elements, giving them existence; in plants, giving them life; in the animals, giving them sensation; in human beings, giving them intelligence; and finally, how in this way he dwells also in myself, giving me existence, life, sensation, and intelligence; and even further, making me his temple, since I am created as a likeness and image of the Divine Majesty." (c) By considering "how God labors and works for me in all the creatures on the face of the earth; that is, he acts in the manner of one who is laboring. For example, he is working in the heavens, elements, plants, fruits, cattle, and all the rest—giving them their existence, conserving them, concurring with their vegetative and sensitive activities, and so forth." (d) By considering "how all good things and gifts descend from above; for example, my limited power from the Supreme and Infinite Power above; and so of justice, goodness, piety, mercy, and so forth—just as rays come down from the sun, or the rains from their source" (§234-237). All such considerations should serve to stir up in me a true expression of my love for God.

18.5 "For those who are called to his purpose" (8:28b). Paul expresses the basis of his affirmation about the implementation of the divine plan of salvation. God has called us to be Christians, to be followers of his Son, and to live a life empowered by the Spirit. We have thus been summoned in accord with "his purpose." For the divine design that has called has been conceived in eternity. "Those who are called" is a phrase that is complementary to "those who love God." For Paul human love of God is, consequently, a result of God's initiative, of a prevenient "call" to such love. Those who are called have been accosted by the gospel and its preachers. Yet even before that, they have been lured on by divine grace. All of that is part of God's purpose or plan for the salvation of humankind.

18.6 "Those whom he foreknew, he also predestined" (8:29a). Paul introduces for the first time the idea of predestination, a notion that he will use again in chap. 9. He speaks of it in a *corporate* sense, in contrast to the individual sense introduced by Augustine, with whom came the restriction of "those who are called" to individuals who were predestined for glory (*De correptione et gratia* 7.14 [PL 44.924-25]). That is a later precision that Paul's text does not envisage. He sees the call of human beings as related to a destiny of salvation, and his stress is on divine prevenience. He notes five steps, which are described in anthropomorphic language. The first is "foreknowledge," which is a development of the Old Testament idea of God's "knowledge" (Gen 18:19; Jer 1:5; Amos 3:2), his knowing with affection and predilection, and not merely knowing in an intellectual sense. The Essenes of Qumran acknowledged in their hymns: "Before you created them, you knew all their deeds forever. [For without you no]thing is made, and apart from your will nothing is known" (1QH 1:7-8). The second step is "predetermination," God's gratuitous election (to the status to be described in the next phrase). Because teaching about predestination has often created problems in the history of the church, one is at times reluctant to stress it too much, but it is an important notion of Pauline spirituality, and one from which we can gain a genuine perspective. What happens to us is all governed by God's foreknowledge and permissive will.

18.7 "To be conformed to the image of his Son" (8:29b). Paul plays on the noble conception that he has of Christian destiny. Christians are not only called to a share in glory, or to a share in the life of the risen Christ, but they are also called to be assimilated to the image of God's Son. According to the divine plan, they are called to reproduce in themselves with the aid of divine grace an image of God's Son. This is done by the progressive share in his risen life that they receive even in this life (8:17; Gal 4:4-6). For "all of us, with unveiled face, are beholding the glory of the Lord (and) being changed into his likeness from one degree of glory to another" (2 Cor 3:18; cf. 4:4-6). In other words, through faith and baptism the sinner becomes a Christian, who has been destined to bear the shape and image of God's unique Son. Paul's description advances beyond what he said in 8:15: for Christians are not just adopted children of God, but are being continually transformed and metamorphosed into an *eikōn*, "image, likeness" of his Son. Paul thinks of the face of the risen Christ as a mirror, on which the glory of God has shone (in raising him from the dead, Rom 6:4), and which in turns reflects that glory on the Christian, who gazes upon him in faith (2 Cor 4:4-6). Thereby the Christian is transformed. This is the sublime conception that Paul has of the destiny of Christians.

18.8 "That he might be the firstborn among many brothers" (8:29c). The divine transforming power is God's "glory," which changes Christians, making them look like Christ and shaping them as members of the same family. Christ is the "firstborn," because he is the first raised from the dead by the Father's glory and power; it thus emphasizes his preeminence. But it also implies the sharing of that glorious status by Christians. Through it they become his (adopted) brothers and sisters, now transformed by association with him, who is the firstborn in God's family.

18.9 "Those whom he predestined, he also called" (8:30). The third step is a "call" to faith in the gospel and to baptism into Christ's body. This is the beginning of the implementation of the divine salvific plan. "Those whom he called he also justified" (8:30b). The fourth step is "justification," the aftermath of the call, which is the status of rectitude in God's sight. Again Paul echoes the basic thesis of the epistle. Cf. 1 Cor 6:11, "You have been washed, you have been sanctified, you have been justified in the name of the Lord Jesus Christ and in the Spirit of our God." Behind the call lies God's uprightness summoning human beings to rectitude in his sight. "Those whom he justified, he also glorified" (8:30c). The fifth step is still another effect of the Christ-event: glorification, which is the term and final destiny of the Christian. Paul speaks of this effect proleptically: Christ Jesus has already glorified the Christian, even though the definitive form of that status is not yet attained. It "is going to be revealed in us" (8:18); it is guaranteed by the divine plan and decision. "The Lord, Jesus Christ, will transform our lowly body to become like his glorious body, by the power that enables him even to subject all things to himself" (Phil 3:21).

18.10 To this panorama of the divine plan of salvation and its mode of implementation or realization, Paul now adds a hymn to the love of God for human beings manifested through Christ Jesus (8:31-39). Paul has discussed various aspects of the new life of Christians lived in union with Christ Jesus and his Spirit, which provides the basis of Christian hope. Now Paul concludes this second doctrinal section of the epistle with a rhetorical, even hymnic, passage about the love of God manifest in what Christ Jesus has done for humanity. He has shown in this section that through Christ Christians have been set free from sin and death, self and sin, and the law, from those forces that tyrannize human life and tend to drag human beings down and doom them to frustration, even to death and destruction. Instead, "the one who is upright shall find life through faith" (1:17). In a jubilant mood Paul ends this section by praising God anew for what he has done.

18.11 For the proper understanding of this concluding passage one has to imagine a lawcourt setting, as in Job 1-2 or Zechariah 1, in which a prosecutor accuses a defendant. The latter is the justified Christian, who now has nothing to fear ("With the Lord on my side I fear not," Ps 118:6). About such a person Paul asks a series of rhetorical questions, which usually answer themselves. The first verses (31b-35) emphasize the theocentric and christocentric aspects of salvation and justification that have come through Christ. Verse 36 establishes these aspects on the basis of Ps 44:23, and v. 37 draws a conclusion.

18.12 "What then shall we say about this? If God is for us, who can be against us?" (8:31). God's "love" was first mentioned in 5:5 and is now seen as the basis of all that the intervening chapters have spelled out. God's love has brought it about that the Christian lives in Christ. God is "for us," is on our side, and no one can undo that relationship. This is the God whom Paul worships, the God of Israel of old, the God who saves those who believe (1 Cor 1:21). This means a "God for us." With God on our side, any forces marshalled against us are nothing; they cannot prevail. The prosecutor has no case against us.

18.13 "He who did not spare his own Son, but handed him over for all of us—how will he not give us everything else along with him?" (8:32). Thus God has given us the best that he could, "his own Son." This was no mean or banal gesture; Paul elsewhere says that we were bought "at a price" (1 Cor 6:20). It was God's "own Son" who was given for us, not just one of his adoptive children. Ever since the time of Origen (*In Genesim hom.* 8; PG 12. 208), it has been thought that Paul uses phraseology here that alludes to the story of Abraham willing to sacrifice his only son Isaac. Whether there is an echo of that story or not in the first clause, and commentators debate it, one cannot miss the vicarious soteriological aspect of Paul's addition in the second, "handed him over *for* all of us." What God did, he did for "all of us," and Paul intends never to let us forget that. Indeed, he argues *a maiori ad minus*: "How will he not give us everything else along with him?" Will God not grace us with "everything" along with that gift of his Son? Christian destiny is once again implied: we are to be "with him."

18.14 The lawcourt scenario continues. "Who will bring a charge against God's chosen ones?" (8:33), i.e. against us who have been predestined, called, justified, and glorified. The implication is that no one can level a charge against a Christian so defended by God. Paul may be alluding here to an Old Testament passage, where the Servant of Yahweh exclaims, "He who vindicates me is at hand. Who is it that prosecutes me?" (Isa 50:8-9)—part of the Third Servant Song (50:4-11). Just as the Servant there was expressing his confidence in God, his vindicator, so too the chosen Christian. Paul continues his query: "God himself, who justifies?" Again, the rhetorical question implies, "Of course not!" It cannot be God, the judge, who himself has acquitted those who put faith in Christ Jesus, for the justifying God and the judge are the same. "Who will condemn them?" (8:34). The logic of the query moves from charge to condemnation. "Christ Jesus, who died? Rather who was raised, who is at God's right hand and even intercedes for us?" Again, the rhetorical question answers itself, as the argument moves from God to Christ. The one to "condemn" us cannot be the Christ who through his death, resurrection, exaltation, and heavenly intercession has brought it about that we stand acquitted before the divine tribunal. Noteworthy here is the introduction of Christ's heavenly intercession on our behalf. It is not only the Spirit that intercedes for us (8:26-27), but also the risen Christ in his heavenly status. Such an exalted intercessor cannot assume the role of an accuser or be the one who will condemn us. With both God and Christ on our side, our eternal destiny is assured.

18.15 "Who will separate us from the love of Christ?" (8:35), i.e. from the love that Christ has for us (as vv. 37, 39 make clear), his self-surrender on behalf of us. All that Christ has done for humankind stems from the love that he has for us. "The love of Christ impels us" (2 Cor 5:14), i.e. motivates and sustains our lives and our conduct. Paul's argument has moved from the idea of an accuser to a divider, someone or something that would try to sever the link between Christians and Christ. So intimate is that bond that nothing can dissolve it.

18.16 "Will distress or anguish or persecution or famine or nakedness or danger or the sword?" (8:35). None of the dangers or troubles of earthly life, even the worst of them, can make true Christians forget the love that Christ has made known for them in his death and resurrection. In effect, Paul is spelling out the "sufferings" of which he spoke in 8:18, sufferings that are incomparable with the glory that awaits us. To bolster up his contention, the apostle further quotes Ps 44:23, "For your sake we are being put to death all day long; we are considered as sheep to be slaughtered" (8:36). The psalmist was uttering a plaint of the community, bemoaning the injustice done to Israel by its enemies, as it recalled its loyalty to Yahweh and sought aid and deliverance. "Yet in all of it we are more than victors because of him who loved us" (8:37). Christ has won the case for us! We are victors in court; we have been vindicated in a superabundant way because of what he has done for us.

18.17 "I am convinced that neither life nor death, neither angels or principalities, neither the present nor the future, nor any powers, neither height nor depth, nor any other creature will be able to separate us from the love of God, which is in Christ Jesus our Lord" (8:38-39). Paul adds his personal conviction as the climax of the hymn. No natural, cataclysmic, or cosmic power or force, no spirit of any sort, nothing created can rupture the union of Christ and the Christian. Paul's rhetoric builds up to express his conviction. For God's love was poured out in the Christ-event, and that love has become the basis of Christian life and the unshakable hope that marks Christian existence and destiny. So Christians must learn to trust in it.

18.18 Here one might consider Ignatius' consideration of the Third Degree of Humility: "When options equally further the praise and glory of God, in order to imitate Christ our Lord better, to be more like him here and now, I desire and choose poverty with Christ poor rather than wealth; contempt with Christ laden with it rather than honors. Even further, I desire to be regarded as a useless fool for Christ, who before me was regarded as such, rather than as a wise or prudent person in this world" (§167). For all such things, wealth, honor, and fame should never allow me to be separated from the Christ who so loves me. To be like him, I shall prefer poverty, contempt, and dishonor. Such demands of discipleship parallel the sufferings which cannot separate the Christian from the love of Christ who calls us to be like him.

18.19 Questions. Am I convinced of this love of God and this love of Christ for me? Does it motivate my existence and my conduct? How can it better achieve in my life what it was meant to accomplish for me?

COLLOQUY: PSALM 63:1-9

> O God, you are my God,
>   for you I long!
> For you my body yearns;
>   for you my soul thirsts.
> Like a land parched, lifeless,
>   and without water.
> So I look to you in the sanctuary
>   to see your power and glory.
> For your love is better than life;
>   my lips offer you worship!
> I will bless you as long as I live;
>   I will lift up by hands, calling upon your name.
> My soul shall savor the rich banquet of praise,
>   with joyous lips my mouth shall honor you!
> When I think of you upon my bed,
>   through the night watches I will recall
> That you indeed are my help.
>   and in the shadow of your wings I shout for joy.
> My soul clings fast to you;
>   your right hand upholds me.

See further *Romans*, 521-38.

Justification through Faith Does Not Contradict God's Promises to Israel, Which Stem from His Gratuitous Election of It (9:1-29)

9:1 I am speaking the truth in Christ; I am not lying, as my conscience bears witness to me in the Holy Spirit, 2 that my sorrow is great and the anguish in my heart is unrelenting. 3 For I could even wish to be accursed and cut off from Christ for the sake of my brothers, my kinsmen by descent. 4 They are Israelites, and to them belong the sonship, the glory, the covenants, the giving of the law, the cult, and the promises; 5 to them belong the patriarchs, and from them by natural descent comes the Messiah, who is God over all, blest forever! Amen.

6 It is not as though the word of God has failed. For not all descendants of Israel are truly Israel; 7 nor because they are offspring of Abraham are they all his children. Rather, "*It is through Isaac that your offspring will be named.*" 8 That is, it is not the children of the flesh who are the children of God, but the children born of the promise who are reckoned as Abraham's offspring. 9 For so runs the promise, "*At the time appointed I shall return and Sarah will have a son.*" 10 Not only that, but even when Rebecca had children by one and the same man, our father Isaac—11 even before they had been born or had done anything good or evil, in order that God's purpose in election might persist, 12 not because of deeds but because of his call—it was said to her, "*The older shall*

serve the younger." [13] As it stands written, *"Jacob I loved, but Esau I hated."* ˅

[14] What then shall we say? Is God unjust? Certainly not! [15] *For he says to Moses, "I will show mercy to whomever I will, and I will have compassion on whomever I will."* ʷ [16] So it depends not on human willing or effort, but on God's mercy. [17] For Scripture says to Pharaoh, *"For this very reason have I raised you up, that I might display my power through you and that my name might be proclaimed over all the earth."* ˣ [18] Therefore he has mercy on whomever he wills and hardens the heart of whomever he chooses. [19] Will you therefore say to me, "Then why does God still find fault? Who has ever resisted his will?" [20] But who are you, a mere human being, to answer back to God? *Will what is molded say to its molder, "Why did you make me like this?"* ʸ [21] Has not the potter the right to make out of the same lump of clay one vase for a noble purpose and another for common use? [22] Yet what if God, wishing to display his wrath and make known his power, has endured with much long-suffering those vases of wrath, fashioned for destruction? [23] This he did to make known the riches of his glory for the vases of mercy, which he had fashioned beforehand for such glory.

[24] Even for us, whom he has called, not only from among the Jews, but also from among the Gentiles, [25] as indeed he says in Hosea,

> *"Those who were not my people*
> *I shall call 'my people';*
> *and her who was not loved*
> *I shall call 'my beloved'";* ᶻ

[26] and

> *"in the very place where it was said to them,*
> *'You are not my people,'*
> *they shall there be called 'children of the living God."* ᵃ

[27] And Isaiah cries out about Israel,

> *"Should the number of the Israelites be as the sands*
> *of the sea, a remnant shall be saved.* ᵇ
> [28] *"For the Lord will carry out his sentence on the earth with*
> *rigor and dispatch."* ᶜ

[29] And as Isaiah has predicted,

> *"If the Lord of hosts had not left us offspring,*
> *we would have fared like Sodom and been made like*
> *Gomorrah."* ᵈ

^s Gen 21:12	^t Gen 18:10
^u Gen 25:23	^v Mal 1:2-3
^w Exod 33:19	^x Exod 9:16
^y Isa 29:16	^z Hos 2:25
^a Hos 2:1	^b Isa 10:22-23
^c Isa 28:22	^d Isa 1:9

19.1 Paul now invites us to meditate on a different aspect of his gospel: the relationship of Israel to this new mode of justification and salvation through faith. In a sense he has been preparing for this discussion all along, especially in 3:1-9 and 3:31. For his teaching about this new mode must have encountered the obvious objection even in his day that the mass of his fellow coreligionists had resisted his gospel and had not espoused the freedom that it announced: "Your own fellow Jews have not accepted your gospel!" Paul himself admitted that his gospel was a message of salvation "for the Jew first" (1:16), but it has become the classic problem of the rejection of Israel (so formulated in 11:15, *apobolē autōn*, "their rejection"). What does this "rejection" mean in view of the election of Israel as God's Chosen People and of the irrevocable promises made by God to the patriarchs of Israel? Another way of asking the question is, How is the gospel as promise related to the law? or How is the new revelation of the uprightness of God related to the divine promises of old? In effect, chaps. 9–11 become the climax of Paul's discussion of justification by grace through faith.

Because Paul is here reflecting on a historic aspect of that teaching, it may seem that there would be little in this part of Romans that would lend itself to our meditation. And yet there is more than a little, because what happened to Israel can be the lot of any human being. It is well, then, that we reflect on that problem and Paul's reaction to it.

19.2 Paul begins his discussion with a personal lament about his fellow coreligionists. He speaks as a Jewish Christian, as a Jew who has come to belief in Jesus as the Messiah and risen Lord. He poignantly formulates his sadness over the lot of his brother and sister Jews, whose prerogatives he readily acknowledges. These are the seven God-given privileges accorded to the Jewish people, to which Paul adds one of his own. In expressing his anguish, he reckons with the problem that confronted him in his personal preaching of the gospel. He has been at pains to teach about God as the source of new human justification and salvation; now he seeks to teach about the same God who has granted privileges to the people chosen of old, but who now also calls Gentiles to share in the destiny of that Chosen People. "My sorrow is great and the anguish in my heart is unrelenting" (9:2). The sorrow and anguish come from the loss that he senses is theirs. "I could even wish to be accursed and cut off from Christ for the sake of my brothers, my kinsmen by descent" (9:3). So Paul would pray, echoing the prayer that Moses uttered on behalf of unruly Hebrews, when he asked "to be blotted out of the book of life" so that they might be forgiven (Exod 32:32). Paul, the herald of Christ, prays even to be cut off from Christ for the sake of his own people. He thus becomes the model of concern for us who care about other brothers and sisters who we may know are experiencing a similar loss in their relation with God.

19.3 "They are Israelites" (9:4). Paul bestows on his "brothers" and kinsfolk a honorific title, the very name given to them by Yahweh himself, when Jacob's name was changed to "Israel" (Gen 32:29). In that name they rightly gloried, and Paul recognizes it. "To them belong the sonship, the glory, the covenants, the giving of the law, the cult, the promises, the patriarchs" (9:4). Seven were the classic prerogatives in which the Jewish people could boast, for they were regarded as God's "firstborn son" (Exod 4:22), and theirs were the "glorious" presence of God among them in the Tabernacle (Exod 15:6,11; 16:10), the "covenants" made with Abraham (Gen 15:18), Isaac (Gen 26:3-5), Moses (Exod 24:7-8), the giving of the *tôrāh,* "instruction," whereby Israel came to know God's will (Exod 20:1-17), the awesome cult of Yahweh in the Temple (Exodus 25–31), the promises made by Yahweh to Abraham (Gen 12:2), Isaac (Gen 26:3-5), Jacob (Gen 28:13-14) about the great people that they would become, and the patriarchs themselves, Abraham, Isaac, and Jacob. To the classic septet of prerogatives Paul adds an eighth: "from them by natural descent comes the Messiah" (9:5), a prerogative that he recognizes, but that his brother and sister Jews undoubtedly would not have admitted.

"Who is God over all, blest forever!" This highly contested ending of the verse is problematic because of the way one has tried to punctuate the clause (see *Romans*, 548-49 for details). It may mean that Paul has even come to acknowledge the divinity of Christ Jesus, a rare occurrence in his letters.

The lesson in all of this for us is the concern that Paul has for other members of the human race, for those who were closely related to him, his "brothers," his "kinsmen by race or descent." Despite all their prerogatives they have not come to accept God's gospel, and this is the cause of Paul's sorrow and anguish.

19.4 If, however, Israel has been so favored by God and yet has not responded to the gospel, and if God has opened up to Gentiles a share in Israel's status, does it not really mean that God has been unfaithful to chosen Israel? Paul's answer to such a question is a firm no. "It is not as though the word of God has failed" (9:6). In explanation, he proceeds to distinguish the meaning of the name "Israel" and the title "offspring of Abraham." "Not all descendants of Israel are truly Israel; nor because they are offspring of Abraham are they all his children" (9:6b-7). For both "Israel" and Abraham's "children" had been constituted by God's free election. Hence the trouble lies not with God who freely chose them. Paul seeks to explain why. "It is through Isaac that your offspring will be named" (9:7b, quoting Gen 21:12), and not through Ishmael and the six other children born to Abraham (Gen 16:15; 25:2). God has freely chosen Isaac to bear Abraham's name and heritage. Similarly, God freely chose Jacob to bear that heritage, and not Esau (Gen 25:21-26), even though both were born of one and the same mother and father (Rebecca and Isaac), and neither had done anything to merit such a status. "Jacob I loved, but Esau I hated" (Mal 1:2-3), i.e. "I loved less," according to an ancient near eastern hyperbole (compare Gen 29:30-31; Deut 21:15-17). Hence "the children born of the *promise* are reckoned as Abraham's offspring" (9:8), a promise freely made by God. Paul alludes to the promise made to Abraham that Sarah would bear him a son, who would be his heir and through whom his offspring would continue. He likewise interprets the election of Jacob over Esau. He thus uses these Old Testament examples of God's freedom in election to show that God has only been dealing with his Jewish contemporaries as he did with the patriarchs of old. It may seem that God is unjust or shows partiality, but Paul will not tolerate that implication. God freely chose Israel and has sovereignly established Abraham's progeny through Isaac and Jacob; to that promise he remains faithful. So the fidelity of God is not in question. Paul thus reassures us of the very source of our salvation. It rests with a sovereign and free God, who has graced us with his favor.

19.5 Indeed, God's sovereign freedom can even use indocility to his purpose. To make a further point in his discussion, Paul adds two further examples that he draws from the Old Testament. The first example of such freedom is taken from the story of the Pharaoh (Exod 3:10-12:36), who, in the time of Moses, hardened his heart against releasing the Hebrews from their bondage and slave labor. So Paul quotes the words Moses was instructed to say to the Pharaoh in Exod 9:16, "For this very reason have I raised you up, that I might display my power through you and that my name might be proclaimed over all the earth." In other words, God even used the stubborn pagan Pharaoh to his purpose, and through him God's free use of his power was manifested. So Paul adds: "Therefore he has mercy on whomever he wills and hardens the heart of whomever he chooses" (9:18). In the Old Testament the hardening of Pharaoh's heart was attributed at times to God (Exod 4:21; 7:3) and at times to Pharaoh himself (Exod 7:14; 8:11). In the first of such instances, we have another example of protological thinking (see p. 33 above), to which Paul alludes as he ascribes to God the hardening of Pharaoh's heart and thereby illustrates God's sovereign freedom. Paul's example teaches us how we are to think about God, the source of our justification and salvation. God is not one to act arbitrarily despite the way we might be tempted to envisage divine activity in our regard. Pharaoh was reluctant to let the Hebrews go forth from Egypt; he opposed the divine plan for their release from servitude and slave-labor. Yet God brought good out of such opposition to him. He used the Pharaoh's indocility to achieve his purpose for the fashioning of his Chosen People. Paul insists, this divine use of Pharaoh's indocility reveals how God showed favor to Israel; it was a free choice of God who favored Israel and not the Pharaoh.

Given the fact that Paul has already mentioned predestination in 8:30, one cannot help but think of the example of Pharaoh as an instance in which God's providence and foreknowledge has brought good out of evil. God has shown mercy to Israel and hardened Pharaoh's heart to his own purpose. So we too are dependent on God's good pleasure. The evil that happens to us in our lives is not without God's good purpose. The sufferings that Paul mentioned in 8:18, a necessary part of human existence, are also things that happen to us in his wise disposition of our lives. They too come from his free choice in our regard.

19.6 The other example that Paul draws from the Old Testament is the image of the potter, who deftly shapes elegant vases or ordinary pots from a lump of clay on the potter's wheel, one to a noble purpose, the other to common, everyday use. The point in the example is that the lump of clay has no say as to whether it will be shaped for elegant or common use. "Will what is molded say to its molder, 'Why did you make me like this?'" (9:20, quoting Isa 29:16). The potter's wheel and deft craftsmanship had become the springboard from which the ancients derived the idea of a creator god, who not only fashioned the earth and all that is in it, but also controlled and governed it at will. Ancient Egyptian wall-drawings depict various gods so fashioning human beings, especially kings. This example, then, serves Paul in his effort to depict the sovereign freedom of God in his dealings with Israel. God is not unfaithful. Rather, God has rather freely chosen to fashion Israel as his people. "This he did to make known the riches of his glory for the vases of mercy, which he had fashioned beforehand for such glory" (9:23). In his mercy God chose Israel and fashioned it for glory. Paul adds this sentence to forestall an objection, because he realizes that God has tolerated "vases of wrath" in order to manifest his mercy to those whom he has freely called, "the vases of mercy." This explains too how God could use the indocility and reluctance of Israel even to his own purpose, i.e. in his dealings with Christians who have come from Judaism as well as from paganism. Israel's reaction to God's gospel is thus not the result of God's election of it as his people.

Again, this image of the creator God as a ceramist enables Paul to sharpen the image of God that he wants his readers to understand. The God who has made us is a God of benevolence, who freely fashions vases of wrath and vases of mercy; both serve his purpose. The good that has come to us in our lives reveals that we may be "vases of mercy," but the evil that we do and the evil that may still come from us may also reveal in what sense we may become "vases of wrath."

19.7 It might seem that God acts arbitrarily. He has chosen Israel to be his people, but now he summons Gentiles to share its destiny. This too Paul rejects, because the infidelity of Israel has been foreseen in God's plan. He will cite the testimony of the Hebrew Scriptures to prove this very point, but also to show that God has provided for a remnant of Israel that would be responsive to the challenge of the gospel. This God did "even for us, whom he has called, not only from among the Jews, but also from among the Gentiles, as indeed he says in Hosea, 'Those who were not my people I shall call "my people"; and her who was not loved I shall call "my beloved"'" (9:24-25, quoting Hos 2:25; cf. Hos 1:9). Paul thus cites the Scriptures of the Jewish people to show that in God's providence, as thus made known, others than Jews would be called to share the inheritance of Israel. So this call was not only not arbitrary, but even foreseen of old.

Moreover, even Isaiah the prophet uttered about Israel, "Should the number of Israelites be as the sands of the sea, a remnant shall be saved" (9:27, quoting Isa 10:22; cf. Hos 2:1). In Isaiah the "remnant" referred to those who would survive the doom that was coming upon Israel in its Babylonian captivity. But the remnant that would "be saved" denotes for Paul those Jewish people who, like himself, have responded positively to the challenge of the gospel. Thus he invokes the Scriptures of Israel against Israel, showing that even its own sacred writings noted and recorded its infidelity in the past; hence the reaction of Israel now to the gospel is nothing new. God will provide a remnant, the salvation of which is foreseen. Otherwise Israel would have become like the cities destroyed by divine wrath, Sodom and Gomorrah. "If the Lord of hosts had not left us offspring, we would have fared like Sodom and been made like Gomorrah" (9:29, quoting Isa 1:9). So Paul vindicates the fidelity of God in the instance of Israel's infidelity.

19:8 Questions. Should not I too pray for the Jewish people, as did Paul? Should I not thank God for the free and gracious call he extended to such people to be his Chosen Ones? Should I not praise God for the Jewish heritage of Christianity? Should I not again thank God for calling me to be a Christian and to be one among his new people? Should I not thank God for the mercy that he has shown me, in reality a vessel of wrath? What lesson can I learn from Pharaoh's indocility?

COLLOQUY: PSALM 130

> Out of the depths I call to you, LORD;
>> Lord, hear my cry!
> May your ears be attentive
>> to my cry for mercy.
> If you, O LORD, mark our sins,
>> LORD, who can stand?
> But with you is forgiveness,
>> and so you are revered.
> I wait with longing for the LORD,
>> my soul waits for his word.
> My soul looks for the LORD
>> more than sentinels for daybreak.
> More than sentinels for daybreak,
>> let Israel look for the LORD,
> For with the LORD is kindness,
>> with him is full redemption,
> And God will redeem Israel
>> from all its sins.

See further *Romans*, 539-75.

Israel Has Stumbled in Its Pursuit of Righteousness (9:30–10:21)

[30] What then shall we say? That Gentiles who did not pursue uprightness have attained it, an uprightness based on faith, [31] whereas Israel, which was pursuing a law of uprightness, did not achieve it? [32] Why was this? Because they pursued it not with faith, but as if it were by deeds. They stumbled over "the stumbling stone," [33] as it stands written: "*Look, I am setting in Zion a stone to stumble against, a rock to trip over; and no one who believes in him shall be put to shame.*" [e]

[10:1] Brothers, my heart's desire and my prayer to God for them is their salvation. [2] Indeed, I can testify for them that they have zeal for God; but it is not well informed. [3] For being unaware of God's uprightness and seeking to set up their own uprightness, they have not submitted to the uprightness of God. [4] For Christ is the end of the law so that there may be uprightness for everyone who believes.

[5] For Moses writes thus of the uprightness that comes from the law: "*The one who does these things will find life in them.*" [f] [6] But the uprightness that comes from faith speaks thus: "*Do not say in your heart, 'Who can go up to heaven?'* [g] (that is, to bring Christ down); [7] or '*Who will go down into the abyss?*' [h] (that is, to bring Christ up from the dead)." [8] But what does it say instead? "*The word is near to you, on your lips and in your heart*" [i] (that is, the word of faith that we preach): [9] If you profess with your lips that 'Jesus is Lord' and believe in your heart that God has raised him from the dead, you will be saved. [10] Such faith of the heart leads to uprightness;

such profession of the lips to salvation. [11] For Scripture says, *"No one who believes in him shall be put to shame."* [j] [12] No distinction is made between Jew and Greek: the same Lord is Lord of all, bestowing his riches on all who call upon him. [13] *For "everyone who calls upon the name of the Lord shall be saved."* [k]

[14] But how will people call upon him in whom they have not believed? How can they believe in him to whom they have not listened? How can they hear of him unless through a preacher? [15] And how can people preach unless they are sent? As it stands written, *"How timely the arrival of those who bring good news!"* [l] [16] Yet everyone has not heeded the gospel. But even Isaiah says, *"Lord, who has believed our message?"* [m] [17] Faith then comes from what is heard, and what is heard comes through the word of Christ. [18] But I ask, can it be that they have not heard of it? Of course they have! *"Their voice has gone forth over all the earth, and their words to the bounds of the world."* [n] [19] But again I ask, Can it be that Israel did not understand? First of all, Moses says, *"I shall make you jealous of those who are not a nation; and with a foolish nation shall I provoke your anger."* [o] [20] And Isaiah made bold to say, *"I was found by those who were not seeking me; I showed myself to those who were not asking for me."* [p] [21] Yet of Israel he says, *"All day long have I held out my hands to a disobedient and defiant people."* [q]

[e] Isa 28:16	[f] Lev 18:5
[g] Deut 30:12	[h] Ps 107:26
[i] Deut 30:14	[j] Isa 28:16
[k] Joel 3:5	[l] Isa 52:7
[m] Isa 53:1	[n] Ps 19:5
[o] Deut 32:21	[p] Isa 65:1
[q] Isa 65:2	

20.1 In the preceding passage Paul concluded that what has happened to Israel does not mean that God has been unfaithful to it. God has been displaying mercy and grace toward it. Now Paul will insist that Israel itself is responsible for its misstep. What has happened to Israel is not contrary to God's direction of history, because its infidelity had been foreseen and even recorded in its Scriptures. Having considered Israel's problem from the standpoint of God, Paul now turns to it from the viewpoint of

Israel itself. Now he restates the reasons for his sorrow and anguish (9:2): pagans who have not even been trying to attain the status of uprightness before God have reached that goal, whereas Israel, which was pursuing such a goal, has failed to reach it. Pagans have responded to "God's gospel" (1:1), whereas most of God's Chosen People have resisted it and preferred their own way of uprightness. "They pursued it not with faith, but as if it were by deeds" (9:32). In their pursuit of uprightness by doing deeds prescribed by the law, they have not pursued it with faith. What has gone wrong in this misguided pursuit has caused Paul such sorrow and anguish.

20.2 The Jewish people have "stumbled over 'the stumbling stone,' of which Isaiah (28:16 + 8:14) once wrote, "Look, I am setting in Zion a stone to stumble against, a rock to trip over, and no one who believes in him shall be put to shame" (9:33). Paul understands Christ Jesus to be a stumbling stone set by God. Running madly and with zeal in pursuit of a certain kind of uprightness, Israel has failed to see the obstacle on its rough road: It has failed to acknowledge Christ and the role that he has come to play in God's providence for humanity. It has thus stumbled over the stumbling stone that God laid in Zion. "Being unaware of God's uprightness and seeking to set up their own uprightness, they have not submitted to the uprightness of God" (10:2). Israel has ignored the divine uprightness revealed in the gospel and made manifest against all human wickedness (3:5, 21), and so it has not come to a real knowledge of what divine uprightness involves. This is why Paul maintains that Israel has stumbled over Christ. For "no one who believes in him shall be put to shame" (9:33).

There is a lesson here for all of us. For we too often pursue our own goals and ignore the goal of upright living. We too can "stumble" over the stumbling stone, which is Christ. We can ignore the place that he should be playing as Lord in our lives and in our conduct. Our faith in him can become faint, and we can forget that only the one who lives out one's life in faith "shall not be put to shame."

20.3 "For Christ is the end of the law so that there may be uprightness for everyone who believes" (10:4). Christ as "the end of the law" has been understood in two ways: (a) As the "termination" of the law; *telos* is understood temporally. Recall the stages of salvation history as viewed by Paul through Jewish spectacles (p. 111 above). The age of the Messiah has come; this has happened in our day, "upon whom the ends of the ages have met" (1 Cor 10:11). So Paul writes as he sees that the end of the age of *Tôrāh* has met the beginning of the age of the Messiah (Christ). We are part of the new aeon, in which Christ is the Lord, who should now dominate our lives instead of the tyrannizing law. (b) As the "goal" or *finis* of the law; *telos* is understood as expressing purpose, that toward which the law itself tended (as many patristic writers understood it). The latter is preferred by many commentators who relate this verse to 9:31-33, where the "pursuit" of uprightness implies a "goal" to be reached. It would mean that Christ as the goal of the law has brought it about that those who believe in him are accredited with achieving the "goal" of the law, that which the law was intended to achieve, God's way of uprightness. Thus faith brings it about that the goal of the law is attained.

20.4 Having presented Christ as the "end" or "goal" of the law, Paul moves on to discuss what faith means in the pursuit of such uprightness. Many of the following verses in this chapter spell out aspects of the Pauline meaning of "faith." The apostle begins by stressing the ease of this new uprightness "that comes from faith" (10:6). To appreciate this aspect of faith in the following verses, one has to recall the difficult task confronting those who were "under the law" (3:19-20); it was no easy task to keep it, as Ps 143:2, which was quoted there, admitted.

Ironically enough, to explain the ease with which this new mode of attaining uprightness in God's sight, Paul alludes to the words of Moses who sought to instruct Israel about how easy it would be to observe the law: "For this command that I enjoin on you today [to keep the commands and statutes written in the book of the law] is neither too mysterious nor too remote for you. It is not up in the heavens, that you should have to say, 'Who will go up into the heavens to get it for us and tell us about it, so that we may carry it out?' Nor is it across the sea, that you have to say, 'Who will cross the sea to get it for us and tell us about it, that we may carry it out?' No, it is something very near to you, already in your mouths and in your hearts; you have only to carry it out" (Deut 30:11-14). Paul does not cite these words explicitly, but he alludes to them, commenting in midrashic fashion on those that he uses, even applying some of them directly to Christ. His point is: the way of uprightness through faith is easy; you do not have to scale the heights of the heavens or plumb the depths of the abyss in order to believe. To have faith you do not have to pull off the incarnation or the resurrection of Christ Jesus–nothing so arduous! You have only to believe, to put your faith in Christ Jesus. You have only to utter the Christian confession, "Jesus is Lord." "The word is near to you, on your lips and in your heart" (10:8, quoting Deut 30:14). This is the ease of the new way of uprightness. So Paul borrows the argument of Moses and applies it to faith in Christ Jesus, the new way of achieving righteousness in God's sight.

20.5 For Christian faith as a response to the gospel has to begin with an affirmation, with an assent given to a proposition: "If you profess with your lips that 'Jesus is Lord'" (10:9a). Thus Paul recalls to us the role that the lordship of Christ must play in our lives. But faith does not stop with such a mere intellectual acknowledgement; it must engage the whole person: "And believe in your heart that God has raised him from the dead, you will be saved" (10:9bc). Salvific faith must come from the heart and involve one in a commitment to God who raised Christ from the dead. It also involves a recognition of the risen Lord, "who was handed over (to death) for our trespasses and raised for our justification" (4:25). For this is "the word of faith that we preach" (10:8c), the "gospel of God."

20.6 "Such faith of the heart leads to uprightness; such profession of the lips to salvation" (10:10), i.e. through such faith one is accredited as righteous in God's sight and through it one will be saved. To this explanation Paul again adds reference to Isa 28:16, as in 9:33: "No one who believes in him shall be put to shame." No one who believes will stumble over the stumbling stone laid in Zion. This is said of all, Jew and Greek alike, for Christ Jesus is "Lord of all" (10:12). And "everyone who calls upon the name of the Lord shall be saved" (10:13, quoting Joel 3:5 [Engl. 2:32]). In the original the prophet Joel spoke of the awesome day of Yahweh, when deliverance and survival would come to those who call upon Yahweh. Paul extends the meaning of this promise to those who now call upon *Kyrios* in the Christian sense.

What Paul has just said about faith is absolutely fundamental for him in Christian life. It is the response to the gospel of God preached or announced to us, which challenges us to allegiance expressed by lips and heart, by the whole of our being. That gospel which proclaims that "Jesus is Lord" evokes from us a commitment of faith, a dedication to God in Christ Jesus, which should radically transform our lives.

20.7 Paul now adds to his presentation of the meaning of Christian faith a series of objections of an imaginary interlocutor, which seek to excuse Israel because of its reaction to the gospel. Israel has not taken advantage of this new and easy way to justification offered in the gospel and foreshadowed in the prophets of old. By his answers to these objections, which he gives in the form of quotations from the Old Testament, Paul will clarify in what sense Israel is responsible for its misstep. He does this in answer to four objections: (a) How can people believe such a gospel unless it has been fully preached by messengers duly sent? (vv. 14-15). (b) But it has not been accepted by everybody! (vv. 16-17). (c) Perhaps Israel did not hear it! (v. 18). (d) Perhaps Israel did not understand it! (v. 19). He briefly answers each of these objections and quotes the Old Testament to support his contention about the responsibility of Israel.

20.8 "Faith comes from what is heard" (10:17). Paul insists that Christian faith begins with a listening to the preached gospel, to the proposition that is proclaimed, "Jesus is Lord!" For "what is heard comes through the word of Christ." This could mean "through the message that Christ himself has brought" (a genitive of origin) or it could mean "through the message about Jesus as the Messiah" (an objective genitive). Thus Christ would be speaking his message through the mouths of authorized heralds.

This is the last time that "Christ" is mentioned in the epistle until its hortatory section begins (12:5). Nor does "Jesus" or "Lord" (= the risen Christ) appear again in chaps. 10–11. The significance of this absence of his name will emerge later (see 11:25-26 on p. 181).

20.9 "Moses says, 'I shall make you jealous of those who are not a nation; and with a foolish nation shall I provoke your anger" (10:19, quoting Deut 32:21). Paul quotes part of the Song of Moses, in which Yahweh, through Moses, tried to educate Israel and make known that it will be humiliated by heathen nations. In effect, Paul is comparing contemporary Israel with what it had been in the time of its wandering in the desert. If it was humiliated for its infidelity then, how much greater should its humiliation be now? Gentiles, the "nonpeople" and "a foolish nation," understand and accept the gospel message, yet Israel remains uncomprehending. What happens to the Gentiles is meant to provoke Israel to a reaction.

20.10 "'I was found by those who were not seeking me; I showed myself to those who were not asking for me.' Yet of Israel he says, 'All day long have I held out my hands to a disobedient and defiant people'" (10:20-21, quoting Isa 65:1-2). To the testimony of Moses, Paul adds that of Trito-Isaiah. Thus Paul ends his indictment of Israel as a "disobedient and defiant people." He depicts God holding out his hands, not in supplication, but in a gesture of invitation and welcome, a gesture that Israel refuses. Paul insists, God had never stopped reaching out to Israel, even in all of its resistance of old.

Again, the lesson is obvious for all who read this stern summary: God is still holding out his hands to us, even when we resist his welcome and invitation.

20.11 Questions. Have I been going my own way and not measuring up to the uprightness of God that summons me? Is my zeal for God rightly informed and motivated? Have I reckoned with how easy the living out of faith can be in my life? Do I realize my own culpability when I fail to respond to the divine invitation in my life? Do I resist the call of God? Am I one who even defies the invitation and welcome of God?

COLLOQUY: PSALM 44

> O God, we have heard with our own ears;
>   our ancestors have told us
> The deeds you did in their days,
>   with your own hand in days of old:

You rooted out nations to plant them,
>   crushed peoples to make room for them.
Not with their own swords did they conquer the land,
>   nor did their own arms bring victory;
It was your right hand, your own arm,
>   the light of your face, for you favored them.
You are my king and my God,
>   who bestows victories on Jacob.
Through you we batter our foes;
>   through your name, trample our adversaries.
Not in my bow do I trust,
>   nor does my sword bring me victory.
You have brought us victory over our enemies,
>   shamed those who hate us.
In God we have boasted all the day long;
>   your name we praise forever.
But now you have rejected and disgraced us;
>   you do not march out with our armies.
You make us retreat before the foe;
>   those who hate us plunder us at will.
You hand us over like sheep to be slaughtered,
>   scatter us among the nations.
You sell your people for nothing;
>   you make no profit from their sale.
You make us the reproach of our neighbors,
>   the mockery and scorn of those around us.
You make us a byword among the nations;
>   the peoples shake their heads at us.
All day long my disgrace is before me;
>   shame has covered my face
At the sound of those who taunt and revile,
>   at the sight of the spiteful enemy.
All this has come upon us,
>   though we have not forgotten you,
>   nor been disloyal to your covenant.
Our hearts have not turned back,
>   nor have our steps strayed from your path.
Yet you have left us crushed,
>   desolate in a place of jackals;
>   you have covered us with darkness.
If we had forgotten the name of our God,
>   stretched out our hands to another god,

Would not God have discovered this,
>God who knows the secrets of the heart?
For you we are slain all the day long,
>considered only as sheep to be slaughtered.
Awake! Why do you sleep, O LORD?
>Rise up! Do not reject us forever!
Why do you hide your face;
>why forget our pain and misery?
We are bowed down to the ground;
>our bodies are pressed to the earth.
Rise up, help us!
>Redeem us as your love demands.

See further *Romans*, 576-601.

Israel's Failure Is Partial and Temporary (11:1-36)

11:1 I ask, then, Has God rejected his people? Certainly not! I am an Israelite myself, a descendant of Abraham, from the tribe of Benjamin. 2 No, *God has not rejected his people,* r whom he foreknew. Do you not know what Scripture says in the passage about Elijah, how he pleaded with God against Israel: 3 "Lord, *they have killed your prophets and torn down your altars; and I am left alone, and they are seeking my life."* s 4 And what was the divine reply to him? "*I have reserved for myself seven thousand men who have not bent the knee to Baal."* t 5 So too at the present time a remnant, chosen by grace, has come into being. 6 And if by grace, it is no longer by deeds, since grace would cease to be grace. 7 So then what? What Israel sought for, it did not achieve; the chosen ones achieved it, whereas the others were made obtuse. 8 As it stands written, "*God granted them stupor of spirit, eyes that see not and ears that hear not—even to this day."* u 9 *David too says, "May their table be a snare and a trap, a stumbling block and a retribution for them;* 10 *may their eyes be dimmed so that they cannot see! Bend their backs continually!"* v

11 Now then I ask, Did they stumble so as to fall irremediably? Certainly not! Yet because of their trespass salvation has come to the Gentiles to make Israel jealous. 12 Now if their trespass has meant the enrichment of the world, and their loss the enrichment of Gentiles, how much more will their full number mean! 13 I turn now to you Gentiles: Inasmuch as I am the apostle of the Gentiles, I make much of this ministry of mine 14 in the hope that I may

stir up my own people to jealousy and save some of them.
[15] For if their rejection has meant the reconciliation of the
world, what will their acceptance mean? Nothing less than
life from the dead! [16] If the first fruits are holy, so too is the
whole batch of dough; if the root is holy, so too are the
branches. [17] If some of the branches have been lopped off,
you, though a branch from a wild olive tree, have been
grafted into their place and have come to share in the rich
sap of the olive root. [18] Do not boast over those branches. If
you do, remember this: you do not support the root; the
root supports you. [19] You may indeed say, "Branches were
lopped off so that I might be grafted in." [20] True, but they
were lopped off because of a lack of faith, whereas you are
there because of faith. So do not become haughty for that
reason; be fearful. [21] For if God did not spare the natural
branches, perhaps he will not spare you either. [22] Consider
then God's kindness and severity; severity to those who
have fallen, but kindness to you, if you only remain in his
kindness. For you too may be cut off. [23] And those others, if
they do not remain in their lack of faith, will be grafted
back in. God indeed has the power to graft them in again.
[24] For if you were cut from an olive tree that is wild by nature
and grafted contrary to nature into a cultivated one, how
much more readily will these, the natural branches, be
grafted back into their own olive stock!

[25] I do not want you to be unaware of this mystery,
brothers, lest you become wise in your own estimation: a
partial hardening of heart has come upon Israel until the
full number of the Gentiles comes in; [26] and so all Israel
shall be saved, as it stands written, *"From Zion shall come the
deliverer; he shall turn godlessness away from Jacob.* [27] *This is
my covenant with them, when I take away their sins."* ˇ [28] As far
as the gospel is concerned, they are enemies for your sake;
but as far as election is concerned, they are beloved of God
because of the patriarchs. [29] For irrevocable are God's gifts
and his call. [30] As you were once disobedient to God but now
have been shown mercy as a result of their disobedience,
[31] so too they have now become disobedient so that they too
may now be shown mercy as a result of the mercy shown to
you. [32] For God has imprisoned all people in disobedience
that he might show mercy to all!

**³³ Oh the depth of the riches, of the wisdom, and of the
knowledge of God!**

How inscrutable are his judgments!

How untraceable his ways!

³⁴ *Who has known the mind of the Lord?*

Who has been his counselor? ˣ

**³⁵ Who has ever given him a gift
to receive a gift in return?**

³⁶ For from him and through him and for him are all things.

To him be glory forever! Amen.

ʳ Ps 94:14	ˢ 1 Kgs 19:10
ᵗ 1 Kgs 19:18	ᵘ Isa 29:10; cf. Deut 29:3
ᵛ Ps 69:23-24	ʷ Isa 59:20-21; 27:9
ˣ Isa 40:13; cf. Wis 9:13	

21.1 Paul continues his discussion of Israel's misstep. His description of it so far is not pleasant, because he has said that the problem rests not with God, but with Israel itself. Yet he has indicated that God has provided that there would be at least a "remnant," among which he includes Jews like himself. Now he seeks to explain that what has been called Israel's "rejection" is only partial and temporary, and that "all Israel shall be saved," which he calls a "mystery," and for which he praises the "wisdom" of God's plan.

21.2 Paul begins by framing an objection, "Has God rejected his people?" deriving the wording of his objection from Ps 94:14. It formulates a suggestion that he resolutely rejects. In effect, he says, How can I, a genuine Israelite, admit such a thing? He insists that he, a member of God's holy people, is at least one who has welcomed God's gospel and acknowledged Christ as his Messiah. Moreover, he knows too that Israel's reaction to that gospel is not a sign of the divine rejection of his own kinsfolk. He not only implicitly boasts of his Jewish heritage, but sees that he and other Jewish Christians are signs to the contrary. For he, just as the rest of Israel, is a "descendant of Abraham." He boasts of his relation to "the tribe of Benjamin," the tribe that was often considered the most Israelite of the twelve, "beloved of the Lord" (Deut 33:12). His answer to the question is, "No, God has not rejected his people," changing the future tense of the verb in Ps 94:14 to a past tense. Moreover, he significantly adds, "Whom he foreknew." By predilection Israel has been assured a place in the divine plan of salvation. The Apostle ascribes to God's foreknowledge the very election of Israel as his people. "For the sake of his own great name the Lord will not cast away his people, since Yahweh himself has taken it to heart to make you a people for himself" (1 Sam 1:22; cf. Amos 3:2). Recall what Paul said in 8:29: "Those whom he foreknew, he also predestined to be conformed to the image of his Son." Among those Paul would now include Jewish Christians like himself.

21.3 Paul, however, is aware that he and other Jewish Christians are not numerous. He cites, then, the example of Elijah, the ninth-century prophet from Tishbe in Gilead, who alone opposed the introduction of Baalism into the kingdom of Israel from Tyre under Jezebel and who alone pleased God in contrast to all Israel: "Lord, they have killed your prophets and torn down your altars; and I am left alone, and they are seeking my life" (11:3, quoting and abridging 1 Kgs 19:10). God's answer to Elijah was that he had preserved a remnant of "seven thousand men who have not bent the knee to Baal" (11:4, a free paraphrase of 1 Kgs 19:18). Thus Paul implies that Jewish Christians like himself are few; they know that their status also comes from God's predilection and that they are part of the remnant so favored: "A remnant, chosen by grace, has come into being" (11:5); they have been selected by divine favor and owe their status not to fidelity to the law. Hence for Paul "Israel" exists in the remnant, and it is all owing to God's grace: "If by grace, it is no longer by deeds; for grace would cease to be grace" (11:6). So Paul, in a generalizing statement, emphasizes the role of God's favor, not only in the life of this remnant, "Israel," but of all human life. Divine favor and grace reign supreme.

21.4 "What Israel sought, it did not achieve" (11:7). Paul refers to the majority of the Jewish people, to ethnic Israel, which did not attain the uprightness it pursued (reiterating what he had said in 9:30-31)—the source of Paul's sadness about his kinsfolk. But "the chosen ones achieved it," i.e. the "election," an abstract way of saying "those whom God has chosen," i.e. not only Jewish Christians, the remnant of 9:27, but also the Gentiles so favored by divine predilection. But "the others were made obtuse," i.e. by

God. Paul again uses a theological passive and indulges in proto-logical thinking (see p. 33 above), as he ascribes to God himself the hardening of Israel's heart. To bolster up this contention, he conflates phrases from Deut 29:3; Isa 29:10; Ps 69:23-24: "God granted them stupor of spirit, eyes that see not and ears that hear not—even to this day." He further cites Ps 69:23-24: "May their table be a snare and a trap, a stumbling block and a retribution for them." "Table" refers to a table-cloth spread on the ground in order to eat from it, but over which one might easily trip. In other words, what was closest to Israel has become the source of its misstep and its stumbling. They have not seen what lay right before their eyes, as Deut 29:3 and Isa 29:10 make clear: "May their eyes be dimmed so that they cannot see!" and "Bend their backs continually," i.e. may their back be weak under the burden they bear because of the rejection of the gospel. So Paul concludes his contrast of the "remnant" and the rest of Israel and has explained how the rejection is only partial.

21.5 Now he turns to the temporary and providential character of Israel's rejection. "Did they stumble so as to fall irremediably? Certainly not! Yet because of their trespass salvation has come to the Gentiles to make Israel jealous" (11:11). What has happened to Israel has suited God's providential plan of salvation, because it has enabled preachers of the gospel to proclaim it to Gentiles. It may seem unworthy that Paul would introduce the idea of Israel's jealousy, but we shall see how in the rest of this paragraph he will pit over against Israel's jealousy the smugness of chosen Gentiles. In other words, there is method in his madness, as he uses such banal and superficially unworthy motives.

21.6 "If their trespass has meant the enrichment of the world, and their loss the enrichment of Gentiles, how much more will their full number mean!" (11:12). What Israel has failed to do in its misstep has affected not just Gentiles, but even the *kosmos*, which has come into a situation of "wealth," in being able to share in the bounty of messianic salvation. Paul hints at the untold benefits for the world that would come about with the acceptance of the gospel by the "full number" of ethnic Israel. Here Paul dreams: suppose all Israel were to accept the challenge of the gospel of Jesus Christ!

21.7 Paul turns now to address Gentile Christians, because he is "the apostle of the Gentiles" (11:13) and because he makes much of his ministry as such, "in the hope that I may stir up my own people to jealousy and save some of them" (11:14). Even as a Christian, Paul still regards the Jewish people as his own "flesh." He has been called by God to evangelize the Gentiles, but he is nevertheless concerned about the salvation of Israel, his own people. In saying this, he echoes what he said in 10:1; cf. 1 Cor 9:22.

21.8 Paul continues his explanation of the "rejection" of Israel. "If their rejection has meant the reconciliation of the world, what will their acceptance mean? Nothing less than life from death" (11:15). Although some commentators think that Paul means by "their rejection" the rejection of Israel by God, sometimes explained as temporary and with an appeal to Sir 10:20, the phrase is better taken as a subjective genitive, Israel's rejection of the Christian gospel, because of what Paul himself has written in 11:1, where he refused to admit that God has rejected his own Chosen People. Paul reformulates what he said in 11:12 about the consequence of that rejection on the "world." Now he understands it as a "reconciliation of the world," echoing what he wrote in 2 Cor 5:19, "God was in Christ reconciling the world to himself" (or: "God was reconciling the world to himself through Christ"). This underlines the providential aspect of what has happened to Israel, and Paul expresses it even in term of a cosmic effect of the Christ-event. Such a reconciliation would have the effect of making ethnic Israel jealous and also of drawing it closer to God's new mode of salvation.

If, however, Israel were to come to accept the gospel, that would mean for it a passage from death to life. It would mean an identification of the Jewish people with Christ Jesus and a share in the new life that comes with such identification (recall 6:4 and the effects of baptism). They too would begin to live by this "new life" and experience the "new creation" (Gal 6:15). (Those who explain "their rejection" as a rejection of Israel by God would explain "their acceptance" as the acceptance of them by God. This is a possible meaning, but rather unlikely in the general context.)

Since the time of Origen, however, both medieval and modern commentators have thought that in this part of v. 15 ("nothing less than life from the dead") Paul would be alluding to the general resurrection of the dead at the parousia. Such an interpretation has given rise to the idea that the conversion of all Jews to Christ would precede the end of the world. This is a dubious conclusion at best, because Paul does not speak here of *anastasis nekrōn,* the phrase that he uses elsewhere when he wants to speak of the "resurrection of the dead" (6:5; 1 Cor 15:12, 13, 21, 42). For this reason the phrase is better understood of Israel's own passage from death to life, from the status in which it now is to life in Christ.

21.9 Paul now comments on the "remnant" in another way, but he mixes his metaphors in doing so. "If the firstfruits are holy, so too is the whole batch of dough; if the root is holy, so too are the branches" (11:16). At first he uses the idea of "firstfruits," the first portion of the harvest or the first portion of a meal, which being dedicated to God renders the whole harvest or meal holy, giving it a legal purity and making it fit to be consumed by God's people (cf. Lev 19:23-25; 23:14 Num 15:17-21). Holiness denotes consecration to the awesome service of God. Paul now applies the figure to a batch of dough, but then he goes further and compares Israel with a tree, the root of which nourishes the branches, individual Israelites that belong to it and live by its sap and life. In both instances there is the dependence of the whole on what was at the origin of the whole. Though some commentators, ancient and modern, have tried to understand the "firstfruits" and the "root" as referring to Christ, the better meaning for both is the patriarchs, to whom Paul refers in the following context, or the "remnant," i.e. the "elect" (11:7), to whom Paul refers in the preceding context.

21.10 "If some of the branches have been lopped off, you, though a branch from a wild olive tree, have been grafted into their place and have come to share in the rich sap of the olive root" (11:17). Paul continues the image of the tree and its root and compares Gentile Christians with branches of wild olive tree cut from its own stock and grafted into a cultivated olive tree, which is Israel. The stock from which Gentile Christians derive their life is now that of Israel of old. Thus "the church of the Gentiles is an extension of the promises of God to Israel and not Israel's displacement" (J. C. Beker, *Paul the Apostle,* 332). Gentiles are made to share in the bounty that God has shown to his Chosen People of old; they have thus become *sperma Abraam,* "offspring of Abraham." The "lopped off" branches do not denote all Israel, because Paul diplomatically speaks of "some" (*tines*) branches, i.e. individual Jews who have not accepted God's gospel. Paul does not say that the old cultivated olive tree has been cut down in divine providence; it still stands and is the source of vitality for the Gentile Christians who now share in the richness of its life. For this reason Paul counsels Gentile Christians not to be smug about their situation: "Do not boast over those branches. If you do, remember this: you do not support the root; the root supports you" (11:18). Israel of old still occupies the privileged position of the carrier of life and salvation to the world. "You may say, 'Branches were lopped off so that I might be grafted in.' True, but they were lopped off because of a lack of faith, whereas you are there because of faith. So do not become haughty for that reason; be fearful. If God did not spare the natural branches, perhaps he will not spare you either" (11:19-20). Thus Paul calls once again for "faith," but links with it a call for requisite humility and a sense of where one belongs in the plan and process of divine salvation. For this whole matter of the "rejection" of Israel and the ingrafting of Gentiles has been meant to bring all human beings to the recognition of God's "kindness and severity" (11:22). For "those others, if they do not remain in their lack of faith, will be grafted back in. God indeed has the power to graft them in again" (11:23). Paul argues *a fortiori:* if God was able to graft a wild olive branch onto an old cultivated olive tree, then he can also graft in again a branch lopped off from that cultivated olive tree. Implied in his message is the conviction that the lopped off branches have not yet been cast onto the rubbish heap. The contrast suggests the transcendent nature of the call of Gentiles to Christian faith, but it also stresses that the restoration of Israel may be easier even than the call of the Gentiles. Yet Paul's message is a warning to all of us about not being smug about our own relation with God or about our salvation.

21.11 Finally, Paul comes to admit the coming salvation of "all Israel." He realizes that his solution to the problem of Israel may not be wholly satisfying; so he begins to speak of the "mystery" of Israel. By this he means not that the problem is insoluble or opaque to human understanding, but that it has been part of a secret hidden in God for ages and now made known, even if it is not yet wholly comprehensible. What makes Paul conceive it in this way is his preoccupation with God's mercy and salvific purpose now made known. The Roman Christians to whom he is writing have to learn that they cannot rely on their own speculation about the fate of Israel or its relation to God's salvific plan. Having counseled Gentile Christians about not being smug, he now stresses that Israel is not unprivileged in God's sight, even though it may not have been fully responsive to the gospel. He hastens to add that "all Israel shall be saved" (11:26a), because in God's plan mercy is to be shown to all, including Israel itself.

21.12 That statement of Paul in 11:26a, "all Israel shall be saved," has invoked a variety of interpretations over the centuries. Today the two most important interpretations are the theological and the christological. According to the first, the verb *sōthēsetai* is taken as a theological passive, "shall be saved (by God)." Paul continues, "As it stands written, 'From Zion shall come the deliverer; he shall turn godlessness away from Jacob. This is my covenant with them, when I take away their sins'" (11:26bc-27). This would mean, then, that God will be the "deliverer" and display an act of mercy toward Israel independently of any acceptance of Jesus as Messiah or of any mass conversion to the gospel. Israel would thus be delivered from its partial hardening by a "deliverer" (11:26c, quoting and adapting a Greek form of Isa 59:20-21a, coupled with Isa 27:9), who would be none other than Yahweh himself. The main reason given for this interpretation is the fact that Christ has not been been mentioned so far in chap. 11, and indeed not since 10:17 (see p. 169 above). Christ is not being envisaged, then, as the deliverer. Thus the solution to the problem of Israel is sought in an act of God's mercy manifested toward the Chosen People of old. The "covenant" (11:27) would still be the everlasting covenant between Yahweh and Israel (2 Sam 23:5). So these words of Paul have been interpreted by K. Stendahl, M. A. Getty, P. Lapide and P. Stuhlmacher.

According to the second interpretation, the verb *sōthēsetai* is taken as in 1 Cor 9:22, where it has the connotation of "be converted," and the salvation of Israel will come about through Christ

Jesus, who will be its "deliverer," through whom God will turn all godlessness from Jacob. This is sometimes understood of Christ at the parousia (as in 1 Thess 1:10) and the "covenant" is understood as the "new covenant" of Jer 31:33 in its definitive stage. Thus the parousiac Christ will save all Israel without a preceding conversion of Jews to the gospel. So F. Mussner understands it. But the majority of commentators who use the christological interpretation insist that there can be no *Sonderweg* or "separate way" for Israel, in view of the general thrust of the epistle itself. For Paul has insisted on the justification and salvation of "all" human beings through faith in Christ Jesus (see 1:16; 4:25; 10:9; and implicitly in 11:14). By "all" Paul must mean Jews and Gentiles alike (1:16; 3:21-22, 30). Thus Christ will be the "deliverer," and "from Zion" would refer possibly to his Davidic descent or merely that he too came from the Chosen People of old, and the "covenant" will be that of Jer 31:33, as realized in the ministry, death, and resurrection of Jesus Christ and not limited to an act at his parousia, about which there is no mention in the paragraph. For Paul there is only one way: faith in Christ Jesus. Through him and him alone "all Israel shall be saved," even if this remains opaque to our normal human understanding.

21.13 "As far as the gospel is concerned, they are enemies for your sake" (11:28ab), i.e. enemies of God, cut off from relationship with him. Israel as an ethnic group has put itself in opposition to God by its reaction to the gospel. But this has been providential for the Gentiles, because they have come to share in the salvific destiny originally promised to Israel. "But as far as election is concerned, they are beloved of God because of the patriarchs" (11:28cd). The "election" of Israel is irrevocable in human history, manifest in the favor shown to its patriarchs (Lev 26:42), a claim that the Gentiles lack. "They will be my people, and I shall be theirs forever; I shall dwell with them forever and ever" (11QTemple 29:7-8)—so the Qumran community was convinced, as it echoed the promises of old.

What Paul admits in this verse creates a problem for his generic thesis about justification and salvation through faith, which he is defending globally in chaps. 9–11, because he seems to admit another principle of salvation, one somehow tied to an ethnic condition and based on God's love of the patriarchs. But he phrases the matter in this way because he is interested in the contrast of Israel as "enemies" and as "beloved." Paul insists that the former condition does not wipe out the latter. Both of these elements are part of God's salvation history. Paul's explanation of the way of salvation for Israel goes through disbelief to faith, through stumbling and fall to restoration, through partial rejection to final full acceptance. Thus God leads Israel through rejection to salvation.

21.14 "Irrevocable are God's gifts and his call" (11:29). God has not regretted or gone back on his word and promises to Israel or all the good things that he has provided for his Chosen People; he has not gone back on his "call" of Israel, the initial summons of Abraham (Gen 12:1-2), which became in time the election of Israel as God's "chosen" people (Deut 7:6-7: "You are a people sacred to the Lord, your God; he has chosen you from all the nations on the face of the earth to be a people peculiarly his own"; cf. Isa 41:8-10; Ezek 20:5; Ps 135:4).

21.15 "As you were once disobedient to God but now have been shown mercy as a result of their disobedience, so too they have now become disobedient so that they too may now be shown mercy as a result of the mercy shown to you. For God has imprisoned all people in disobedience that he might show mercy to all!" (11:30-32). Paul addresses the Roman Christians as predominantly Gentile in background, and his view of their former status agrees with what his Jewish kinsfolk would have thought. Their disobedience has become the opportunity for the manifestation of divine mercy to Gentiles in order to incorporate them into the salvation promised to Israel. That disobedience of Israel has not been disbelief in God, but a failure to accept his gospel and Christ Jesus, the agent sent to them to bring them salvation in a new way. Paul sees the matter as one of reciprocity: God's mercy and grace were originally manifested toward Israel, his Chosen People; those qualities continue to favor it. Sinful Gentiles have been brought in to share in the blessings once promised to Abraham and his offspring. Divine mercy has thus been shown in a special way to them, who have accepted the gospel. Now the mercy shown to Gentiles becomes the basis of mercy to be displayed to Israel in its enmity.

Universal salvation thus proceeds from God's mercy. Paul indulges yet again in protological thinking (see p. 33 above), as he asserts that God has locked up all human beings in disobedience. His stress falls on "all," both Jew and Greek alike, who have been unfaithful to God and have become objects of his merciful deliverance. These are salutary words for all of us. Even in our disobedience we too can still be objects of divine mercy and deliverance from such a status.

21.16 Paul ends his discussion of the problem of Israel with a hymn in praise of God's inscrutable wisdom and mercy. In 11:25 Paul referred to the problem as a "mystery," something now made known to humanity, even if it is not wholly comprehensible. God's goodness is not at fault, even if the matter surpasses human comprehension. The doxology sums up Paul's discussion in chaps. 9–11 and echoes the hymn that he used to conclude his discussion in chap. 8. In effect, it forms a fitting conclusion to the entire doctrinal section of the epistle to the Romans. It is addressed to God, who has accomplished all through Christ Jesus, who remains, however, unnamed. "Oh the depth of the riches, of the wisdom, and of the knowledge of God! How inscrutable are his judgments! How untraceable his ways!" (11:33). Everything that happens in this world depends on God's wisdom, knowledge, and judgment. The key verse in the hymn follows: "Who has known the mind of the Lord? Who has been his counselor? (11:34, quoting Isa 40:13). The answer, of course, is, "No one!" See 1 Cor 2:16, where Paul asks the same question and answers it by saying, "We have the mind of Christ." Neither in plans devised nor in gifts to humanity is God a debtor; all proceeds from gracious divine bounty. "Who has ever given him a gift to receive a gift in return?" (11:35). God needs no one to anticipate his bounty; so rich are his gifts. God seeks no cooperation from human beings as a condition for his bounty, even though he may expect cooperation with the prevenient graces that he grants. To such prevenient grace human faith and cooperation correspond, but his goodness is not a payment for services rendered.

"For from him and through him and for him are all things. To him be glory forever! Amen" (11:36). God is acknowledged as the source and origin of all, the provider and sustainer of all, and the end or goal of all. Thus Paul recognizes the absolute dependence of everything in the created universe on God, along with the prerogatives of Israel and the bounteous call of Gentiles, of which he has just been speaking. Everything shares in the divine bountiful providence and wise care. Everything is destined to glorify and praise him. Thus, in effect, Paul reiterates his teaching about all humanity created to "glorify" and "thank" God, notions with which he began his epistle (1:21)—or to use the terminology of Ignatius, "to praise, reverence, and serve God our Lord" (§23.2).

21.17 Questions. Should I not pray once again that all Israel may be saved? Should I not ask for a deeper understanding of this mystery of Israel, how God in his bounty toward his Chosen People has still tolerated their rejection of his gospel, and yet not turned from them or hidden his face from them? Do I fully understand my relation to Israel of old, how my very status as a Christian depends on a relation to this people of election? Do I really understand my status as a wild olive branch grafted into the stock of Israel of old? What does this say about my own reaction to God's providence on my behalf? Do I praise God's wisdom and knowledge for the status that I enjoy in this world?

COLLOQUY: PSALM 33

> Rejoice, you just, in the LORD;
> > praise from the upright is fitting.
> Give thanks to the LORD on the harp;
> > on the ten-stringed lyre offer praise.
> Sing to God a new song;
> > skillfully play with joyful chant.
> For the LORD's word is true;
> > all his works are trustworthy.
> The LORD loves justice and right
> > and fills the earth with goodness.
> By the LORD's word the heavens were made;
> > by the breath of his mouth all their host.
> The waters of the sea were gathered as in a bowl;
> > in cellars the deep was confined.
> Let all the earth fear the LORD;
> > let all who dwell in the world show reverence.

For he spoke, and it came to be,
    commanded, and it stood in place.
The LORD foils the plan of nations,
    frustrates the designs of peoples.
But the plan of the LORD stands forever,
    wise designs through all generations.
Happy the nation whose God is the LORD,
    the people chosen as his very own.
From heaven the LORD looks down
    and observes the whole human race,
Surveying from the royal throne
    all who dwell on earth.
The one who fashioned the hearts of them all
    knows all their works.
A king is not saved by a mighty army,
    nor a warrior delivered by great strength.
Useless is the horse for safety;
    its great strength, no sure escape.
But the LORD's eyes are upon the reverent,
    upon those who hope for his gracious help,
Delivering them from death,
    keeping them alive in times of famine.
Our soul waits for the LORD,
    who is our help and shield.
For in God our hearts rejoice;
    in your holy name we trust.
May your kindness, LORD, be upon us;
    we have put our hope in you.

See further *Romans,* 602-36.

Spirit-Guided Christian Life Must Be Worship Paid to God (12:1–13:14)

^{12:1} I urge you, then, brothers, by God's mercy to offer your bodies as living sacrifices, holy and acceptable to God, as a cult suited to your rational nature. ² Do not conform yourselves to this present world, but be transformed by a renewal of your whole way of thinking so that you may discern what is God's will, what is good, acceptable to him, and perfect.

³ In virtue of the grace given to me I say to everyone of you: Do not think more highly of yourself than you ought to; rather, think of yourself with sober judgment according to the measure of faith that God has apportioned each of you. ⁴ For just as we have many members in one body and all of the members do not have the same function, ⁵ so we, though many, are one body in Christ, and individually members of one another. ⁶ We have gifts that differ according to the grace given to us. If prophecy, let it be used in proportion to one's faith; ⁷ or ministry, let it be used in service; or if one is a teacher, let him use it for instruction; ⁸ if one is an exhorter, for encouragement; if one is a contributor to charity, let him use it with simple generosity; if one is a leader, with diligence; if one does works of mercy, let it be with cheerfulness.

⁹ Love must be unfeigned. You must detest what is evil and cling to what is good. ¹⁰ Be devoted to one another with brotherly love; outdo one another in showing honor. ¹¹ Serve the Lord, unflagging in diligence, fervent in spirit, ¹² rejoicing in hope, patient in affliction, persistent in prayer.

[13] Contribute to the needs of God's dedicated people, and practice hospitality. [14] Bless those who persecute you, bless and do not curse them. [15] Rejoice with those who are rejoicing; mourn with those who are mourning. [16] Think in harmony with one another. Put aside haughty thoughts and associate with the lowly. Do not become wise in your own estimation. [17] Repay no one evil for evil; take thought for what is noble in the sight of all human beings. [18] If it possibly lies in your power, live at peace with everyone. [19] Take no revenge, dear friends, but leave room for God's wrath, for it stands written: *"Vengeance is mine; I will repay,"* [y] says the Lord. [20] But *if your enemy is hungry, feed him; if he is thirsty, give him something to drink. In doing this, you will heap coals of fire upon his head.* [z] [21] Do not be overcome by evil, but overcome evil with good.

[13:1] Let every person be subject to the governing authorities, for there is no authority except from God, and those which exist have been set up by God. [2] Consequently, anyone who resists authority opposes what God has instituted; such opponents will bring judgment on themselves. [3] For rulers are not a terror to good conduct, only to evil. Would you be free from fear of the bearer of authority? Then do what is right, and you will gain his approval. [4] For he is God's servant working for your good. But if you do wrong, then be afraid, for he does not carry the sword for nothing. He is God's servant, an avenger, bringing wrath upon the wrongdoer. [5] Therefore, one must be subject, not only because of such wrath, but also because of one's conscience. [6] For this reason you also pay taxes. Authorities are God's servants, persistently devoted to this very task. [7] Pay all of them their due—taxes to whom taxes are due, revenue to whom revenue is due, respect to whom respect is due, and honor to whom honor is due.

[8] Owe nothing to anyone, save that of loving one another; for the one who loves another has fulfilled the law. [9] The commandments, *You shall not commit adultery, You shall not kill, You shall not steal, You shall not covet*—or any other commandment—are summed up in this one, *"You shall love your neighbor as yourself."* [b] [10] Love does no wrong to a neighbor, for love is the fulfillment of the law.

[11] Do this, then, realizing how critical the moment is—that it is already time for you to be roused from sleep; for our

salvation is now closer than when we first believed. [12] The
night is far spent, and day has drawn near. Let us cast off,
then, the deeds of darkness and don the armor of light,
[13] that we may conduct ourselves with decency as befits the
daylight, not in orgies or drunkenness, not in debauchery or
sexual excess, not in quarreling or jealousy. [14] Put on rather
the Lord Jesus Christ and give no more thought to the
desires of the flesh.

[y] Deut 32:35	[z] Prov 25:21-22
[a] Deut 5:17-21; Exod 20:13-17	[b] Lev 19:18

22.1 Paul now begins the hortatory section of the epistle to
the Romans; it is a catechetical unit, such as he was accustomed to
add to the doctrinal discussion in his various letters. In this case,
when he is addressing Christians of a church that he has not
founded or as yet even evangelized, his exhortation is generic. But
in 14:1–15:13 he will include advice for a problem in the Roman
community, about which he has apparently heard. This hortatory
section, however, is not exactly an ethical treatise, for it is quite
unsystematic and rambles. As it stands in this epistle, it implies
that Mosaic legal prescriptions may no longer be the norm for
Christian conduct, but there are, nonetheless, demands made of
Christians. The principle at work in all of them is love or charity
(13:8-10), which flows from the faith evoked by the gospel. The
details that he will mention are examples of how Christian faith
works itself out through love.

Having developed his idea about Christian life lived in the
Spirit (8:1-39), Paul now seeks to draw from that basic teaching
some consequences that should guide Christians. In this first part
of the hortatory section Paul concentrates on six aspects of
Christian life: (1) Life in the world as worship of God (12:1-2); (2)
Sober existence using God's gifts for all (12:3-8); (3) Counsels for
Christians living together in community (12:9-21); (4) The relation
of Christians to civil authorities (13:1-7); (5) The debt of love that
fulfills the law (13:8-10); and (6) An eschatological exhortation:
Christian life as vigilant conduct (13:11-14). Most of these topics
are only loosely linked; they are generalities, reflecting perhaps
problems with which the Apostle had to cope in the past in

churches founded by him, perhaps even in the church of Corinth, from which he sends this letter to Rome.

22.2 Paul begins with advice about how Christians are to conduct their lives, especially the demands of living together in a community, where the common pursuit of the good is expected. The unity and harmony of the community demand that individuals realize that they are living in a new aeon and are to strive to overcome evil with good.

He begins with a basic consideration: Christians should live in "this world" as if their Christian mode of life were offering worship to God. "I urge you, then, brothers, by God's mercy to offer your bodies as living sacrifices, holy and acceptable to God, as a cult suited to your rational nature" (12:1). Paul compares Christians with animals sacrificed or slaughtered in Jewish or pagan cults, but he corrects the comparison by adding "living" to the "sacrifices," along with other phrases. Christian life is not a cult that offers to God dead animals, but Christians who strive to do what is right give a cultic or sacrificial meaning to the very lives that they lead. It is a worship of God that befits their "rational nature" (*tēn logikēn latreian hymōn*, which is often translated as "your spiritual worship") and is therefore "holy and acceptable to God." In Gal 5:24 Paul says, "Those who belong to Christ Jesus have crucified the flesh with its passions and desires." Here the important thing is that such a spiritual cult, suited to one's rational nature and entailing the offering of the Christian's body, is precisely what Paul means by living under the uprightness of God. Spiritual worship is thus the realization of God's eschatological work, whereby he is claiming for himself the world that belongs to him. It implies the offering to God of the human self in an act of obedience stemming from faith.

To such a recommendation Paul adds two imperatives: "Do not conform yourselves to this present world, but be transformed by a renewal of your whole way of thinking so that you may discern what is God's will, what is good, acceptable to him, and perfect" (12:2). Such a way of life is an expression of the very rational nature of the Christian, and it involves the transformation or metamorphosis of the Christian, which is really an effect of the Christ-event. As he says in Gal 5:25: "If we live by the Spirit, let us also walk by the Spirit." Basic to this transformation is the grace of God and the leading of the Holy Spirit. It is not a mere external metamorphosis, but a renewal of the *nous*, "mind," a renewed way of thinking about life and conduct. For knowledge of what God desires becomes the norm of Christian life and conduct.

22.3 Since everyday life is the realm in which Christians are to pay such homage and worship to God the Father, the cult to be rendered should manifest itself concretely in a life in community based on humility and charity. Paul recommends to the Christians of Rome that they are not to pretend to be more than they are. "If anyone is in Christ, that one is a new creation" (2 Cor 5:17). To be in Christ is to be a member of the body of Christ. Life in the body of Christ calls for a proper, unselfish use of one's talents and spiritual gifts for the good of all. "In virtue of the grace given to me I say to every one of you: Do not think more highly of yourself than you ought to; rather, think of yourself with sober judgment according to the measure of faith that God has apportioned each of you" (12:3). Thus Paul addresses the Christians of Rome in his capacity as a commissioned apostle, called and graced by God. However gifted Christians are, they are all members of the body of Christ and called to serve one another. Again he invokes the role of "faith" in Christian life; it is to be the norm of how Christians think of themselves. Lesser persons in social status may be the recipients of greater graces and may live lives of deeper faith. Paul speaks here of what later theologians called *fides qua creditur*, the active response of the individual to God's gospel.

"For just as we have many members in one body and all of the members do not have the same function, so we, though many, are one body in Christ, and individually members of one another" (12:4-5). Paul does not say here, "You are the body of Christ," as he does in 1 Cor 12:27, but he is stressing the mutual unity of Christians in "one body," their mutual dependence on one another, and consequently the concern that they should have for others in that body. "We have gifts that differ according to the grace given to us. If prophecy, let it be used in proportion to one's faith; or ministry, let it be used in service; or if one is a teacher, let him use it for instruction; if one is an exhorter, for encourage-ment; if one is a contributor to charity, let him use it with simple generosity; if one is a leader, with diligence; if one does works of mercy, let it be with cheerfulness" (12:6-8). The diversity of the graces given should evoke responsible activity on behalf of all in the body. Inspired preaching, communal service, teaching, counseling, philanthropy, leadership, and works of mercy should all be used to promote the common good in a Christian community. Paul gives seven examples, and his use of seven suggests totality; in other words, all gifts, no matter what they are, should be so used. Skill in any of these diverse functions entitles no one to think more highly of himself or herself than is due. For all these charisms result from divine grace, and not from individual efforts alone; they are all granted for the good that they can promote within the Christian community. Thus Paul plays on the relation between *charisma* and *charis*, "favor, grace." What should be noted here is the absence of any reference to *ekklēsia*, "church," in this discussion of the one body. It stands in contrast to what one finds in 1 Cor 12:27-28. For some strange reason Paul has not mentioned the "church" in this important writing (save in chap. 16, where it occurs several times in the sense of the local church or house church).

22.4 Paul now continues with a series of general counsels for the Christians of Rome, who, he knows, are living in such a community. He stresses the generic role that love must govern all and in diverse ways emphasizes the obligation to do good and avoid evil: "Love must be unfeigned. You must detest what is evil and cling to what is good" (12:9). His advice could not be more basic.

This generic counsel is further spelled out: "Be devoted to one another with brotherly love; outdo one another in showing honor. Serve the Lord, unflagging in diligence, fervent in spirit, rejoicing in hope, patient in affliction, persistent in prayer. Contribute to the needs of God's dedicated people, and practice hospitality" (12:10-13). But even in the Christian community there can be dissension and opposition, and so Paul continues: "Bless those who persecute you; bless and do not curse them" (12:14). His counsel may echo that of Jesus (Matt 5:44-47; Luke 6:27-28), which is a rare instance, if he were aware that Jesus himself so counseled his followers. "Rejoice with those who are rejoicing; mourn with those who are mourning. Think in harmony with one another. Put aside haughty thoughts and associate with the lowly. Do not become wise in your own estimation" (12:15-16). Paul realizes the detriment that pride and ambition can cause in a community, and Origen caught the import of the Pauline counsel when he wrote, "The one who is wise in his own estimation is foolish in arrogance; the one who cherishes his own foolishness as wisdom cannot know the real wisdom of God" (*In ep. ad Romanos* 9.18; PG 14. 1222). "Repay no one evil for evil; take thought for what is noble in the sight of all human beings. If it possibly lies in your power, live at peace with everyone" (12:17-18). Paul is aware that life in community is not easy, and the demand to live at peace with all may be heroic.

22.5 "Take no revenge, dear friends, but leave room for God's wrath, for it stands written: 'Vengeance is mine, I will repay,' says the Lord. But 'if your enemy is hungry, feed him; if he is thirsty, give him something to drink. In doing so, you will heap coals of fire upon his head'" (12:19-20, quoting Deut 32:35 and Prov 25:21-22a). So Paul adopts Old Testament teaching to extend it to life in the Christian community. Revenge is not the mark of the Christian disciple, who should rather leave that to God himself. The meaning of Prov 25:21-22 has always been obscure. Origen, Augustine, Jerome and some modern commentators have thought that the "coals of fire" were symbolic of burning pangs of shame. The enemy would be moved by such kindness to shame and remorse; it would burn like coals of fire upon his head. Other Greek patristic writers, such as John Chrysostom and Theophylact, rather understood the "coals of fire" as a symbol of a more noble type of revenge: if one feeds an enemy and he remains hostile, such kindness makes him liable to more serious punishment from God, i.e. in effect, one heaps on his head coals of divine punishment. The trouble is that there is no clear extrabiblical use of the figure; so one cannot be sure of its meaning. Whatever the meaning of this mysterious expression, Paul clearly is not recommending Stoic passive resistance to such hostility, but rather the Old Testament treatment of an enemy: the overcoming of evil with kindness or some charitable action, as the last verse of this paragraph suggests: "Do not be overcome by evil, but overcome evil with good" (12:21). The Christian's victory over evil consists in refusing to promote it by returning evil for evil or to become like the person who wickedly injures. In all these counsels there is much food for thought for the modern Christian.

22.6 Paul continues his exhortation of the Roman Christians with an instruction that must answer questions that they often had in their relation to those who govern them as civil authorities. In effect, it offers a specific instance of the advice already given. Yet it is a strange instruction, which reads more like a philosophical paragraph than anything specifically Christian; it makes no mention of Christ Jesus or of the God of Israel, and derives all its motivation from "God" alone. In no other of his letters does Paul treat of this topic. It may be that he was aware of some specific problem that Christians in Rome, the capital of the empire, were having in their relation to imperial authority. In view of what Paul has already written about the "freedom" of Christians (Gal 5:1) and about their heavenly citizenship (Phil 3:20: "our common-wealth [*politeuma*] is in heaven"), some of them may have come to a skewed view of their relation to civil authorities, which he now considers important to correct. He recommends to Roman Christians order in civil society, respect for authority, civic obedi-ence, payment of taxes and revenue, and honor for authorities, who are "God's servants" (13:6). The passage has often created problems in recent times, because what Paul asserts in it has often been used to justify obedience to any kind of human government, e.g. in Nazi Germany. The supposition in vv. 1-7 is that civil authorities are good and promoting the common good of society; Paul does not envisage the possibility of a totalitarian or tyrannical government or one that fails to cope with the just rights of individual citizens or minority groups. The concept of civic disobedience does not enter into his discussion. Paul must have known of the connivance of the Roman prefect, Pontius Pilate, in the death of Jesus of Nazareth, but even that did not deter him from writing as he does in this paragraph. Given the perspective that he thus adopts, one can derive profit from what he says about the proper relation of Christians to civil authorities.

22.7 "Let every person be subject to the governing authorities, for there is no authority except from God, and those which exist have been set up by God. Consequently, anyone who resists authority opposes what God has instituted; such opponents will bring judgment on themselves" (13:1-2). Some commentators have queried the meaning of *exousiai,* "authorities," whether they might be invisible angelic powers understood as standing behind state government or even "the empirical state *and* angelic powers," comparing 1 Cor 2:8; 15:24; 1 Pet 3:22; Col 1:16; 2:10. But most of them understand it as human authorities (such as those to whom taxes are paid, 13:6), for Paul is otherwise using the vocabulary characteristic of Hellenistic political administration. More important, however, is his rooting of all such authority in God himself. Even as a Christian, Paul thus acknowledges that God is the source of all the welfare, prosperity, and peace brought by human civil rule, even if the ruler is a pagan. This is the reason why he calls for obedience, which is in reality an Old Testament teaching (2 Sam 12:8; Prov 8:15-16; Jer 17:5-6; Isa 45:1; Dan 2:21, 37). The Jewish historian Josephus shared such a view: "Not apart from God does anyone rule" (*J.W.* 2.8.7 §140).

"For rulers are not a terror to good conduct, only to evil. Would you be free from fear of the bearer of authority? Then do what is right, and you will gain his approval. For he is God's servant working for your good" (13:3-4a). Paul enunciates what he understands to be the purpose of civic authority: the promotion of what is the common good in such a society. It reformulates what he said in 13:1 and stresses two ideas: the delegated character of civil authority in its relation to God, and the final cause of such an institution. "But if you do wrong, then be afraid, for he does not carry the sword for nothing. He is God's servant, an avenger, bringing wrath upon the wrongdoer" (13:4bc). The bearer of civic authority thus becomes the instrument whereby God pours out his wrath on civic wrongdoers. "Therefore, one must be subject, not only because of such wrath, but also because of one's conscience" (13:5). Submission to civic authority involves not only the possibility of a reaction of divine wrath, but also one's conscience, which is in reality a philosophical consideration. Yet even so, both divine wrath and conscience must be guides of Christian conduct.

22.8 "For this reason you also pay taxes. Authorities are God's servants, persistently devoted to this very task. Pay all of them their due—taxes to whom taxes are due, revenue to whom revenue is due, respect to whom respect is due, and honor to whom honor is due" (13:6-7). Paul proceeds to a further instance in which Christians owe submission to civil authorities, in the payment of taxes. In this he echoes in his own way what Jesus said about paying tribute to Caesar (Mark 12:13-17). For the third time in this paragraph he stresses the delegated nature of civic authority, "God's servants." But he does not end with taxes or revenue; rather he generalizes: "Pay all of them their due." It is the principle that governs his entire discussion in vv. 1-7. This paragraph puts before us a singular consideration. Because Paul has never treated such a topic elsewhere in his writings, it becomes here an important aspect of the way in which he envisages Christian life. It thus becomes a prime example of how his principles must guide our lives in the concrete situation in which we live, even as Christians. We owe our allegiance to God in Christ Jesus, but we must also conduct ourselves responsibly even in civil society.

22.9 Having expressed his view of the obligation of Christians in civil society, Paul moves on to another duty incumbent on them: the obligation of love. This is also an important aspect of Christian life, because it supplies Christians with a fundamental principle to cope with legality, but also sums up the Christian reaction to the Mosaic law in the new dispensation. The uprightness that must govern earthly and civil life is only a form of the uprightness of the new aeon, in which life is lived as love of one's neighbor. For Paul Christians must conduct themselves "in Christ" and "in love." So far Paul has spoken of God's love (*agapē*) for human beings (5:5, 8; 8:35, 37, 39; 9:13, 25) and will speak (possibly) of the Spirit's love (15:30); he has also spoken of the love of human beings for God (8:28). Now he introduces human love for other human beings (13:8-10; 14:15; cf. 12:9; possibly also in 15:30). In Gal 5:22 it is mentioned as a fruit of the Spirit. He begins strangely enough by speaking of love as a "debt," undoubtedly because he has just been speaking of what is "due" in the preceding paragraph. He is using oxymoron, for love cannot be "owed," since it is by nature freely bestowed. It is the open, outward concern of one person for another that takes one out of oneself and does not depend on what the other has done or will do in return. So love cannot be "owed." It is not like a debt. Christian life, therefore, must be marked by mutual love. "Owe nothing to anyone, save that of loving one another; for the one who loves another has fulfilled the law. The commandments, 'You shall not commit adultery, You shall not kill, You shall not steal, You shall not covet'—or any other commandment—are summed up in this one. 'You shall love your neighbor as yourself.' Love does no wrong to a neighbor, for love is the fulfillment of the law" (13:8-10).

All important here is Paul's view of love as the fulfillment of the law. If love dominates human existence, then the do's and don'ts of the law are automatically fulfilled, and the law is thereby sustained and upheld (3:31). Moreover, love is the way that faith works itself out (Gal 5:6), and it thus becomes the "deeds" of which Jas 2:18 speaks, "I by my deeds will show you my faith." This Pauline idea might seem to suggest, however, that law in the long run has the last say, if love fulfills the law. What Paul means, however, is that Christians, living by faith that works itself out through love, fulfill the very aspiration of those who have tried to live by the Mosaic law. He is not proposing the fulfillment of the Mosaic law as an ideal for Christian life. He is only reformulating what he already said in 8:4, Christian love does what the law requires. Paul gives a more elaborate treatment of the details of Christian love in 1 Corinthians 13.

22.10 Paul concludes the first part of this hortatory section of the epistle with an eschatological exhortation: Christian life must be a form of vigilant conduct. "Do this, then, realizing how critical the moment is—that it is already time for you to be roused from sleep; for our salvation is now closer than when we first believed" (13:11). Christians must realize that they are living in the *eschaton*, for the two ages (that of the Torah and that of the Messiah) have met (as Paul puts it in 1 Cor 10:11). Christ Jesus, by his passion, death, and resurrection, has inaugurated the new aeon: Salvation is at hand. So Christians must respond to the age in which they now live. This is the explanation of why Christians must not conform themselves to this world (12:2), but must be in harmony with the new aeon. They must be looking forward to the day when salvation fully arrives. Salvation is said to be nearer, but it is still a thing of the future. Yet the time in which Christians live is critical, and Paul seeks to awaken them from slumber and exhorts them to vigilance. "The night is far spent, and day has drawn near. Let us cast off, then, the deeds of darkness and don the armor of light, that we may conduct ourselves with decency as befits the daylight, not in orgies or drunkenness, not in debauchery or sexual excess, not in quarreling or jealousy" (13:12-13). Paul indulges in apocalyptic writing, using "night" and "day," "darkness" and "light" as symbols of evil and good conduct. In this he borrows motifs from his Jewish background: see Isa 45:7; 1QS 2:7; 1QM 15:9 ("in darkness are all their deeds," i.e. the deeds of the sons of darkness, who are dominated by the prince of demons, Belial). In contrast, "the armor of light" is depicted in 1 Thess 5:8 as faith, charity, and hope, the supreme virtues or characteristics of Christian living (cf. 2 Cor 6:7; 10:4). For those justified by Christ cannot conduct themselves as though they were still in darkness. Recall the influence of these verses on Augustine (see p. 13 above). "Put on rather the Lord Jesus Christ and give no more thought to the desires of the flesh" (13:14). Let Christ himself be your armor. In baptism the Christian has already "put on" Christ (Gal 3:27), as armor or a heavenly garment. But that identification of the Christian with Christ must bear fruit in conscious life. Such a psychological awareness, once cultivated, will stifle all the desires of the Ego subject to sin and its allurements. So Paul sums up his eschatological exhortation.

22.11 Questions. How aware am I of living my Christian life as an act of worship of God? Is my way of thinking still that of this world? Does cooperation with divine grace seek to transform it to discern better the will of God on my behalf? How often do I try to use God-given talents for the good of others in the body of Christ, of which I am a member? How consciously do I strive to judge soberly about myself according to the measure of faith that God has apportioned me? To what extent do I let Paul's individual counsels about Christian living influence my life? How do I react to those in the community who oppose me, my enemies? Do I ever pray for civil authorities to whom I owe submission? Do I look down upon them instead of giving them their due respect and honor? To what extent does my Christian faith really work itself out in love, in deeds that seek the good of my fellow Christians? What does it mean in my life that my salvation is now closer than when I first came to faith?

COLLOQUY: PAUL'S MORE EXCELLENT WAY (1 CORINTHIANS 13)

> If I speak with the tongues of human beings and of angels,
>> and have not love,
>> I am a noisy gong or a clashing cymbal.
> If I have prophetic powers and comprehend all mysteries,
>> possess all knowledge and even faith to move mountains,
>> and have not love,
>> I am nothing.
> If I give away all that I have and hand my body over to be burned,
>> and have not love,
>> I gain nothing.
> Love is longsuffering and is kind;
>> love is not jealous or boastful;
>> it is not arrogant or rude.
> Love does not insist on its own way;
>> it is not quick-tempered or resentful;
>> it does not rejoice in wickedness, but delights in fidelity.
> Love bears all things, believes all things;
>> it hopes for all things, endures all things
> Love never fails. As for prophecies, they will be brought to nothing;
>> as for tongues, they will come to an end;
>> as for knowledge, it will be brought to nothing.
> For we know only in part, and we prophesy only in part.
>> But when what is full comes, the partial will come to an end.
> When I was a child, I spoke as a child,
>> I thought as a child, I reasoned as a child;
>> when I became a man, I put an end to the things of a child.
> For now we see dimly, as in a mirror, but then face to face.
>> Now I know only in part; then I shall understand fully,
>> even as I have been fully understood.
> Now then faith, hope, love remain, these three;
>> and the greatest of these is love.

See further *Romans*, 637-85.

Duty of Love Owed by the Strong in the Community to the Weak (14:1–15:13)

^{14:1} Welcome among you anyone who is weak in conviction, but not to quarrel about disputable matters. ² One may be convinced that one may eat anything, but the one who is weak eats only vegetables. ³ Let the one who eats not despise the one who abstains; let the one who abstains not pass judgment on the one who eats, for God has welcomed him. ⁴ Who are you to sit in judgment on the servant of another? Before his own master he stands or falls. And stand he will, for the master is able to make him stand. ⁵ One person regards one day as more important than another; yet another regards every day as the same. Each one, however, should be fully convinced of this in his own mind: ⁶ the one who observes a set day, observes it for the Lord; and the one who eats, eats for the Lord, for he gives thanks to God. The one who abstains, abstains for the Lord and also gives thanks to God. ⁷ Yet none of us lives for himself, and none of us dies for himself. ⁸ If we live, we live for the Lord; and if we die, we die for the Lord. So whether we live or die, we belong to the Lord. ⁹ For this reason too Christ died and came to life again in order that he might exercise lordship over both the dead and the living. ¹⁰ Why then do you sit in judgment over your brother? Or why do you despise your brother? We shall all have to appear before God's tribunal, ¹¹ for it stands written, "*As I live, says the Lord, to me every knee shall bend, and every tongue shall give praise to God.*" ^c ¹² Everyone of us, then, will give an account of himself before God.

¹³ So let us no longer pass judgment on one another. Make

rather this decision, never to put a stumbling-block or an obstacle in your brother's way. [14] As one who is in the Lord Jesus, I know and am convinced that nothing is unclean in itself; but for the one who considers something to be unclean, that becomes so for him. [15] If your brother is indeed distressed because of what you eat, you are no longer conducting yourself in love. Let not the food you eat bring ruin to such a one for whom Christ died. [16] Do not let what is good for you be reviled as evil. [17] For the kingdom of God is not eating and drinking, but uprightness, peace, and joy in the holy Spirit. [18] Anyone who serves Christ in this way is pleasing to God and esteemed among human beings. [19] Let us then pursue what makes for peace and for mutual edification. [20] Do not demolish the work of God for the sake of food. All things are indeed clean, but it is wrong for a human being to eat something that creates a stumbling-block for another. [21] It is better not to eat meat or drink wine, or do anything that causes your brother to trip over, to stumble, or be weakened. [22] The conviction you have keep to yourself before God. Blessed, indeed, is the one who does not condemn himself for what he approves. [23] But the one who has doubts is already condemned if he eats, because the eating does not proceed from conviction. For whatever proceeds not from conviction is sin.

[15:1] We who are strong ought to bear with the failings of those who are weak and not merely suit our own pleasure. [2] Each of us should please his neighbor for his good, to build him up. [3] For not even Christ suited his own pleasure, but as it stands written, *"The insults of those who insult you have fallen upon me."* [4] And what was written of old was written for our instruction that through endurance and the encouragement of the Scriptures we might have hope. [5] May God, the source of such endurance and encouragement, grant you a spirit of mutual harmony in accord with Christ Jesus, [6] so that with one mind and one voice you may glorify the God and Father of our Lord Jesus Christ.

[7] Welcome one another, then, as Christ welcomed you, for the glory of God! [8] For I tell you, Christ became a servant to the circumcised to show God's fidelity, to confirm the promises made to the patriarchs, [9] and Gentiles have glorified God for his mercy, as it stands written,

"Therefore, I will proclaim you among the Gentiles

　　　and sing praise to your name." [e]
[10] **Again it says,**
　　　"Rejoice, you Gentiles, along with his people." [f]
　　　[11] *"Praise the Lord, all you Gentiles,*
　　　and let all peoples sound his praise." [g]
[12] **Once again Isaiah says,**
　　　"There shall appear the Root of Jesse,
　　　the one who rises to rule the Gentiles;
　　　in him the Gentiles shall find hope." [h]
　　[13] **So may the God of hope fill you with all joy and peace in believing, so that you may abound in hope by the power of the holy Spirit.**

[e] Isa 49:18; 45:23	[d] Ps 69:10
[e] Ps 18:50; 2 Sam 22:50	[f] Deut 32:43
[g] Ps 117:1	[h] Isa 11:10

23.1 In the second part of the hortatory section of the epistle to the Romans, Paul takes up a specific problem that he has learned about in the Christian community in Rome. It is concerned immediately with questions about the eating of meat, drinking of wine, and observance of holy days; but more fundamentally with the age-old problem of the scrupulous versus the enlightened conscience in the Christian community–what Paul calls the "weak" and the "strong."

There is no reason to think that this problem did not exist in the Roman community, even if Paul has had no firsthand knowledge of it himself; but his treatment of it may also reflect his experience of dealing with such a problem in other churches in the eastern Mediterranean area, the evangelization of which he has just completed. For instance, it may be reflected also in 1 Corinthians 8–10.

It is not unlikely that Paul, in speaking of the "weak" and the "strong," is referring to a historical situation that had recently emerged in the Christian community of Rome. According to the historian Suetonius, the emperor Claudius had "expelled from Rome Jews who were making constant disturbances at the instigation of Chrestus" (*Claudii Vita* 25.4). This is most likely a reference to *Christos*, "Christ," which was misunderstood by Suetonius as the name of some common instigator (*Chrēstos* being a common name for slaves in his day). Suetonius undoubtedly had learned something about disturbances between Jews and Jewish Christians in Rome, who differed over Jesus as the *Christos,* and mistakenly wrote the name as "Chrestus," since the Greek form of the latter (*Chrēstos*) would have been pronounced as *Christos* in his day. The result of the disturbances was the expulsion by the emperor of "Jews" from Rome in A.D. 49, undoubtedly of Jewish Christians as well (see Acts 18:2). When Claudius died in A.D. 54 and Nero became emperor, Jews and Jewish Christians probably returned to Rome. The latter would then have found that the Gentile Christian community that had remained in Rome was no longer so observant of Jewish dietary and calendaric customs as in the days before A.D. 49. This undoubtedly caused a rift in the Roman Christian community to which Paul now writes (in the winter of A.D. 57-58). The "weak" would be Christians of Jewish background, still observant of such dietary and calendaric customs, and the "strong" those of Gentile background, who had come to live without them, indifferent as they were.

23.2 Paul's counsel to the Christians of Rome is that they should welcome all, the "strong" and the "weak" alike, but especially that the "strong" should let their Christian love show respect for the consciences of the "weak." For the latter also stand before the Lord, no matter what they eat or drink and no matter what days they celebrate. All, weak and strong alike, must one day stand before God's tribunal. The matter over which they now differ are *adiaphora,* "indifferent" matters.

Paul's principle is stated in 14:7-8: "None of us lives for himself, and none of us dies for himself. If we live, we live for the Lord; and if we die, we die for the Lord. So whether we live or die, we belong to the Lord."

23.3 "Welcome among you anyone who is weak in conviction, but not to quarrel about disputable matters" (14:1a). The "welcome" may refer to the returning Jewish Christians, and Paul's counsel is that all should learn to live generously with the brother or sister who is "weak," or scrupulous about observing diets and holy days. He uses the word *pistis,* which elsewhere in this epistle refers to basic Christian "faith," now in the sense of "conviction," a meaning that will return toward the end of chap. 14. It is not used here of someone who is weak in basic Christian faith, but rather of someone whose "conviction" about "disputable matters" is not what it should be. Such matters concern eating meat or vegetables (14:2, 21), drinking wine or not (14:21), or celebrating certain days or not (14:6). These are trivial indifferent matters that should not stand in the way of Christian love.

23.4 "Who are you to sit in judgment on the servant of another?" (14:4a). The weak brother or sister is a servant of the Lord as much as the strong, and God will be the judge of both. For even the weak person serves the Lord, and all, whether weak or strong, "shall have to appear before God's tribunal" (14:10). Once again eschatological judgment is invoked to motivate Christian readers. Recall 2:1-11. "Every one of us, then, will give an account of himself before God" (14:12).

23.5 Paul presses further. It is not merely a question of eschatological judgment that faces both the weak and the strong, but the example of Christ himself must rule in the community. "As one who is in the Lord Jesus, I know and am convinced that nothing is unclean in itself; but for the one who considers something to be unclean, that becomes so for him" (14:14). Paul's robust conscience recognizes that one of the consequences of God's gospel is that no foods are "common" or "unclean" in themselves (recall the words of Jesus recorded in Mark 7:14-23). But Paul's principle is reformulated: "If your brother is indeed distressed because of what you eat, you are no longer conducting yourself in love" (14:15ab). So Paul brings his basic estimation of the role of love in Christian life to bear on an indifferent matter such as this dietary question: "Love does no wrong to a neighbor" (13:10). That is why he continues, "Let not the food you eat bring ruin to such a one for whom Christ died" (14:15c). If an action of mine becomes a source of scandal for a fellow-Christian, then I should be ready to reconsider it out of love for him or her, but also because Christ died for him and her. "Anyone who serves Christ in this way is pleasing to God and esteemed among human beings" (14:18). In all such indifferent matters, "the conviction you have keep to yourself before God" (14:22). Since conviction in such a matter is not crucial to one's salvation, one should contain it out of love for a fellow-Christian. "Blessed, indeed, is the one who does not condemn himself for what he approves. But the one who has doubts is already condemned if he eats, because the eating does not proceed from conviction. For whatever proceeds not from conviction is sin" (14:22b-23). One sees now the importance of *pistis* in this chapter as "conviction," for in this question of indifferent matters it refers to actions that one may perform against one's own conscience. To go against that would be sinful. In all of this quetion one sees how Paul grants to love the primacy that it must have in Christian action and conduct. For that love is none other than the recognition of Christ's influence in our lives especially as it should mark our relations with fellow-Christians, and all human beings.

23.6 At the beginning of chap. 15 Paul presses on to propose to the "strong" the very example of Christ Jesus himself. "Each of us [who are strong] should please his neighbor for his good, to build him up. For not even Christ suited his own pleasure, but as it stands written, 'The insults of those who insult you have fallen upon me'" (15:2-3, quoting Ps 69:10). Paul identifies himself with the strong and urges them to consider the example of Christ and the encouragement that comes from Scripture itself. In all, the goal of every Christian should be the edification of fellow-Christians, the upbuilding of them in holiness of life and conduct, their growth in dedication to God. Christian activity should for that reason be a manifestation of love in imitation of the love that Christ himself displayed, who sought not to avoid the insults and reproaches addressed to God by those who opposed his life and ministry. Those who put him to death were indeed reviling God, who sent his Son on their behalf. In citing Psalm 69, Paul makes use of the classic psalm that the early church used to describe the passion of Jesus. For him it has now become a biblical passage with significance for Christian disciples in their dealings with one another. It underlines that what Christ did for us did not suit "his own pleasure." So Paul proposes to us Christ as a model, even in daily actions that are of indifferent character. He teaches us further to draw encouragement and motivation from the written Word of God: "What was written of old was written for our instruction" (15:4). Aspects of Old Testament teaching still have relevance for Christian life. Recall what Paul said about Abraham's faith in 4:23 (p. 67 above). What was composed as God's word was written not just for people of old, but through it God still speaks to us, as he has been speaking to generations of Jews and Christians ever since. Cf. 1 Cor 9:10; 10:1-6.

23.7 "May God, the source of such endurance and encouragement, grant you a spirit of mutual harmony in accord with Christ Jesus" (15:5). So Paul prays for the Roman Christian community, realizing that such mutual harmony is a gift from God, as are also the understanding and encouragement of Scripture. Christ Jesus is again proposed as the model of Christian solidarity: when Christians live not for themselves, but for others, then such solidarity is achieved. The purpose of such mutual harmony and unity is the praise and glorification of God: "so that with one mind and one voice you may glorify the God and Father of our Lord Jesus Christ" (15:6).

23.8 Paul ends his exhortation about the "weak" and the "strong" with a repeated call to welcome all, Jews and Gentiles, who turn to Christ, for in the divine plan it was foreseen that Gentiles would come to join Israel in the praise and glorification of its God. "Welcome one another, then, as Christ welcomed you, for the glory of God! For I tell you, Christ became a servant to the circumcised to show God's fidelity, to confirm the promises made to the patriarchs, and Gentiles have glorified God for his mercy" (15:7-9). Christ Jesus, as a Jew, was sent first to his own people; in his ministry, passion, and death he served them. God used that testimony, which his Son bore to his own people, as a means of manifesting divine faithfulness to the Chosen People of old, as a means of confirming the promises made to their patriarchs, and as a means of relating Gentiles to the goal of Israel's existence, viz. the glory of God.

23.9 To bolster up his contention, Paul again appeals to the Old Testament and introduces another *testimonia* list (recall his use of such a list in 3:10-20). Now he will quote the Torah, the Prophets, and the Writings, and in each case the catchword bond is "Gentiles" (*ethnē*) or "peoples" (*laoi*). The contrast of the "root of Jesse" and "Gentiles" reveals now why the "strong" have been understood as Gentile Christians and the "weak" as Jewish Christians in the preceding context.

"Therefore I will proclaim you among the Gentiles and sing

praise to your name" (Ps 18:50 = 2 Sam 22:50). As Israel of old was called in this royal thanksgiving psalm to praise and glorify Yahweh for the king's victory over his enemies, the "nations," so now, as Paul uses the verse, Jewish Christians are called to praise God not only in the midst of Gentile Christians, but even along with them. All are to unite in a harmonious glorification of the God who saves.

"Rejoice, you Gentiles, along with his people" (15:10, quoting a form of Deut 32:43, which agrees exactly with none of the preserved Hebrew or Greek forms). The words come from the last verse of the Song of Moses, which calls upon the heavens and the "nations" to break out in song and praise God along with his people. Paul applies the invitation to Gentile Christians to sing God's praise alone with Jewish Christians.

"Praise the Lord, all you Gentiles, and let all peoples sound his praise" (15:11, quoting Ps 117:1). The psalm summoned the praise of all peoples to the worship of Yahweh, stressing the universality of the summons. Paul cites it to recommend the praise of God to all, Gentile as well as Jewish Christians, in the Roman community.

"There shall appear the Root of Jesse, the one who rises to rule the Gentiles; in him the Gentiles shall find hope" (15:12, abridging the Septuagint text of Isa 11:10). The Septuagint form of the Isaian verse introduced the idea of the Root of Jesse "ruling" the nations; a descendant of the Davidic dynasty (Jesse being the father of David) would be the rallying point for the "nations." Paul accommodates the Isaian verse, understanding Jesus as the anointed descendant of David, welcoming Jew and Gentile alike. Thus Jesus, sprung from the root of Jesse, has become the source of hope for both Jewish and Gentile Christians.

"So may the God of hope fill you with all joy and peace in believing so that you may abound in hope by the power of the holy Spirit" (15:13). So Paul ends his exhortation of the Christians of Rome with a prayer for joy and peace that will enhance their faith and hope.

23.10 Questions. What is my reaction to scrupulous members of the community in which I reside? Do I act toward them with the love that Paul would ask of me? Do I seek to understand indifferent matters in Christian life as I should? Does the model of Christ, who did not suit his own pleasure, influence my Christian life? What is my reaction to liberal or conservative Christians in the community in which I live? How can I learn to respect the conscience of others? Do I seek to build up the mutual harmony of the community? Do I allow the word of God to be a source of endurance and encouragement in my life?

COLLOQUY: PSALM 118

Give thanks to the LORD, who is good,
> whose love endures forever.
Let the house of Israel say:
> God's love endures forever.
Let the house of Aaron say,
> God's love endures forever.
Let those who fear the LORD say,
> God's love endures forever.
In danger I called on the LORD;
> the LORD answered me and set me free.
The LORD is with me; I am not afraid;
> what can mortals do against me?
The LORD is with me as my helper;
> I shall look in triumph on my foes.
Better to take refuge in the LORD
> than to put one's trust in mortals.
Better to take refuge in the LORD
> than to put one's trust in princes.
All the nations surrounded me;
> in the LORD's name I crushed them.
They surrounded me on every side;
> in the LORD's name I crushed them.
They surrounded me like bees;
> they blazed like fire among thorns;
> in the LORD's name I crushed them.
I was hard pressed and falling,
> but the LORD came to my help.
The LORD, my strength and might,
> came to me as savior.
The joyful shout of deliverance
> is heard in the tents of the victors.

"The LORD's right hand strikes with power;
　　The LORD's right hand is raised;
　　the LORD's right hand strikes with power."
I shall not die but live
　　and declare the deeds of the LORD.
The LORD chastised me harshly,
　　but did not hand me over to death.
Open the gates of victory;
　　I will enter and thank the LORD.
This is the LORD's own gate,
　　where the victors enter.
I thank you for you answered me;
　　you have been my savior.
The stone the builders rejected
　　has become the cornerstone.
By the LORD has this been done;
　　it is wonderful in our eyes.
This is the day the LORD has made;
　　let us rejoice in it and be glad.
LORD, grant salvation!
　　LORD, grant good fortune!
Blessed is he
　　who comes in the name of the LORD.
We bless you from the LORD's house.
　　The LORD is God and has given us light.
Join in procession with leafy branches
　　up to the horns of the altar.
You are my God, I give you thanks;
　　my God, I offer you praise.
Give thanks to the LORD, who is good,
　　whose love endures forever.

See further *Romans*, 686-708.

Paul's Plans, Coming Task, Request for Prayers; Letter of Recommendation for Phoebe (15:14–16:27)

[14] I myself am convinced about you, brothers, that you are full of goodness, equipped with all knowledge, and capable of admonishing one another. [15] Yet I write to you quite boldly, partly to remind you in virtue of the grace given to me by God [16] to be a minister of Christ Jesus to the Gentiles, with the priestly duty of preaching God's gospel, so that the offering of the Gentiles might become acceptable and consecrated by the holy Spirit. [17] Therefore, in what pertains to God I have this boast in Christ Jesus. [18] For I shall not dare to speak of anything save what Christ has accomplished through me for the commitment of the Gentiles, either in word or in deed, [19] by the power of signs and wonders, or by the power of God's Spirit. So I have fully preached the gospel of Christ from Jerusalem all the way round to Illyricum. [20] Thus it has been my ambition to preach the good news where Christ has not been named, lest I build on the foundation of someone else. [21] But as it stands written, *"Those who have had no news of him will see, and those who have not heard of him will understand."* [i] [22] This is why I have so often been hindered from coming to you. [23] But now I no longer have room for work in these regions and have been longing for many years to come to you; (I plan to do so) [24] as I proceed on my way to Spain. I hope to see you as I travel

along and be sped on my way there by you, once I have enjoyed your company for a while.

²⁵ At present, however, I am making my way to Jerusalem to bring aid to God's dedicated people there. ²⁶ For Macedonia and Achaia kindly decided to make some contribution for the poor among these people in Jerusalem. ²⁷ They kindly decided to do so, and indeed they are indebted to them. For if Gentiles have come to share in the spiritual blessings of Jerusalem Christians, they ought to be of service to them in material things. ²⁸ So when I have completed this task and have delivered this contribution under my own seal, I shall set out for Spain, passing through your midst. ²⁹ I know that, when I arrive among you, I shall be coming with the full blessing of Christ.

³⁰ I urge you, then, brothers, by our Lord Jesus Christ and by the love of the Spirit to join me in my struggle, by praying to God on my behalf, ³¹ that I may be delivered from unbelievers in Judea and that my service in Jerusalem may be acceptable to God's dedicated people, ³² and that by God's will I may come to you with joy and be refreshed together with you. ³³ May the God of peace be with all of you! Amen.

¹⁶:¹ I commend to you our sister Phoebe, a minister of the church of Cenchreae. ² Please receive her in the Lord in a manner worthy of God's dedicated people and help her in whatever she may require of you; she has been a patroness of many here, and of myself too.

³ My greetings to Prisca and Aquila, fellow-workers of mine in Christ Jesus. ⁴ They risked their necks for me; not only I, but all Gentile churches are grateful to them. ⁵ Greet too the church that meets at their house. Greetings to my dear friend Epaenetus, the first convert to Christ in Asia. ⁶ Greetings to Mary, who has worked hard for you. ⁷ Greetings to Andronicus and Junia, my fellow-countrymen, who were imprisoned with me and who are outstanding among the apostles. They were in Christ even before me. ⁸ Greetings to Ampliatus, my dear friend in the Lord. ⁹ Greetings to Urbanus, my fellow-worker in Christ, and to my dear friend Stachys. ¹⁰ Greetings to Apelles, who is approved in Christ's service, and to the household of Aristobulus. ¹¹ Greetings to my fellow-countryman Herodion, and to those who belong to the Lord in the household of Narcissus. ¹² Greetings to those workers in the

Lord, Tryphaena and Tryphosa. Greetings to my dear friend Persis, who has toiled hard in the Lord. [13] Greetings to Rufus, the chosen one of the Lord, and to his mother—whom I call mother too. [14] Greetings to Asyncritus, Phlegon, Hermes, Patrobas, Hermas, and the brothers who are with them. [15] Greetings to Philologus and Julia, Nereus and his sister, Olympas, and all God's dedicated people who are with them. [16] Greet one another with a holy kiss. All the churches of Christ send you their greetings.

[17] I urge you, brothers, to watch out for those who create dissension and scandal in opposition to the teaching you have learned. Keep away from them. [18] For such people do not serve our Lord Christ, but their own appetites; for by smooth talk and flattery they deceive the minds of the simple. [19] Your commitment, however, is known to all; so I am happy about you. But I want you to be wise about what is good, and innocent about what is evil. [20] The God of peace will soon crush Satan under your feet. The grace of our Lord Jesus be with you!

[21] Timothy, my fellow-worker, and Lucius, Jason, and Sosipater, my fellow-countrymen, send their greetings to you. [22] I, Tertius, who write this letter, also greet you in the Lord. [23] Gaius, my host, and the whole church here, send greetings too. Erastus, the treasurer of this city, and Quartus, our brother, also greet you.

[25] Now to him who is able to strengthen you according to my gospel and the preaching of Jesus Christ, in accord with the revelation of the mystery kept secret for long ages, [26] but now disclosed and made known by command of the eternal God in prophetic writings so that all the Gentiles may come to the commitment of faith—[27] to the only wise God, be glory forever through Jesus Christ! Amen.

[i] Isa 52:15

24.1 This last exercise is devoted to the end of the epistle to the Romans, in which Paul tells of his plans of coming to visit the Christians in Rome and includes a letter of recommendation for Phoebe, a deacon of the church Cenchreae, one of the ports of nearby Neo-Corinth, from which he has been writing this epistle. Most of the text is thus taken up with factual details, plans, and greetings to numerous persons, but mixed in with such items are others that provide a basis for some reflection and prayer. After all, we have been meditating on a Pauline letter, one, however, which is unique in that it is ostensibly a letter with which Paul seeks to introduce himself to the Christians of Rome, a church with which he has had so far little to do. But along with the introduction Paul has included an exposé of his understanding of God's gospel and of the Christ-event that it proclaims. As we come to the end of it, we get a glimpse into the way Paul, the apostle of the Gentiles, reacted to various concrete details in his own Christian life.

24.2 Paul begins this concluding part of the epistle with an admission of what he knows about the Christians of Rome: "I myself am convinced about you, brothers, that you are full of goodness, equipped with all knowledge, and capable of admonishing one another. Yet I write to you quite boldly, partly to remind you in virtue of the grace given to me by God to be a minister of Christ Jesus to the Gentiles, with the priestly duty of preaching God's gospel, so that the offering of the Gentiles might become acceptable and consecrated by the holy Spirit" (15:14-16). His boldness will be displayed in 16:17-19.

Here we see Paul reflecting once again on his own vocation: he has been called by God to be a "minister of Christ Jesus to the Gentiles," and he perceives his preaching of the gospel as an act of cultic service to God. He calls himself not *diakonos*, "servant," or *oikonomos*, "steward," terms that he uses elsewhere (2 Cor 3:6; 1 Cor 4:1), but *leitourgos*, "cultic minister." He thus sees his evangelization of Gentiles as an act of worship, explicitly comparing his preaching of God's gospel with the cultic service of Yahweh rendered by the priests in the Jerusalem Temple of old. This he does by using the participle *hierourgounta*, "functioning as a priest," employing the very verb that Josephus and Philo have used of those "offering sacrifice." Cf. Exod 28:35, 43; 29:30, where Aaron and his sons are referred to as "priests." What Paul sees himself offering to God by his preaching and his priestly service is the Gentiles themselves, who are said to have become "acceptable and consecrated by the holy Spirit." All of this, Paul acknowledges, comes from "the grace given to me by God." It is not that Paul has somehow rendered the Gentiles "acceptable" to God, but their consecration by the Spirit has brought this about. So Paul acknowledges the work of the holy Spirit in his own priestly ministry. The Gentiles have been "made holy" by God's own Spirit through Paul's evangelization of them.

24.3 Indeed, Paul insists on God's part in what he has been able to accomplish in his ministry. "For I shall not dare to speak of anything save what Christ has accomplished through me for the commitment of the Gentiles, either in word or in deed, by the power of signs and wonders, or by the power of God's Spirit. So I have fully preached the gospel of Christ from Jerusalem all the way round to Illyricum" (15:18-19). He has carried the word of God's gospel from its matrix, Jerusalem, to the bounds of the eastern Mediterranean world, which he calls "Illyricum" (the area of modern Albania and southern Yugoslavia). He realizes that the evangelization of this eastern area has been accomplished by Christ himself "through" him. Even the miracles that were wrought, the "signs and wonders," those that he calls in 2 Cor 12:12 "the signs of a true apostle," are recognized to have been done "by the power of God's Spirit." Thus Paul gives us a telling picture of his own apostolate: his readiness to trace to God's grace whatever he has been able to accomplish in his preaching of the gospel.

24.4 "It has been my ambition to preach the good news where Christ has not been named, lest I build on the foundation of someone else. But as it stands written, 'Those who have had no news of him will see, and those who have not heard of him will understand'" (15:20-21, quoting Isa 52:15). In the Isaian context the words refer to "nations" and "kings" who come to learn of the Servant of Yahweh. In using Isaiah's words, Paul implies that through his ministry those who had previously not even heard about Christ have come to knowledge about him and belief in him. This Paul says to explain why he has not yet come to Rome, the capital of the empire in which he has been working. His principle has been to preach the gospel where Christ has not yet been proclaimed; yet in this very epistle he has announced to those who are already Christians in Rome that he is desirous of coming there "in order to reap some fruit among you as among the other Gentiles" (1:13); hence his "eagerness to preach the gospel also to you who are in Rome" (1:15). This is not to be understood as a contradiction; nor is it that Paul has forgotten what he had written in chap. 1. His real goal is to evangelize gospel-less Spain, and en route he would like to "preach the gospel also" to those who are in Rome. It tells us how much he esteems the gospel of Christ Jesus. In fact, he has been evangelizing them already through this very epistle. And we have been profiting from such evangelization.

24.5 First, however, Paul must carry to Jerusalem the collection that he has had taken up in the Greek churches of Achaia and Macedonia for the poor of the mother-church in Jerusalem. The Gentile Christians of these churches "kindly decided to do so, and indeed they are indebted to them. For if Gentiles have come to share in the spiritual blessings of Jerusalem Christians, they ought to be of service to them in material things" (15:27). We find here the motivation that Paul used to make the Gentiles whom he had evangelized aware of their indebtedness to the mother-church, in whose "spiritual blessings" they have come to share, prime among which is the blessing of Christian discipleship. This is, moreover, a concrete sign of the solidarity of Christians in the body of Christ, of which Paul has already spoken (12:5). It is further a concrete sign of how Christian faith can work itself out through love— through love for fellow-Christians, who are not so well off as the more prosperous Gentile Christians of Achaia and Macedonia.

Moreover, we see how Paul himself sought to carry out the recommendation made to him at the time of the so-called Council of Jerusalem, when the early disciples approved of his mission "to the Gentiles" and instructed him to "remember the poor, which very thing I was eager to do" (Gal 2:10). "To remember the poor": Paul writes this epistle to the Christians of Rome from Corinth, to the Christians of which he once likewise recommended that a collection for the poor of Jerusalem be taken up, as he had also done to the churches of Galatia (1 Cor 16:1). With all of this collection Paul now intends to set out for Jerusalem, before he makes his way to the capital of the Roman empire on his way to the West and to Spain.

24.6 Paul ends the discussion of his plans by requesting that the Christians of Rome pray for him as he plans to go to Jerusalem with the collection for the poor. "I urge you, then, brothers, by our Lord Jesus Christ and by the love of the Spirit, to join me in my struggle by praying to God on my behalf, that I may be delivered from unbelievers in Judea and that my service in Jerusalem may be acceptable to God's dedicated people, and that by God's will I may come to you with joy and be refreshed together with you" (15:30-32). Paul reveals his apprehension about the trip to Jerusalem and the reception that he will find there. The Christians of Rome are asked to pray for three things: that he will not encounter difficulties from "unbelievers," i.e. from fellow Jews who have undoubtedly come to regard him as an apostate; that he will be rightly welcomed by the Jewish Christians of Jerusalem, who may have come to be suspicious of him because of his evangelization of Gentiles and because of the gospel of justification by grace through faith in Christ Jesus apart from deeds of the Mosaic law that he is known to have been preaching; and that he may succeed in coming to Rome to be with them. In such a request we see again a basic characteristic of the Apostle Paul. In his humility he realized not only that the good things, such as the collection for the poor of Jerusalem that he was able to take up, came from God, but also that constant communing with God the Father in prayer was necessary as the source of the blessings that he might still be able to pass on. His concern for the poor of Jerusalem is evident, but he wants to make sure that his bringing of aid to them will be accompanied by God's blessing. He is not above asking his fellow Christians to pray for him and for the success of his endeavor. He thus realizes the value of Christian intercession for one another.

24.7 Paul ends the major part of his epistle with a prayer for the Christians of Rome: "May the God of peace be with all of you! Amen" (15:33). It is a prayer that corresponds to the greeting that he sent in 1:7 at the beginning of the epistle. Paul now calls upon God as the source of such peace as he desires for the Christians of Rome (cf. 16:20; 1 Thess 5:23; 1 Cor 14:33; 2 Cor 13:11). He desires that God the source of such peace be with them and endow them with it.

24.8 Paul appends to the epistle proper a letter of recommendation for Phoebe, a deacon of the church of Cenchreae, who has deserved well of Christians in the Corinthian church, for she has been "a patroness of many here, and of myself too" (16:2). She may be the one who was to carry this letter to the Roman community. In this letter Paul includes greetings to various persons in the Roman church, mentioning at least twenty-four of them by name. Some of them he has known in the eastern Mediterranean area, and some of them have worked with him; others are undoubtedly those whose names have come to his attention as resident in Rome. He singles out some for special mention and praise: "Prisca and Aquila...who risked their necks for me" (16:3-4), perhaps at Ephesus during the riot of the silversmiths (Acts 19:23); "Andronicus and Junia, my fellow countrymen, who were imprisoned with me and who are outstanding among the apostles. They were in Christ even before me" (16:7). This pair, probably husband and wife, were Christians even before Paul had become one, and he may even regard them as "outstanding" apostles. To all of the Christians of Rome he sends his greetings "with a holy kiss" (16:16a, as in 1 Thess 5:26; 1 Cor 16:20; 2 Cor 13:12). "All the churches of Christ send you their greetings" (16:16b). So Paul greets them in the name of the churches he has founded—a fitting global greeting to a church that he is about to visit for the first time.

24.9 Strangely enough, Paul adds to his letter of recommendation a stern warning: "I urge you, brothers, to watch out for those who create dissension and scandal in opposition to the teaching you have learned. Keep away from them. For such people do not serve our Lord Christ, but their own appetites; for by smooth talk and flattery they deceive the minds of the simple. Your commitment, however, is known to all; so I am happy about you. But I want you to be wise about what is good, and innocent about what is evil" (16:17-19). It seems strange, because Paul, writing to a community that he has not founded or evangelized, undertakes to admonish it so strongly. In 15:15 above Paul had said, "I write to you quite boldly," but little boldness was displayed at that juncture. Now it appears. It is, however, only a half-admonition, because he also commends the Roman Christians for their faith commitment (16:19), as in 1:8 and 15:14. His warning concerns the influence of strangers who might introduce dissension and scandal. Because the admonition is so short and cryptic, it is hard to say specifically what he had in mind. But it reveals another aspect of the apostle, one who did not fear to admonish his fellow-Christians.

"The God of peace will soon crush Satan under your feet" (16:20a). So Paul recasts the blessing that he uttered in 15:33, now alluding to Gen 3:15, as he interprets the serpent of Genesis as Satan, the personification of all evil, disorder, dissension, and scandal. He prays that God, who shapes human ways in peace, may do away with such dangers that threaten the community. He thus implies that those who create dissension are under the domination of Satan, and not on the side of God. "The grace of our Lord Jesus be with you!" (16:20b). So runs his usual final blessing (cf. 1 Cor 16:23; 1 Thess 5:28).

24.10 Greetings follow from Paul's companions (16:21-23), and the epistle ends with a doxology (16:25-27): "Now to him who is able to strengthen you according to my gospel and the preaching of Jesus Christ, in accord with the revelation of the mystery kept secret for long ages, but now disclosed and made known by the command of the eternal God in prophetic writings so that all of the Gentiles may come to the commitment of faith—to the only wise God, be glory forever through Jesus Christ! Amen." Even if the doxology is not an authentic Pauline composition, it is a fitting conclusion to the epistle, for it catches the spirit of the Apostle's message in it: from of old God in his wisdom has bound up salvation with Christ Jesus, and the mystery of this wise decision has now been disclosed. The God who rules over human beings of all ages has now caused his gospel to be proclaimed among the nations to bring about the commitment of faith among them as well: "To the only wise God be glory forever through Jesus Christ!"

24.11 Questions. Am I as convinced as Paul was of the grace given to me to serve the Lord? Is what I do in life an act of worship, as Paul understood his evangelization of the Gentiles? Do I think of my work as being consecrated by the holy Spirit? Is my concern for the poor among God's people what it should be? Can I find some way in which I can imitate Paul's concern for them? Do I ever seek to reward in a material way those who have benefited me spiritually? Do I ever ask fellow-Christians to pray for me? For the success of what I am trying to accomplish in my Christian life? Do I thank God for the Christian friends who have labored with me or suffered with me? Am I ready to end these exercises with fitting praise for the only wise God who has spoken to me in these days?

COLLOQUY: PSALM 150

> Praise God in his holy sanctuary;
>> give praise in the mighty dome of heaven.
> Give praise for his mighty deeds,
>> praise him for his great majesty.
> Give praise with blasts upon the horn,
>> praise him with harp and lyre.
> Give praise with tambourines and dance,
>> praise him with flutes and strings.
> Give praise with crashing cymbals,
>> praise him with sounding cymbals.
> Let everything that has breath
>> give praise to the LORD! Hallelujah!

See further *Romans*, 709-56.

Select Bibliography

Becker, J., *Paul: Apostle to the Gentiles* (Louisville, KY: Westminster/ John Knox, 1993).

Beker, J. C., *Paul the Apostle: The Triumph of God in Life and Thought* (Philadelphia, PA: Fortress, 1980).

Brown, R. E., J. A. Fitzmyer, and R. E. Murphy, *The New Jerome Biblical Commentary* (Englewood Cliffs, NJ: Prentice-Hall, 1990), esp. 830-68 ("The Letter to the Romans"), 1329-37 ("Paul"), 1382-1416 ("Pauline Theology").

Byrne, B., *Reckoning with Romans: A Contemporary Reading of Paul's Gospel* (Good News Studies 18; Wilmington, DE: Glazier, 1986).

Cranfield, C. E. B., *The Epistle to the Romans* (International Critical Commentary; 2 vols.; Edinburgh: Clark, 1975).

———— *Romans: A Shorter Commentary* (Edinburgh: Clark; Grand Rapids, MI: Eerdmans, 1985).

Dunn, J. D. G., *Romans 1-8* and *Romans 9-16* (Word Biblical Commentary 38A-B; Dallas, TX: Word Books, 1988).

Fitzmyer, J. A., *Romans: A New Translation with Introduction and Commentary* (Anchor Bible 33; New York: Doubleday, 1993).

Ganss, G. E., *The Spiritual Exercises of Saint Ignatius: A Translation and Commentary* (Chicago, IL: Loyola University, 1992).

Käsemann, E., *Commentary on Romans* (Grand Rapids, MI: Eerdmans, 1980).

Lietzmann, H., *An die Römer* (Handbuch zum Neuen Testament 8; 5th ed.; Tübingen: Mohr [Siebeck], 1971).

Michel, O., *Der Brief an die Römer* (MeyerKommentar 4; 14th ed.; Göttingen: Vandenhoeck & Ruprecht, 1978).

Mussner, F., *Tractate on the Jews: The Significance of Judaism for Christian Faith* (London: SPCK; Philadelphia, PA: Fortress, 1984).

Nygren, A., *Commentary on Romans* (Philadelphia, PA: Muhlenberg, 1949).

Robinson, J. A. T., *Wrestling with Romans* (Philadelphia, PA: Westminster, 1979).

Segal, A. F., *Paul the Convert: The Apostolate and Apostasy of Saul the Pharisee* (New Haven/London: Yale University, 1990).

Stendahl, K., *Paul among Jews and Gentiles and Other Essays* (London: SCM; Philadelphia, PA: Fortress, 1976).

Notes

1. See M. Downey (ed.), *The New Dictionary of Catholic Spirituality* (Collegeville, MN: Liturgical Press, 1993).

2. They have often been translated into English: e.g., L. J. Puhl, *The Spiritual Exercises of St. Ignatius: A New Translation Based on Studies in the Language of the Autograph* (Westminster, MD: Newman, 1951); D. L. Fleming, *The Spiritual Exercises of Saint Ignatius: A Literal Translation and a Contemporary Reading* (St. Louis, MO: Institute of Jesuit Sources, 1978); G. E. Ganss, *The Spiritual Exercises of Saint Ignatius: A Translation and Commentary* (Chicago, IL: Loyola University, 1992).

3. *Romans: A New Translation with Introduction and Commentary* (Anchor Bible 33; New York: Doubleday, 1993).

4. The crown at the Olympian Games was made of olive; at the Pythian Games (Delphi), of laurel; at the Nemean Games, of celery; and at the Isthmian Games, two crowns were used, one of pine, and one of celery. Se O. Broneer, "The Isthmian Victory Crown," *AJA* 66 (1962) 259-63.

5. "Christ our Lord" or "Christ" is mentioned in §47-48, but those instances are part of Ignatius' general explanation of what the first and second preludes of a meditation or a contemplation might be.

6. See also Rom 9:28, where Paul conflates Isa 10:23 with a form of Isa 28:22b; 10:16, where Paul quotes a Greek form of Isa 53:1, which has added *Kyrie;* 11:3, where Paul himself uses *Kyrie* as he introduces a Greek form of 1 Kgs 19:10; 11:34, where he quotes a Greek form of Isa 40:13. In 14:6 Paul himself uses *Kyrios* of God (despite the christological use of it in 14:8), but in 14:11 he conflates a Greek form of Isa 9:18 and 45:23. In 15:11, he quotes a Greek form of Ps 117:1.

7. See my article, "The Semitic Background of the New Testament *Kyrios*-Title," *A Wandering Aramean: Collected Aramaic Essays* (SBLMS 25; Missoula, MT: Scholars Press, 1979) 115-42.

Index

226

PARABIBLICAL PASSAGES

SECULAR WRITINGS